# Islamophobia in European Cities



The demise of socialism in Southeast Europe coincided with the breakout of wars and genocidal violence against local Muslim populations. After being displaced and forced to migrate to different European countries, those former socialist citizens quickly developed institutions of sociability and unobtrusively enacted postulates of solidarity. This book brings a spotlight on the "generations after" born to Balkan Muslim families whose repatriation could not take place due to the continuous political instability and insecurity in their homelands. It investigates the new modes of these "second generations" to respond to the current crisis of liberal democracy and rampant Islamophobia in their places of residence. By relating spatial issues to broader religious and political questions, this study shines a light on the civic engagement, religious practices and political sensitivities of young Muslims with Balkan roots in Belgium, Germany, Italy and Poland. The book will be of interest to academics, researchers and policy-makers working in the areas of Islamic Studies, Migration Studies, Anthropology of Religion and Memory Studies.

**Francesco Trupia** is Assistant Professor at the Faculty of Humanities at the Nicolaus Copernicus University in Toruń, Poland. His research interests range from identity and memory politics to minority inclusion, from post-socialist democratisation to study of civil society in Southeast and Eastern Europe.

## Routledge Advances in Minority Studies

Routledge Advances in Minority Studies (RAMS) provides a platform for outstanding state-of-the-art research on interdisciplinary and intersectional understandings of minorities, globally. Monographs and edited volumes in the series advance scholarly and practitioner insights from Anthropology, Law, Politics, Sociology, History and beyond. The series foregrounds pluralism and diversity of both authors and subjects of study, with a particular focus on emerging fields and marginalized voices.

Under the editorial supervision of Dr Stavroula Pipyrou and Dr Kyriaki Topidi, the series will be a primary source for students, scholars and practitioners in minority studies while presenting authors with a valuable means to reach a wide and growing readership.

Series Editors

*Stavroula Pipyrou is a Senior Lecturer in Social Anthropology at the University of St Andrews, UK, and Founding Director of the cross-disciplinary Centre for Minorities Research (CMR). She has published widely on minority politics, governance, and civil society in Italy and Greece.*

*Kyriaki Topidi is Head of the Research Cluster on Culture and Diversity and a Senior Researcher at the European Centre for Minority Issues, Germany. Her research interests focus on diversity management, minority protection rights and mechanisms, with a special interest in religion, and human rights law. She has published extensively on these and related areas.*

Titles in the series:

**Islamophobia in European Cities**
Solidarities, Responses and Dilemmas for Young Balkan Muslims
*Francesco Trupia*

For more information about this series, please visit: www.routledge.com/Routledge-Advances-in-Minority-Studies/book-series/RAIMSv

# Islamophobia in European Cities

## Solidarities, Responses and Dilemmas for Young Balkan Muslims

**Francesco Trupia**

Routledge
Taylor & Francis Group
LONDON AND NEW YORK

First published 2025
by Routledge
4 Park Square, Milton Park, Abingdon, Oxon OX14 4RN

and by Routledge
605 Third Avenue, New York, NY 10158

*Routledge is an imprint of the Taylor & Francis Group, an informa business*



*British Library Cataloguing-in-Publication Data*
A catalogue record for this book is available from the British Library

*Library of Congress Cataloging-in-Publication Data*
Names: Trupia, Francesco, author.
Title: Islamophobia in European cities : solidarities, responses and dilemmas for young Balkan Muslims / Francesco Trupia.
Description: Abingdon, Oxon [UK] ; New York, NY : Routledge, 2025. | Series: Routledge advances in minority studies | Includes bibliographical references and index. | Contents: Being (with) the Other — The Ummah and the "Balkan Rest" — Echoes of War — Believing without Belonging? — Halal or Haram? — Political Sensitivities and Civic Responses to Islamophobia — City(zens) of Silence.
Identifiers: LCCN 2024056573 (print) | LCCN 2024056574 (ebook) | ISBN 9781032964805 (hardback) | ISBN 9781032964829 (paperback) | ISBN 9781003589624 (ebook)
Subjects: LCSH: Muslims—Legal status, laws, etc.—Balkan Peninsula. | Minorities—Legal status, laws, etc.—Balkan Peninsula. | Islam and state—Balkan Peninsula. | Islamophobia—Balkan Peninsula.
Classification: LCC KJC5144.M56 T78 2025 (print) | LCC KJC5144. M56 (ebook) | DDC 305.6/970811094—dc23/eng/20241125
LC record available at https://lccn.loc.gov/2024056573
LC ebook record available at https://lccn.loc.gov/2024056574

ISBN: 978-1-032-96480-5 (hbk)
ISBN: 978-1-032-96482-9 (pbk)
ISBN: 978-1-003-58962-4 (ebk)

DOI: 10.4324/9781003589624

Typeset in Galliard
by Apex CoVantage, LLC

# Contents

# Acknowledgements

Writing a book is never an easy undertaking. Although I bear full responsibility for this study and its shortcomings, the entire process of writing has been a collective experience. Above all, this book could not have been written without all respondents who voluntarily decided to participate in my research. I was humbled to see their willingness to share family stories and everyday worries after giving me their time and introducing me to their most intimate spaces. This is not a book about them, but *for* them, who peacefully fought – and continue to fight – against the painful and unpleasant circumstances that they have endured while grappling with the burden of the past. I hope I have highlighted their courageous ways of healing and, at times, seeking solidarity and justice in a time of (geo)political upheavals in and beyond Europe.

I am also immensely grateful to a large number of scholars, faculty members and practitioners who have challenged the way I had organised my research. Here, I thank Prof. Adam Kola and Prof. Agata Domachowska for their guidance and critical exchange of ideas during a three-year research period, as well as Dr. Michał Bomastyk, Szymon Bojarski-Syrek and Dr. Rafał Openkowski for the constant administrative assistance at the Nicolaus Copernicus University in Toruń, Poland.

I wish to thank Barbara Tan, Policy Advisor Knowledge Transfer for the Young University for the Future of Europe, for reaching out on my behalf to excellent scholars and faculty members at Antwerp University, Belgium. A special thanks goes to Prof. Marnix Beyen and the whole research community at the Centre for Political History (PoHis) for welcoming me and hosting my talks with students, doctoral and postdoctoral fellows. I also wish to thank Prof. Gritt Klinkhammer and Prof. Yasemin Karakaşoğlu at the Bremen University, Germany, for their generous and helpful comments. I am indebted to Dr. Lumnije Jusufi from the Humboldt University in Berlin, who was very supportive of my research in Dortmund, Germany. Another special thanks goes to Dr. Kamila Fiałkowska and Dr. Ignacy Jóźwiak, who, together with Dr. Weronika Kloc-Nowak, have welcomed me at the Centre for Migration Research (CMR) at Warsaw University and showed tremendous and genuine interest in my research project since the very early stage.

As parts of this book have been presented and discussed in international conferences and academic fora in Europe, my gratitude also extends to all the researchers and friends who have offered critical comments on research findings and suggested different perspectives to improve the final results of the whole research project. I would especially like to thank Naum Trajanovski, Emina Zoletic, Arban Mehmeti, Ema Dzananovic and Karolina Bielenin-Lenczowska. Last but not least, I thank Maggie, my parents, my sister, Fabiana, and other family members – all silent and patient supporters of my academic endeavours.

# Introduction

In the wake of the events of 9/11, descendants of Muslim families born and raised in Western societies have been pressured to comply with secularism and praise religious tolerance. Many still cause alarm due to the geopolitical upheavals across the Muslim world that reverberate throughout Europe, fuelling domestic radicalisation and often overshadowing the positive stories of integration and interfaith dialogue. Yet a generation born to Muslim families seems to be winning people's hearts. Dua Lipa and Rita Ora, both born to Albanian Muslim families who fled Kosovo, packed stadiums for their concerts. Sharing a similar family heritage, Xherdan Shaqiri led the Swiss national team in the football World Cup as no one else had before. Far from celebrity lounges, Jasmina Hostert and Adis Ahmetović, whose parents escaped war-torn Bosnia and Herzegovina in the 1990s, belong to a new generation of politicians in the German Bundestag.[1] Their Muslim heritage remains barely acknowledged, perhaps not fitting the expectation of how Muslims (should) look. Even when some fell victim to labour exploitation, right-wing terrorism and deadly attacks that Muslims themselves perpetrated, their memories were soon consigned to oblivion. The stories of Refat Süleyman, a 26-year-old migrant worker from Bulgaria whose body was found in a designated safety zone servicing toxic waste in Duisburg, as well as that of the victims of the Hanau shootings in 2020, are instructive.[2]

1 In an article published by *The Guardian*, Laura Snapes (2020) describes Dua Lupa's family as Muslim. Safiya Rahman (2023) mentions Dua Lipa's positive review of Riz Ahmed's attempt to improve how Muslims are depicted in movies. Rita Ora's father is a nominal Muslim, and she considers herself a spiritual person. Stephan Uersfeld (2014), Germany correspondent for ESPN, reported that Switzerland's Muslim players like Xherdan Shaqiri, Granit Xhaka and Valon Behrami announced they would not observe Ramadan during the world football championship. In 2021, 24 elected MPs in the German Parliament have Balkan roots. Among them, Jasmina Hostert, who arrived in Germany after being seriously injured during the war in Bosnia, supported the women's struggle against the Iranian Ayatollah's regime (Buyuk and Sinoruka 2021). Likewise, Adis Ahmetović (2021) has actively promoted interfaith dialogue and religious tolerance at the Sami Mosque in Hanover.

2 On February 19, 2020, a racist and right-extremist attack in Hanau took the lives of nine young people, mainly migrants or with migration backgrounds. A few months later, in Vienna

DOI: 10.4324/9781003589624-1

In 2022, Russia's full-scale invasion of Ukraine assumed an inevitable position in political discourse and almost systematically replaced general concerns over the epidemiological crisis. When both events came to dominate headlines and the public debate, Islamophobia seemed to disappear in a puff of smoke. In contrast, a new wave of anti-Muslim sentiment re-emerged from the depths of Western societies after the ensuing terrorist attacks in Paris and Vienna in 2020. The viral footage of the Kremlin-backed Chechen troops deployed in Ukraine and the US's abrupt withdrawal from Afghanistan in 2022 stoked worldwide fear. A point of no return was marked on October 7, 2023, when Hamas's attacks against Jewish civilians brought most Western states to label any manifestation in support of Palestine as colluding with terrorism and anti-Semitism. Before that series of events, however, an all-encompassing discourse over Islam and Muslims had already put security experts on alert. Muslims in and from the Balkans gained attention due to the more than 500 militants who had gone to Syria to join the Islamic State (IS) and the *jihad*. That unending din referred to a long list of events reportedly involving Balkan Muslim radicals, such as the case of the first suicide bomber originally from Kosovo who killed 50 people in March 2014 in Baghdad (Bardos 2014:78). Other pundits referred less alarmingly to the Balkan type of Islam, one that should and could be identified as an exceptional version of Islam after having allegedly developed its own Islamist threats in Yugoslavia during the 1980s (Rexhepi 2017:52).

Although Islam has been part and parcel of European history, heritage and politics, the Western extension of coloniality has reduced indigenous Muslims to a kind of separate ontological category. New speculations about the rise of cultural conflicts were fuelled by residual racism that classified all Muslims the same in both the scientific field and on the grounds of public discourse (Bobako 2015:44). The pitfall of this monoculturalist discourse did not only come to mask the strikingly multifaceted historical heterogeneity of Islam across Europe (Cesari 2003), but also affected multiculturalists in advocating the accommodation of Muslim cultures as homogenous entities in their own right (Grünenberg 2005:177), and distorting the idea of Muslims from Bulgaria, Romania and the former Yugoslavia's sense of belonging. Paradoxically, they do not come from Europe, Morocco, Türkiye or Pakistan, but "from Islam" (Finkelstein 2023:10). Their religion sets them apart of Europe and, like when "Negro" and "Jew" were the favoured names for Europe's terrifying subjects, today they have other names associated with them: Arabs, the foreigners, the immigrants, the refugees, or simply the intruders (Mbembe 2019:43).

on November 2, 2020, victims and perpetrators of a terrorist attack shared their ethnic and national belonging. Two of the four victims were a 21-year-old Austrian Muslim originally from North Macedonia and a police officer originally from Kosovo. At the same time, Kujtim Fejzullah, the perpetrator, had Albanian origins from North Macedonia.

This misconception became ubiquitous during the 2015 "refugee crisis". Throughout the so-called "Balkan corridor" and beyond, categories of "immigrant" and "Muslimness" overlapped, and mechanisms of othering lumped newcomers from the Middle East with local Muslims (Roy and Elbasani 2015; Jezernik 2004). In Central Europe, a magnitude of Islamophobic attitudes penetrated core societies with no Muslims or with a tiny Muslim population (Pickel and Öztürk 2018), while campaigns in "the West" for more recognition of diversity and cultural rights were limited regarding Muslims (Canan and Foroutan 2016). Young Muslims born and bred in Western Europe from émigré families who had fled the war-torn or economically exploited Balkan region, continued to grapple with what people "say" and "think" about Islam. Regardless of what they had "gone through", they have remained the "European Others" (El Tayeb 2017). Despite living for decades in the same neighbourhoods and occupying similar job positions with other coreligionists (Bougarel and Mihaylova 2005:10; Bougarel 2008:159), they keep their distance from the latter, lest they be misrecognised and associated with other radical Muslims. They often yearn to present themselves as innocent victims of radical Islam (Rexhepi 2023:67) in the hope of counteracting the media discourse that has lumped their moderate, secular and non-radical Islam with that of more radical Muslims from the Middle East and North Africa (Mark et al. 2019:169).

The bulk of this book is not devoted to Balkan Muslims in general, nor does it offer a new perspective on the legacies of so-called "European Islam". It is not about Islamophobia, either. Rather, it explores what happened to the generation born and raised after socialism outside the Balkans, and what is currently happening to this generation after their parents and communities experienced displacement, war and painstaking integration into a "host society". As members of the post-migrant, often post-war and surely post-socialist generation, how do they nurture the unchanging universal core values of Islam and their fallible interpretations in contemporary post-secular societies? How do they hold, care and perform civic responsibility and active citizenship to respond to the anti-Muslim rhetoric embedded in the official discourse of institutions and representatives of their countries? As young Muslim Europeans with migration backgrounds, do they experience "otherness" at the grassroots level? If so, how? What about their connection with the Balkans and the *ummah* worldwide?

All these queries show taxing efforts to employ the right vocabulary without reinforcing stereotypes, markers of non-identity and non-belonging, and also certain privileges among the groups under study. Some scholars employ academic yet dichotomous jargon, often too culturalist, which reinforces different racialised categories. In part, this is a consequence of attempting to untangle Muslims – *from* and *in* the Balkans – from nesting orientalisms (Bakić-Hayden 1995) via a certain language of modernity and progress in which academic endeavours (mostly Western) are cloaked. Against this backdrop, this study refers to the groups under study as "young Muslims with

Balkan family heritage", or, alternatively, "Muslims of Balkan origin", rather than "second-generation Balkan Muslims". By definition, "second generation" is widely used in migration studies to refer to those people born in a different country than their parents. Yet it also obscures the diversity that exists within this broad term, such as the specific experiences and positions of 1.5 generations – namely, those who experienced war and displacement in their birthplace and whose predicament in the "host country" has been unfairly overlooked (Müller-Suleymanova 2024:265). Moreover, "second generation" reinforces a signifier of non-belonging to the national community and lived citizenship (Riniolo and Toivanen 2023:302), thereby mulling over the integration of "secondos" (Ferizaj 2019:81). Such a definition also implies an invisible divide between (white) Europeans and former migrant communities (of colour), which unsurprisingly makes most Muslims feel excluded in northwest Europe (El-Tayeb 2001). Granted, the primary goal is to move beyond the hidden flaw of Westernised academia and its coloniality, which positions Muslims *in* and *from* the Balkans exclusively along post-Ottoman and/or post-socialist spatio-temporalities and related majority-minority dynamics. Inspired by scholars like Asad Talal, Piro Rexhepi, Monika Bobako, Xavier Bougarel and Maria Merdjanova, among others, the core idea behind this book is to refute the hegemonic discourse on European *demos* by integrating this generation of young Muslims of Balkan origin as one of the *demois* that constitute the base of European *demoi-cracy* (Schmidt 2005). Their family (hi)stories and related post-memories, as well as the wealth of political sensitivities and unharvested practices of participation and activism, serve to uncover the many contradictions and challenges of "being Muslim" while carving out a legitimate space within the democratic arena. Through the lens of daily identity dilemmas and horizontal relations of continuous cultural negotiations, this study conceives the idea of comparing uneasy and sometimes contradictory post-socialist and post-colonial trajectories as a means of contributing to the much richer scholarship that explores the (under)developments of European Muslims' civic actorness and religious salience in a time of rampant Islamophobia.

Even though combining rioters and Islamists, folk Muslims and fundamentalists, pietists and jihadis, and immigrants from the Global South with their children is a method of strategic incoherence (Leiken 2012:xiv), this study investigates those who are alienated from politics from those who are not, those who might be associated with, at least in theory, the *ummah* from those who, in practice, keep themselves away from other coreligionists. It does so by examining (sub)urban dynamics where "Muslimness" heightens a sense of belonging and religious salience. The choice to look at these potential transnational entanglements (or lack thereof) is made in an attempt to explore political sensitivities and responses to the current nativist discourse, without reinforcing the nesting variants of the Christian/Muslim dichotomy and its replications of East/West and Balkans/Europe divisions (Bakić-Hayden 1995:931). Consequently, this book aims to mend the sociopolitical and historical caesura between Islam and Balkan Muslims by scrutinizing how this potentially disenfranchised generation of young Muslims with Balkan roots has a stake in their localities and construct postulates of solidarity and respect with other same-age peers, coreligionists and the rest of the core society.

## Overview of the Chapters

The book's analysis and overall argument are developed in seven relatively self-contained chapters. After this introduction, Chapter 1 is devoted to the research approach and the methodology through which the study has been carried out. It develops into smaller descriptive sections that discuss issues of approachability and positionality during the fieldwork, along with a detailed description of the groups under study, the data and information collected, and the four countries this book focuses on.

Chapter 2 examines the urban-nuanced relations between respondents and "the rest" of the *ummah* – namely, the global Muslim community. It consists of two sections. Firstly, a historical overview of Balkan Islam and its *ulema* (Muslim scholars), which, secondly, facilitates an understanding of the different relations and disruptions between young Muslims with Balkan family heritage and other coreligionists from the Middle East and North Africa. Looking at the entanglements of spatial issues with broader political and cultural questions, this chapter addresses "whiteness" and global in/justice as verbalised and discussed during the in-depth interviews. Hence, it explores how the legacies of Balkan Islam restrain or activate religious salience and occasionally heighten the latter due to more sensitive topics such as the "Palestinian Question" and Islamophobia.

Inspired by Marianne Hirsch's work (2012), Chapter 3 focuses on the mnemonic predicament of the *generation after* – meaning, how these young Muslims recollect their parents' experiences of forced migration, war and integration. Throughout, a twofold perspective emerges: first, many associate the current atmosphere of rampant nationalism/populism in Europe with the (hi)stories passed down in their family circle from the time of Yugoslavia and state socialism. Second, they reflect on the most recent geopolitical upheavals in the Middle East and Ukraine, empathising with those refugees who arrived and were welcomed in their places of residence. In doing so, the chapter intercepts how interviewees assess, criticise and complain about the Western solidarity campaigns for newcomers – Ukrainians in particular.

Since this *generation after* began grappling with new national identities and citizenship regimes unlike their parents, Chapter 4 draws on the extensive literature regarding belonging to explore the sense of closeness/remoteness to the Balkans. If the studies on diaspora primarily focused on attachment to the former home and the fantasy of return, this chapter shifts the angle of observation. Based on data and knowledge collected and constructed with(in) small family groups originally from Bosnia and North Macedonia, this chapter sheds light on the extent to which respondents act out a sense of belonging to their countries of birth, i.e. Belgium and Germany, respectively. It precisely investigates how they nurture national identity and citizenship in the cities of Antwerp and Dortmund. From this intra-family perspective, findings permit us to discuss the paradox at the heart of belonging: a condition caused by a sense of unfamiliarity with the parental country of origin and by a sense of liminality for being unrecognised as "full nationals" in Belgium and Germany because of their migration heritage and Muslimness.

Chapter 5 begins with Alija Izetbegović's question, "How far are we Muslims?" (1990:17). The latter is not taken into consideration to mull over religious salience in relation to family-laden beliefs, rituals and religious practices in general. Izetbegović's inquiry is critically introduced to qualify respondents as members of "postmodern epistemic communities" (Sandal 2011). As a follow-up to Chapter 2, most respondents acknowledge modernity while relying on human spirituality, relating themselves to the outside world without being alienated. Therefore, the focus of this chapter is on how young Muslims of Balkan origin are ethically bound to the most critical question of *halal* or *haram* – literally, allowed or prohibited? Everyday life is here the realm of investigation. In it, the religiosity of the young respondents is discussed vis-à-vis a vast array of post-modern identity dilemmas that many grapple with in their place of residence.

Although Chapters 2 and 5 show that Balkan Muslim communities have quickly developed institutions of sociability and solidarity once becoming settled in "the West". Chapter 6 shows how even a moderate and secular Islam has not been sufficient to protect their communities from a climate of hate and hostility. Hence, this chapter investigates how groups of young Muslims under study nurture political participation and (attempt to) counter the widespread misconceptions that declare their role and contributions to democracy null and void. Then, it looks at how post-migrant situatedness and Muslimness can stimulate unconventional and non-institutional political participation on a city level. Bearing also upon Chapter 3, findings here allow for a better discussion of how this *generation after* shares a sense of remoteness with the rest of the *ummah* that often heightens the political atmosphere within specific neighbourhoods. Thus, this chapter uncovers a system of values and practices that facilitate the groups under study to align with the "Western", "liberal" and "secular" values of "being Muslim" in Europe.

Throughout the book, "the city" is identified as an everyday space where anti-migration discourse and Islamophobia are not simply present but also verbalised to target Muslim dwellers. Drawing on Antonio Gramsci's paradox of "cities of silence" (Urbinati 1998), Chapter 7 unveils a series of inconspicuous yet present dynamics in the Muslim-majority neighbourhoods of the cities under observation. Placing the voices of interviewees at the forefront, this chapter advances the paradigm of "city/zens of silence" to explain how the political demands and claims of these young Muslims remain subaltern to the much larger and better-established Muslim diaspora originally from Türkiye and the Global South. To conclude, this chapter explores modes of negotiating two (or more) identities of "being Muslim", deeply embedded within a constantly evolving urban fabric that is driven by gentrification.

## References

Ahmetović, A. (2021) Podiumsdiskussion in der Sami-Moschee: “Wir müssen mit allen Religionsgemeinschaften im Dialog sein” [Panel Discussion in the Sami Mosque: “We Have to Be in Dialogue with All Religious Communities], *SPD*. Available at: https://adis-ahmetovic.de/meldungen/podiumsdiskussion-in-der-sami-moschee-wir-muessen-mit-allen-religionsgemeinschaften-im-dialog-sein (Accessed: 6 March 2023).

Bakić-Hayden, M. (1995) Nesting Orientalisms: The Case of Former Yugoslavia. *Slavic Review*, 54 (4), pp. 917–931. https://doi.org/10.2307/2501399

Bardos, N. G. (2014) Jihad in the Balkans: The Next Generation. *World Affairs*, 177 (3), pp. 73–79.

Bobako, M. (2015) Inventing Muslims in Europe. Religion, Culture and Identity in the Time of Neoliberalism. *Przegląd Religioznawczy – The Religious Studies Review*, 4 (258), pp. 43–55.

Bougarel, X. (2008) ‘Balkan Muslim Diasporas and the Idea of a “European Islam”’, in R. Kostić, T. Dulić, I. Maček, and J. Trtak (eds.) *Balkan Currents. Essays in Honour of Kjell Magnusson*. Uppsala: Uppsala University Press, pp. 147–165.

Bougarel, X. and Mihaylova, D. (2005) Diasporas musulmanes balkaniques dans l’Union européenne [Balkan Muslim Diaspora in the European Union]. *Balkanologie – Revue d’études pluridisciplinaires*, IX (1–2), pp. 59–211. https://doi.org/10.4000/balkanologie.577

Buyuk, H. F. and Sinoruka, F. (2021) German Parliament Gets 24 New MPs with Balkan Roots, *Balkan Insights*. Available at: https://balkaninsight.com/2021/09/27/german-parliament-gets-24-new-mps-with-balkan-roots/ (Accessed: 2 October 2022).

Canan, C. and Foroutan, N. (2016) The Paradox of Equal Belonging of Muslims. *Islamophobia Studies Journal*, 3 (2), pp. 160–176. http://dx.doi.org/10.18452/22484

Cesari, J. (2003) ‘Muslim Minorities in Europe: The Silent Revolution’, in J. Esposito and F. Burgat (eds.) *Modernizing Islam: Religion in the Public Sphere in the Middle East and Europe*. New Brunswick: Rutgers University Press, pp. 251–271.

El-Tayeb, F. (2001) *European Others: Queering Ethnicity in Postnational Europe*. Minneapolis: University of Minnesota Press.

El-Tayeb, F. (2017) European Others, *Eurozine*. Available at: www.eurozine.com/european-others/ (Accessed: 20 December 2021).

Ferizaj, A. (2019) Othering Albanian Muslim Masculinities: A Case Study of Albanian Football Players. *OCCHIALÌ – Rivista sul Mediterraneo Islamico*, 5, pp. 71–93.

Finkelstein, K. (2023) *Moderne Muslimas – Kindheit – Karriere – Klischees* [Modern Muslim Women – Childhood – Carries – Stereotypes]. Berlin: Verlagshaus Jacoby & Stuart.

Grünenberg, K. (2005) Constructing “Sameness” and “Otherness”: Bosnian Diasporic Experiences in a Danish Context. *Balkanologie*, IX (1–2), pp. 173–193. https://doi.org/10.4000/balkanologie.587.

Hirsch, M. (2012) *The Generation of Postmemory. Writing and Visual Culture after the Holocaust*. New York: Columbia University Press.

Izetbegović, A. (1990) *Islamic Declaration*. Available at: https://archive.org/details/3IslamicDeclarationEng/mode/2up?view=theater (Accessed: 3 January 2023).

Jezernik, B. (2004) *Wild Europe: The Balkans in the Gaze of Western Travellers*. London: Al Saqi.

Leiken, R. (2012) *Europe’s Angry Muslims: The Revolt of the Second Generation*. Oxford: Oxford University Press.

Mark, J., Iacob, B., Rupprecht, T. and Spaskovska, L. (2019) *1989. A Global History of Eastern Europe*. Cambridge: Cambridge University Press.

Mbembe, A. (2019) *Necropolitics*. Durham: Duke University Press.

Müller-Suleymanova, D. (2024) Remembering the Dealing with Violent Past: Diasporic Experiences and Transnational Dimensions. *Ethnic and Racial Studies*, 47 (2), pp. 259–273. https://doi.org/10.1080/01419870.2023.2260882

Pickel, G. and Öztürk, C. (2018) Islamophobia Without Muslims? The "Contact Hypothesis" as an Explanation for Anti-Muslim Attitudes – Eastern European Societies in a Comparative Perspective. *Journal of Nationalism, Memory & Language Politics*, 12 (2), pp. 162–191. https://doi.org/10.2478/jnmlp-2018-0009

Rahman, S. (2023) Is Singer Dua Lipa Muslim? *Crescent Days*. Available at: https://crescentdays.com/blogs/celebrity-muslims/is-dua-lipa-muslim (Accessed: 5 March 2023).

Rexhepi, P. (2017) 'Unmapping Islam in Eastern Europe Periodization and Muslim Subjectivities in the Balkans', in I. Kacandes and Y. Komska (eds.) *Eastern Europe Unmapped. Beyond Borders and Peripheries*. New York and Oxford: Berghahn Books, pp. 53–77.

Rexhepi, P. (2023) *White Enclosures. Racial Capitalism & Coloniality along the Balkan Route*. Durham: Duke University Press.

Riniolo, V. and Toivanen, M. (2023) Future Paths in the Study of Migrant Descendants' Citizenship: Engaging with Critical Literature. *Migration Letters*, 20 (2), pp. 301–311. https://doi.org/10.59670/ml.v20i2.2890

Roy, O. and Elbasani, A. (2015) *The Revival of Islam in the Balkans: From Identity to Religiosity*. New York: Springer.

Sandal, N. A. (2011) Religious Actors as Epistemic Communities in Conflict Transformation: The Cases of South Africa and Northern Ireland. *Review of International Studies*, 37 (3), pp. 929–949.

Schmidt, V. A. (2005) Democracy in Europe: The Impact of European Integration. *Perspectives on Politics*, 3 (4), pp. 761–779. https://doi.org/10.1017/S1537592705050437

Snapes, L. (2020) Interview. Dua Lipa: 'You Have to Be Made of Steel Not to Let Words Get to You', *The Guardian*. Available at: www.theguardian.com/music/2020/apr/03/dua-lipa-you-have-to-be-made-of-steel-to-not-let-words-get-to-you (Accessed: 5 March 2023).

Uersfeld, S. (2014) Players Take Ramadan Traveling Exemption, *ESPN*. Available at: www.espn.com/soccer/story/_/id/37370376/mesut-ozil-muslim-footballers-forego-ramadan-2014-world-cup (Accessed: 5 March 2023).

Urbinati, N. (1998) From the Periphery of Modernity: Antonio Gramsci's Theory of Subordination and Hegemony. *Political Theory*, 26 (3), pp. 370–391.

# 1 Being (with) the Other

To start, a vignette. While interviewing Jonas, the son of a German and a Bosnian Muslima, the question of belonging was problematised in this manner:

> "As a researcher myself, my name does not ring a bell. At first, my supervisors and colleagues were taken by surprise by my considerable knowledge and interest in the Balkans and my habitual trips to Bosnia, *as if* a person with a German-sounding name could not fit the profile of those Balkan experts whose names and looks were congruent with their research on the region. Their names and the languages they speak help the academic community to relate them with their personal stories and situatedness at the time of the research. This does not happen to me".

Throughout the fieldwork, a few agreed with Jonas's words. Their comments made me think of my positionality while being (with) "the others" on the ground. As neither a Muslim nor a researcher with Balkan heritage, I have often been in Jonas's shoes. After being invited to an *iftar* evening organised by dozens of young Muslims with Bosnian roots at their local mosque in Antwerp, one asked me: "Did you fast today?" Once inside, a young man enquired: "Are you Muslim?" Both answers in the negative were welcomed with a genuine smile and a wish: "Not yet, *inshallah*!"

In retrospect, my personal history has undoubtedly shaped my research interests over time. Born and raised in Agrigento, Italy's southernmost coastline in Sicily, with some family ties with the Arbëreshë community of Piana degli Albanesi (in Albanian, *Hora e Arbëreshëvet*), my upbringing was deeply influenced by living with newcomers from Arab countries who had settled down on the island. At the same time, I saw friends and family members leaving my hometown due to a shortage of opportunities and later struggling to adapt somewhere else. Some managed to return home, whereas many decided to settle elsewhere. All of these have stirred in me a deep passion for the fields of contested identities, borderlands and multiculturalism in general. As a student I was also influenced by postcolonial studies and critical theory, especially in relation to the political problems of the postsocialist predicament and

DOI: 10.4324/9781003589624-2

democratisation in South-Eastern European peripheries. As a philosopher by degree, my desire and commitment to conduct ethnographic research brought me to ponder my positionality. The latter has always been key in relation to studying "the other" (Abu-Lughod 1996) while being myself "the other" in active sites of engagement (Todd 2014:217). I have always been aware of holding a particular, and somewhat ambiguous, position "out there". While I always escape from the danger of "being too close" to the groups under my studies (Hromadžić 2023), my positionality has deepened a sense of distrust and confusion toward me and what I was up to, often reinforcing certain stereotypes about the male, white, straight, Western-looking researcher taking the risk of "going native".

This study has not been an exception. Building trust with potential interviewees was sometimes a stumbling block, especially when highly sensitive topics overlapping with personal stories were touched upon. While I was often asked whether I worked for the government or any other institution, body or agency, speaking the languages of my potential interlocutors brought the latter to be suspicious of me and my questions. My social capital, to borrow a sociological term here, enabled me to hold interviews after building a relationship with young Muslims with Balkan family heritage, who often have a high level of education and a critical ability to reflect on Islam in different ways than the older generations.

Granted, I knowingly designed the research methodology by bearing in mind the potential pitfalls and shortcomings that I could face. In being (with) the other, my ultimate goal was not simply to build upon a basic, affirmative task and let the unheard and unnoticed voices of young Muslims speak or be heard. Nor did I intend to simply describe the heterogeneity of second-generation Balkan Muslims, to write about their multiple intersecting dependencies and entanglements with the previous generations or other communities. Methodologically, all of the fieldwork was carried out by conceiving the idea that Balkan Muslims would neither reflect a segment of socio-cultural homogeneity nor hold multiple standpoint epistemologies that are inevitably in explicit conflict with another actor (Angrosino 2007:11). Against the potential pitfall of conflating this *generation after* with any quasi-imperial, ideological or economic paradigm (Rexhepi 2023), I instead assumed that the groups under study would share similar opinions and actions with other descendants of Muslim families from Africa, Asia and the Middle East in "the West". The scope was not to lump the latter with the former, but rather to explore whether phenomena regarding Muslims *in* and *from* the Balkans are really as they seem, and, eventually, explicitly challenge traditional assumptions regarding the role of young Muslims in consolidated liberal democracies. To do so, the whole research is based around a "strategic heterogeneity" approach to collect information during participation-observation, construct knowledge about minor and unclear nuances from in-depth interviews, and thereby detect potential changes from as many different perspectives as possible.

**Working in the Field**

To begin with, it should be said that this study is the result of mix-method qualitative research carried out over the course of a year, precisely between October 2022 and November 2023, in Italy (November-December 2022), Belgium (February-April 2023), Germany (May and June, 2023) and Poland (October-November 2023). Throughout, these countries were visited and in-depth interviews were also conducted. Respectively, the fieldwork was carried out in Piacenza and Biella, Antwerp and Ghent, Bremen and Dortmund, Warsaw and Toruń. All these cities were deliberately visited to relate their spatial networks to the uneven distributions of power (King 2004:89), and to explore how Islamophobia manifested itself in an emotional and spatial sense in the groups under study. Hence, I gained better knowledge and first-hand information through directly listening to their voices, observing in which language concerns were being verbalised, what kind of encounters and relations were being experienced in their everyday life, who was worshiping at the local mosque, and so forth.

The tandem of participant-observation and interviews was deemed crucial to pre-empt unnecessary ethnicisation *from the outside* so as to then investigate community-related expectations, sensitivities and concerns *from below* (Millar 2018). This emic approach is part of an ethnographic sensibility approach (Simmons and Smith 2017) considered best to investigate specific issues empirically. In this regard, the latter needs further justification. Although "ethnography" literally means a "description of a people" (Angrosino 2007:1), an ethnographic sensibility relies on a "true anthropology", which, to paraphrase Georges Didi-Huberman's words (2016:81), seeks to look, listen, write and even renounce the apodictic claims of the metaphysical school in order to move beyond the "jargon of identities" and address questions of values, viewpoints and sensibilities. Following Talal Asad (2003:17), anthropology is not only about a method, nor about providing a pseudoscientific notion of fieldwork. For the purpose of this study, the fieldwork was organised around listening and relating to people who live and grapple with common issues (Hromadžić 2023:4), and not employed as a kind of intellectual effort aiming to elaborate a "thick description" of and about humanity in a context subjected to law (Geertz 1973:6; Pader 2006; Schatz 2009). On the contrary, the whole research method was tailored to what was studied by shining a spotlight on each community's views of reality (Given 2008), and scrutinizing a series of concerns, interests, commitments, ways of thinking and practices of Islam, later comparing them with synchronic and similar outcomes already discussed in literature.

In other words, this ethnographic sensibility unravels those forces that rupture the boundaries of one's own taken-for-granted world (McGranahan 2018) and capture interesting perspectives from the social structure of a given society (Fort 2022:350). It was employed because of the lack of "hard" and "thick" data about this generation of young Muslims whose voices, sensitivities and everyday worries are often overshadowed either by the much larger diaspora groups in "the West" or by their own community representatives, political authorities and older generations in general. In fact, the fieldwork was conducted with the idea that only in the field can one truly encounter the dynamics of lived human experiences (Angrosino 2007:2) and look at the existing constellation of historical evidence and ethnographic accounts. Since the adoption of an ethnographic sensibility did not require a long-term immersion in the field to exert control over a number of identified variables (Simmons and Smith 2017:126), in-depth interviews and participation-observation were carried out to explore a complex web of issues unclear to the naked eye. Intercepting elements of heterogeneity from the groups under study vis-à-vis a wealth of reproductions of preconceived definitions of "Muslimness" and "Islam" was of particular importance to refer to experiences or/and self-perceptions of "being Muslim in the West" beyond the specific boundaries of class, social group, ethnicity, educational background and so forth (Sofos and Tsagarousianou 2013:84). Hence, I attempted to turn the angle of investigation from "*how ethno-religious identities are performed and constructed in everyday life*" to "*how a variety of moral-ethical identity dilemmas contribute to revive, engage and/or constrict religious salience and activate political sensitivities that, in turn, motivate postulates of tolerance, responsibility and solidarity*". During the fieldwork, only a "thick involvement" – meaning an active positioning, would allow me to concentrate attention on a wide range of concerns, interests, commitments, emotions and social relationships beyond their surface attributes (Angrosino 2007:16), thereby separating the study from capitalist, patriarchal and Western-centric habits of thinking and seeing (Puig de la Bellacasa 2011:96).

Nonetheless, my positionality came under question yet again. While in the course of fieldwork, I knew that some observational techniques could appear obstructive and provoke discomfort among those who knew they were being observed (Angrosino 2007:38). I was also aware that being (with) the other could not happen without informing my potential respondents in advance about the purpose of my visit, and without having their consent about being participants in my research. Thus, in-depth interviews were organised and conducted through the snowball method. Among a previously established network of scholars and friends, who often played the role of gatekeepers to facilitate breaking the ice with potential respondents, I managed to establish a sufficient level of trust to receive invitations to visit cultural centres, local mosques and religious organisations. As a result, participation-observation was carried out only upon mutual agreement. Before attending *iftar* during Ramadan in Antwerp, for example, the youth organisation (in Bosnian, *Mreža Mladih*) was informed in advance about my research and agreed on having me among them. Similar dynamics happened in the Albanian and Bosnian mosques of Bremen, where the *hodzha* asked his students' permission to have me during Qur'anic classes on the weekend. Other public initiatives and commemoration events were attended, such as the "peace march" in memory of the 1995 Srebrenica Genocide in Dortmund, and recreational activities at the mosque in Warsaw. When a potential respondent voluntarily accepted to participate in an in-depth interview, the latter was held as a one-off conversation to avoid double-reporting (Ahern 2014:3) and was conducted in a safe and familiar environment. Some other colloquial dialogues were also occasionally held with other family members and/or friends during recreational time, especially among young Muslims whose families originally from Bulgaria (See Chapter 6 and 7).

Each in-depth interview was guided by a semi-structured and theme-guided questionnaire, whose specific topics and questions were in briefly laid out in advance to the interviewee. Prior to beginning with the interview, a Participation Information Sheet (PIS) and an Interview Consent Form (ICF) was also provided. While the latter was not signed as a matter of trust, the former was always carefully read and discussed in detail. Here, respondents were assured and made aware of their right to remain anonymous, withdraw at any time and receive the transcripts of the oral conversation a few days after the interview. The latter was often taped with a recording device only after receiving permission from the same respondent. In a few cases, some other personal comments and reflections were verbalised via other means of communication, such as social media and email exchanges. In addition, it should be pointed out that data were also collected through an online questionnaire comprised of openly and flexibly formulated questions that had been raised during the in-depth interviews. This was done for avoiding male-centric results. As a male researcher and an outsider to Balkan Muslim communities, setting up in-depth interviews with young female Muslims could potentially infringe the ethics of approachability. Also, mosques and religious sites are usually physically divided spaces along heteronormative gender lines, and often dominated by hegemonic male norms (Mushaben 2008:516). The online questionnaire was a more accessible means to grant participation and capture the specific needs and experiences that Muslim women may have in comparison with Muslim men (Azabar and Van Aelst 2023; Rippin 2001). Hence, participation was granted online at the convenience of female interviewees in order to guarantee a non-threatening and safe space – both in a physical and emotional sense (Mayorga-Gallo and Hordge-Freeman 2017:381).

Of the total number of interviews (n=120), the large majority were conducted with members of the *generation after* (n=72) who were found to be holding at least a bachelor's degree, or pursuing other certifications in a wealth of disciplines. Others were instead employed in different sectors, from academia to civil society organisations, from IT to the third sector, and so forth. At the time of the interviews, respondents were residents of Belgium, Germany, Poland and Italy, and their parents were originally from Albania, Kosovo, Bosnia and Herzegovina, Bulgaria, North Macedonia and Sandžak, a historically Muslim-majority region between today's Serbia and Montenegro. They were found to be between 19 and 38 years of age. A number of 42 was male and 29 was female, while only one respondent with Albanian roots, who was born in Belgium, self-identified as a member of the LGBT community. Among them, many were found engaged in volunteering in youth associations, cultural centres and local mosques in their place of residence. In some cases, I was able to establish at least a first contact and hold interviews with Muslims from Bulgaria of Roma and Turkish origin in Bulgarian. Italian was used for those born and raised in Italy since the early 1990s, while English was mostly and largely used in Belgium and Germany. Both the education profile and personal aspirations were important factors as critical perspectives and in-depth knowledge of Islam and socio-political dynamics do not align with the typically marginalised positions usually ascribed to post-migrant Muslim communities in "the West".

The rest of the respondents constituted NGO practitioners and scholars, as well as some parents of the generation under study. The rationale behind holding an interview with the latter group (n=32) was twofold: first, a few who expressed their interest in participating in the study were found to be underage; hence, their parents (especially fathers) could provide sobering perspectives as being at the same time the local imam, the *hodža* or the community representatives. NGO practitioners and scholars (n=16) were instead occasionally asked for a colloquial discussion since they themselves worked closely with Muslim communities in the four different urban contexts. Their shifted perspectives have also contributed to gathering information and triangulating data when possible.

As briefly introduced, in-depth interviews were guided by a semi-structured and theme-guided questionnaire consisting of open research questions. Overall, each interview lasted about one hour, and revolved around three main themes of conversation, as follows:

1) How does the *generation after* grapple with the legacies of migration and religious identity in their everyday life? Hence, how do members of this post-migrant generation feel about their place of birth and their parental country of origin?

   This twofold question was posed to scrutinise the degree of respondent's awareness of Europe's misrecognition of the history of Islam and indigenous Muslims through the lens of family (hi)stories and potential transmission of knowledge that would heighten a sense of belonging to (or unfamiliarity with) the Balkans. In this first part of the interview, the main goal was to detect whether personal identity dilemmas and/or quotidian practices could stem from past family traumas related to wartime, the assimilation campaign during late socialism, or from the long-lasting legacies of (forced) migration, labour exploitation and experiences of (or the lack thereof) integration in "the West".
2) How does the *generation after* participate in the political life of their place of residence?

   This very general question invited the interviewee to think of any sort of political participation or civic engagement in the public sphere. The main scope was to investigate how personal opinions and value-judgements about the political climate of hate and hostility toward Muslims and Islam were verbalised in response to phenomena of Islamophobia and political violence, and how this tandem may foster political participation and/or everyday practices in the democratic arena. Simply put, this second part was aimed at investigating how interviewees would occasionally position themselves between three (or even more) seemingly competing and overlapping situations: for instance, being born and/or raised in a country different from their parental country of origin, from where local/regional cultures are replicated and passed down, while being a young Muslim and living in a postmodern and secular society where personal ideas can be easily contested, among others. Moreover, normative elements of rights and the (dual) citizenship regime were discussed along with the evolution of political institutions and the current crisis of consolidated liberal democracies.

3) How does (Balkan) Islam guide the everyday life of the groups under study vis-à-vis the current crisis of liberal democracy and multiculturalism? If at all, to what extent do Muslimness and religious salience diverge from, or conform with, the rest of Muslim communities living in "the West" in response to Islamophobia and far-right violence?

This twofold question did not aim at assessing the level of religious salience of the respondents and writing about it. In contrast, it focused on exploring the personal attachment (or lack thereof) to a religious family background and/or the potential disagreements across generations, space and time. When transnational and trans-peripheral entanglements with other post-migrant same-age coreligionists were verbalised, this last open question was used to investigate how, and to what extent, young Muslims of Balkan origin hold, nurture or even refuse to establish postulates of solidarity and forms of cooperation with the rest of the *ummah* in and beyond their place of residence.

During these three moments of the in-depth interviews, opinions and perspectives were weighted according to existing literature and complementary data. To do so, however, a countless variety of potential nuances and epistemologies were considered in preparation for in-depth interviews. To capture the grey areas that might be missed on the surface (Angrosino 2007:43), each in-depth interview was adjusted to the ethnic, national and migration background of the potential respondent. Unless otherwise noted throughout the text, only gender, age and the place of residence are revealed due to the highly sensitive and personal opinions discussed during interviews in specific urban contexts. For example: "Female respondent, 27 y/o, Antwerp" (see Chapter 4). This data minimisation was also conducted along with pseudonymisation for those cases where ethnographic accounts could not be omitted, hence cited otherwise. In this manner, each respondent's personal identity and his/her/their community was fully protected, and any risk regarding identity disclosure avoided. When interviews were conducted in languages other than English, all translations and transcriptions of interview insights are my own.

## Multiple Embodiments

To add another layer of complexity, a note on the definition of "Muslimness" and its polysemy is paramount to lay out. Before initiating the fieldwork, I took into consideration the possibility of reaching out to, and meeting up with, Turkish-speaking Muslims originally from Bulgaria and/or Romania; Slavic-speaking Muslims who self-identified as Bosnian or Bosniaks from Bosnia and Sandžak; members of Gorani, Torberesh and Pomak groups originally from Kosovo, North Macedonia and Bulgaria, respectively; Albanian-speaking Muslims with parents originally from North Macedonia, Kosovo and Albania.

Spyros Sofos and Roza Tsagorousianou argue that talking about *European Muslims* as a meaningful category of inquiry, requires guidance through the murky waters of political wrangling inspired by different agendas among various community activists, policymakers and politicians (2013:66). While Muslims – be they in "the West" or in the traditional Muslim world – are divided by the same antagonisms as westerners (Byrd 2017:3), the so-called idea of "European Islam" needs to be reconsidered due to the transformations of the Islamic public sphere worldwide; this could enhance the chance for Muslims to better position themselves, or even endanger their status and faith, in (arguably, my emphasis) secularised European society (Bougarel 2008:159). After the arrival of Muslim newcomers from the Global South and Eastern Europe, ethnic and national identities were important indicators to map out the geographies of Islam but poor signifiers to explore their religious traditions that occasionally overlapped with political sensitivities and orientation among the diaspora. Åke Sander identifies *ethnic*, *cultural*, *political* and *religious* dimensions to better delve into the various representatives and leaderships, as well as beliefs and collective practices, to navigate the multidimensionality of "Muslimness" in Europe (2014:213–218). Ina Merdjanova notes (2013:2–49) that Balkan Muslims residing in and beyond Southeast Europe may also show further differences *within* Sander's classification. The latter may occasionally need to move beyond simply historical, geographical, ethnic and linguistic categories to consider other intergenerational changes and majority-minority dynamics caused by (forced) migration, dislocation and adaptation to new social contexts and political influences.

The offsprings of the Balkan Muslim communities residing in "the West" belong to a much larger composition of informal gatherings, official associations and political groups that depend on constantly changing circumstances. The groups under study can be understood along religious, ethnic, cultural lines and historical specificities that have, over time, developed out of a complex web of contents, acts and practices. Out of the final sample of n=104 interviews with members of the generation under study and community members, n=37 have Bosnian heritage and n=4 self-identified as Bosniaks but from the region of Sandžak. While n=13 were originally from Bulgaria and n=17 from North Macedonia, they have no Slavic ethnic background, whatsoever; in fact, n=8 speak Turkish as they were born to Turkish families and n=7 have Roma origin. Out of n=34 Albanian speakers, only n=12 have roots from Albania proper since the rest belong to Albanian families originally from Yugoslav Macedonia and Kosovo and n=3 are Slavic speakers but Muslims. Hence, the use of the term "Muslim" may also be considered either incorrect or qualified as imprecise, if not contested by the same members of the groups under study. Various respondents could be depicted as "sociological Muslims" in general (see Popović 1986; Poulton and Taji-Farouki 1997; Bougarel and Clayer 2000, among others), or "cultural Muslims" and "liberal Muslims" (Roy 2013:6). These definitions can mostly describe those respondents born to families originally from Bosnia and Herzegovina, who pointed out to having been socialised into, or having internalised, the Muslim "ways of doing things" (Sander 2014:213). Others admitted to worshipping Islam as "moderate Muslims", also known as "secular Muslims", such as those belonging to the former Yugoslav Kosovo and Macedonia. They self-identified as emancipated and integrated citizens living in an urban context, unlike their parents who still endure a painstaking integration in "the West" due to their poor education background and their "village mentality". Nonetheless, this group of respondents verbalised conservative positions on political grounds. In general, they were neither zealous Muslims nor mosque-goers, but Islam remains part of their cultural identities on a personal and collective level. The genealogy of their political sensitivities goes back to a time of war, persecution and exploitation in their parental birthplace. Tellingly, they unconsciously employ a coping mechanism to distance themselves from other Muslims living in the same places of residence, lest they be associated with the whole of the *ummah* and face yet more political discrimination and racialisation by the core society (Sander 2014; Tsagarousianou 2016:63; Rexhepi 2023:48). Lastly, "Muslims by name" were also met and interviewed, mainly from Turkish and/or Roma families with Bulgarian roots. Mainly non-religious people (Grünenberg 2005:173; Izetbegović 1990:52) who were given Muslim names or "happened to be Muslims (Harris and Nawaz 2015:30) as their denomination of Islam helped them to self-perceive and constitute their identity as "non-Slavic people" trapped, at a personal and collective level, in former Yugoslavian and post-communist South Slavic countries (Bakić-Hayden 1995:926).

With this in mind, the diversity of faith positions that respondents expressed during the interviews should be tacitly understood whenever the general terms of "Islam" and "Muslim" were verbalised. This study did not take for granted the fact that all potential respondents born to a Balkan Muslim family would have the same level of religious salience as older generations and other Muslim communities. If anything, they were considered members of "postmodern epistemic communities" (see Chapter 3) as they would easily comply with the family religious identity but at the same time occasionally disown community ties to escape the burdening legacies of their parental experiences of migration and integration. In this regard, the definition of "second generation" is not used interchangeably, nor does it assort uncritically all interviewees with other second generations belonging to other post-diasporic Muslim communities originally from the Global South. Similar to "Muslim", "second generation" may turn out to be an empty signifier, or unfit for the theoretical category established in the field of migration studies (Riniolo and Toivanen 2023). Since it was taken for granted that most respondents would neither hold memories of experiences of migration, nor have much consciousness of the political dynamics that caused dislocation, I was inspired by Marinne Hirsch's paradigm of "generation after" (2012) to investigate the predicament of the offspring of those who were forcedly expelled from their countries, those who faced genocidal violence and persecution at home, whose traumas still circulate in the generation after. As Hirsch herself defines it, this generation bears witness to the personal, collective and cultural traumas or transformations of those who came before – to events that they "remember" only by means of stories, images and behaviours among which they grew up with. For the purpose of this study, it was assumed that religious identity, to use Jürgen Habermas's words (2009:59), stems from a web of memories and a set of cultural practices passed down in family circles and potentially challenged in a thoroughly post-secular society. This baggage of knowledge, values and practices may largely stem from Balkan Islamic traditions or, conversely, have little to do, if anything, with its socio-cultural and other historical groundings (Grünenberg 2005:183).

## Shortcomings and Data Saturation

Throughout the chapters of this book, a series of case-studies are discussed. I could not rely on the statistical requirement of significant sample sizes due to the shortage of quantitative data about the "second generation" of Balkan Muslims born and raised in "the West". A large number of mostly qualitative studies have been dedicated to the institutionalisation, cultural practices and issues of belonging of Balkan Muslims (Karabegović 2024; Vathi 2015; Bougarel and Mihaylova 2005, among others). On the other hand, the specific nuances of the generations born outside the Balkans, after the demise of state socialism and the Yugoslavian wars, have been either under-researched or overshadowed by the much broader approach to the study of the former Yugoslavian or the postsocialist diaspora. Given this backdrop, I chose to delve into the micro-level by looking at how intra-city dynamics are driven by the phenomena of Islamophobia and gentrification (see Chapters 5 and 7). A small number of individuals and groups were identified in a particular mode and chosen to carve out a niche for a better research strategy. Just as the emic approach described here was deemed necessary for detecting potential intergenerational changes and transformations, so the urban scene was also important in scrutinising the role of the groups under study from within the realm of everyday life (Gallardo Fernandez 2002).

Granted that awareness and interest in postwar, postsocialist and post-migrant generations of Muslims with Balkan family heritage are still at an early stage, I paid attention to three dichotomous contexts. In line with the three main open questions introduced earlier, in-depth interviews and participation-observation were carried out to explore how respondents experience (1) practices of self-exclusion from/inclusion in the core society after the experiences of their grand/parents' migration; (2) alienation/participation in political terms, at all levels; (3) distance from/closeness to other groups of coreligionists in the (sub)urban context. Hence, the vast heterogeneity of the groups under study complicated the data collection process and its comparative nature; the selection of the target-group did not always imply that potential respondents were zealous Muslim believers or had family ties exclusively with the Balkans. In addition, arranging an unequivocal appointment at a proper date, hour and location, was sometimes challenging and coupled with the difficulty of appeasing potential respondents as the terms "research" and "interview" brought with it either a negative connotation or were approached with diffidence. Despite the use of the PIS, a few respondents were suspicious when questioned about their intimate stories and personal anecdotes that converged with, or diverged from, Islam. At times, touching upon the issues of belonging and self-identification with the respective community brought some respondents to recall diasporic affiliations and related issues incorrectly. Altering historical events, geographical contexts and political issues was also common during the interviews. In Bremen, for instance, a young Muslim with Albanian roots was taken by surprise when he discovered that both parents escaped Serbia, and not Kosovo as he himself believed, since Preševo is the city where they come from.

Although in-depth interviews were always organised dialogically (with the only exception being those carried out online), insufficient information or poorly detailed responses were often verbalised with some "political correctness" or stated in the third person. Nonetheless, most interviews went smoothly and successfully. Only in some cases were interviews delayed, cancelled or postponed at the last moment, and thereby influenced by political changes and different developments at all levels. Much-debated political events, such as the Russian war against Ukraine, were verbalised during the in-depth interviews, and discussed and contextualised at the time of the fieldwork and data analysis. In the city of Antwerp and other locations, most male respondents spontaneously expressed concerns and support for the Palestinian Muslims and Palestine, respectively (see Chapter 3). In this regard, it should be noted that this series of interviews were held before the events of October 7, 2023, and the subsequent invasion of Gaza by Israel.

Yet another issue was the invisibility of some specific groups of the Balkan Muslim diaspora. Young Muslims with ethnic Roma or Turkish background were difficult to reach out to due to their precarious work conditions and their cultural closeness with the much larger Turkish diaspora. By invisibility, I do not mean "hidden" or "undetectable", but I rather allude to the difficulties of identifying potential respondents from these specific groups. Cataloguing their everyday concerns and the phenomena of exclusion are already obscured by the intense, albeit ideologically loaded, European debate on economic migrants and Islam in particular (Sofos and Tsagarousianou 2013:26). At the same time, a certain degree of "religious invisibility" stems from (a) low-profile immigrant religiosity and the common mentality of their parents, recently camouflaged by intra- and non-European diaspora movements; (b) the under-researched relationship between the discrepancies and practices of cultural or religious diversity that may (dis)appear within families with a migrant background, (c) under-researched physical, spatial, symbolic, visual and material environments in which everyday life occurs (among others, see Merdjanova 2013:105; Bougarel 2008:155; Bougarel and Mihaylova 2005; Lecoyer 2020:151–153; King 2004).

Hence, an ethnographic approach to the urban linguistic landscapes (See Chapter 7) was employed to observe, detect and understand social stratigraphy and how the choice of certain attitudes articulate conviviality in a given neighbourhood.

## Introducing the Case-Studies

Belgium, Germany, Italy and Poland are the four countries that this research focuses on. These EU member states have been not chosen randomly, although the selection may look incoherent and puzzling. In fact, Islam differs in the way it has been historically perceived, institutionalised and subsequently approached in each of the four countries. However, some telling parallels can be drawn to pave the way to a comparative analysis. Belgium and Germany provide more similar perspectives on a national level with regard to multiculturalism and the Muslim diaspora; they have also experienced migratory inflows from Southeast and Eastern Europe since the aftermaths of the Second World War. Moreover, Germany's law on citizenship change in 2023, and the electoral success of the far-right party *Alternative für Deutschland* – (in English, Alternative for Germany) – show a similar scenario to Italy and Poland. The latter are considered in the foreground of leveraging Islamophobia as a technique to gain power on political and cultural grounds, yet without showing similar issues of spatialisation like in the German and Belgian cities under observation. Moreover, Belgium's administrative and linguistic divisions between the Wallonia and the Flanders resonate with the old-age North/South division in Italy – both being an important interplay between people's understanding of Muslims and the rise of national regionalism. Germany's attempts to institutionalise a "European Islam" are not found in Poland, but Islamophobia has shown similar paradoxical tendencies in both a domestic context and key phenomena within both political landscapes.

### *Belgium*

Islam has been recognised as a national religion in the country since 1974 and it has been represented at the state level by the *Éxecutif des Musulmans de*

*Belgique* (in English, EMB – Belgian Muslim Executive) (Easat-Daas 2020:28). Islam did not only arrive as a religion as a result of migratory phenomena, but also, if not completely, as the negative connotations of religious practices and cultural modes among newcomers. According to the constitutional law principles regarding the social and political organisations, Muslim communities are required to set up a nationally representative Islamic council to receive state funding for religious purposes. This legal recognition was not realised until 1999 (Sofos and Tsagarousianou 2013:47), thereby leaving Muslims without representation at the institutional level since the time of their first arrival in the country.

Since the 1960s, Belgium's small Albanian diaspora played an active role in the establishment of the *Centre Islamique à Bruxelles* (Bougarel and Mihaylova 2005). At the same time, many other Muslims arrived over the next decade through the Yugoslav labour migration flows. Due to relatively liberal citizenship legislation, the majority of Muslim migrants received citizenship, unlike other coreligionists in Germany during the same period of time. In the city of Ghent, the then-established Turkish diaspora provided help and support to many Muslims originally from the exploited regions of Yugoslavia or escaping from Communist Bulgaria's assimilation policies (See Kamusella 2019). Most newcomers easily adapted to the Turkish-majority neighbourhoods of Brugse Poort, Dampoort, Nieuw-Gent, Sluizeken-Tolhuis-Ham and Rabot (Devaux 2017). It is not surprising that some Turkish cultural associations still attempt to lump Muslim Turks with those coming from "Rumelia", namely, the formerly Ottoman region of the Balkans.[1]

Between 1993 and 1995, thousands of Muslims fled war-torn Yugoslavia and arrived in Belgium via Austria and Germany. Due to the highly contested international and political climate around the war in Yugoslavia (Simms 2022), many could not prove being personally persecuted in their birthplace. While the status of escapees was unacknowledged, a new status was adopted in Belgium for granting asylum for a period of three up to six months. Escapees could also prolong their stay in the country or apply for a "white card", which gave them the chance to travel back to Bosnia and return to Belgium. In the early post-conflict scenario designed by the Dayton Agreement in 1995, the Belgian government and the International Organization of Migration (IOM) set up an information campaign for granting repatriation for those who agreed to return and ease their reintegration back home.[2] Currently, about 400 Bosnian families live in Ghent, while Antwerp hosts a much larger community,[3] becoming the Belgian capital of the Bosnian community.

1 In Brussels, Belgium, the "*Belçika Rumeli Türkleri Dernegi*" [Association of Belgian Turks from Rumelia], was contacted for an interview. No answer followed up.

2 Data shown by Thomas Von Ruj (online class) for the "Virtual Tour of Bosnia – Bosnian Diaspora in Belgium" at Antwerp University (Belgium) on 2 April 2021.

3 Interview with the Bosnian imam at the local mosque in Ghent (Belgium), 27 February 2023.

The creation of the representation of a Muslim organisation in government bodies, namely, l'*Exécutif des Musulmans de Belgique*, elected a Muslim Executive Council in order to set up an institutional framework to ensure equality with the other recognised religions in terms of providing subsidies for places of worship, and financing ministers of religion (Sant'Angelo 2004:34). Nonetheless, the disagreements between this organism and the Belgian state did not facilitate integration and inclusion for all Muslims (Merdjanova 2013:104). During the fieldwork in Antwerp, a community representative of the Muslim Bosnian community pointed out that the cultural centre, which also functions as a mosque, was about to be granted recognition from the central authorities. As the European Union gradually enlarged eastward by placing Bulgaria and Romania on the Schengen White List before the final EU accession (Mancheva and Troeva 2011:15), a national legislation framework for seasonal labour was developed. A large number of Polish, Bulgarian and Romanian seasonal workers arrived in the country thanks to a 65-day work permit and a fixed hourly wage under an exceptional status. Migration phenomena definitely contributed to the rise of Islamophobia, which soon turned into systematic discrimination in the marketplace and housing. Islamophobia shifted gears through direct attacks against mosques and individuals, as well as harassment on the street and elsewhere. Instances of discrimination in job recruitment remain rather common, especially when targeting qualified young women only because they wear a headscarf while looking for their first job.

There is no doubt that Islamophobia has become a major concern in Flanders, where regional nationalism and the spectre of secession haunt society. Antwerp, Flanders' biggest city, with more than half of its local population of immigrant origin, is Europe's most racist city according to the Eurobarometer. Of the 168 different nationalities, Muslims with Bulgarian (4%), Albanian (4%) and Serbian heritage are classified with the rest of the population originally from the Global South (Hoops 2021:92). Islam's nature has been question with regard to its apparent incompatibility with, and potential adjustment to Western and Flemish culture. This problematic request polarises Dutch and Belgian society. In it, nationalists usually employ anti-immigration narratives to wish to (directly) remove Islam, and thus Muslims, from Belgian lands (Smits 2023:90).

### *Germany*

When France and the United Kingdom experienced Islamic radicalism in the 2000s, Germany was already foreseen as the future hotbed of radical Islam and religious intolerance. The ambivalent and decades-long division between Protestants and Christians, capitalists and socialists today vacillates between the nationalist opponents and the multiculturalist proponents of having Muslims in the country (Leiken 2012:108). This polarisation separates those who welcome Muslims unequivocally from those willing to protect a Christian/European Germany (Özyürek 2015:3), and even from those who speak in praise of diversity but without Muslims (Canan and Foroutan 2016:164–165). This paradox has been proven true in 2024 by the institutionalisation of Alternative for Germany at all institutional levels.

Similar to Belgium, Germany began to host millions of Muslim workers from Yugoslavia and other Communist countries from the mid-1950s. After initiating an intensive foreign workforce recruitment with the first treaty of recruitment in 1955, the arrival of about six million "guest workers" (in German, *Gastarbeiter*) was positively met to rebuild Germany in the wake of the Second World War. In general, the public debate over Islam remained long dormant. Many had wrongly assumed that guest workers would eventually return to their countries of origin (Mushaben 2008:512). Conversely, those workers were not eager to go back home but rather keen on settling down and bringing their families to Germany in the wake of the global economic crisis. Because of this, the government decided to impose a ban on recruitment (in German, *Anwerbestopp*) in 1973 (Canan and Foroutan 2016:162).

Germany experienced another wave of Yugoslav labour migration in the 1970s and the 1980s, while ordinary citizens were not consulted in the midst of a series of important decisions pertaining to immigrant recruitment: work permits, residency and visa regulation (Leiken 2012:243). Throughout the post-1989 unification period, "the years of the baseball bats" (in German, *Baseballschlägerjahre*), Nazi gangs dominated the streets (Bangel 2019). After cases of violent and lethal attacks against foreigners increased rapidly, the Bundestag considerably tightened the rules for asylum seekers in December 1992 (Mark et al. 2019:167). The political atmosphere remained tense during the 1990s, especially in East Germany where dark-skinned people and Muslims were targeted. Yet Islamic organisations lacked legal recognition and financial support in comparison with established churches.

Germany's citizenship law was deliberated in 2000, shifting the basis of inclusiveness from *ius sanguinis* (blood) to *ius soli* (territory) and automatically granting German citizenship to all children of foreign dwellers up to the age 23 after completing eight years of legal residence. During this period, the debate over the term *Leitkultur* (in English, leading culture) did not only prove that Islam was, and still is (my emphasis), viewed as a threat to German culture, but it also shed light on most people's concerns about cultural encroachment into German society. In the meantime, some public figures reasserted some form of Christian identity to the country, and affirmed that Muslims could live in it but without being part of the core society (Cesari 2003:258). Since then, newer policies have created barriers for immigrants. Only temporary immigration of qualified individuals and family members after reunification were recognised as legal for receiving German citizenship. After January 2005, new immigrants were also obliged to attend integration courses taught by the new Federal Bureau for Migration and Refugees (BAMF). The courses convey general knowledge on Germany, the state system, the German language and a final test must be passed successfully. Yet again conservatives were not content with easing access to citizenship and accused the then-in-charge Social Democratic

Party (SPD) of jeopardising "German cultural identity" by liberalising immigration. Most right-wingers argued that citizenship was the birthright of the German *Volk* (in English, peoplehood) and that the concept of a multicultural society was unconstitutional. However, obtaining German citizenship for many dwellers with migration heritage was not that easy: probationary residency of at least 15 years in the country was required – a decision that affected the generation born after December 31, 1999. For some Muslims in particular, the cultural test was an issue: topics such as polygamy, female equality, spousal rights and homosexuality were certainly taxing (Leiken 2012:243–249).

Among the groups under study, the naturalisation of Muslims sparked criticism during the interviews. When topics of heated debate were mentioned, many were found to be hopeful about the long-waited bill on the dual nationality law (see Chapter 6), which was later approved by the Germany Cabinet during summer 2023 to simplify the naturalisation process and enable multiple citizenship for immigrants (Şimşek 2023). In some highly contested multicultural cities, however, suspicion repeatedly falls on local Muslims. The phenomena of radicalisation have alarmed state officials, especially in relation to the Turkish Muslim movement *Millî Görüş* (in English, National Vision) due to its religious and political ideology apparently inspired by a series of proxy Islamist parties and Necmettin Erbakan.[4] Other Turkish groups are also perceived as radicals and potential terrorists, such as those constituted by ethnic Turks from Western Thrace that have nonetheless different associations from the Turks from Turkey (Bougarel 2008). The lack of a clearly recognised Muslim leadership was a major concern (Merdjanova 2013:105), which is also coupled by the weaponisation of themes related to Muslims across the country. As Muslim life's positive everyday stories are rarely communicated in the mainstream discourse (Finkelstein 2023:12), most Germans feel threatened by Muslims and immigrants (Cesari 2003:268). A study conducted by the German Centre for Integration and Migration Research (DeZIM) reported that in 2022 almost half of the population has already observed a racist incident (mentioned by Zubair 2023:269). At the same time, Esra Özyürek argues that there is much evidence that Islam and Muslims are treated unequally (2015:8).

Given the great expansion of the country and the large number of Muslims with Balkan heritage, fieldwork was conducted after the deliberate selection of two neighbourhoods: Gröpelingen and Innenstadt-Nord in Bremen and Dortmund, respectively. In the case of the latter, the choice was taken as Dortmund is, at the municipal level, Germany's most segregated city when considering indices of ethnic and social segregation (Sürig and Wilmes 2015:102). In the case of the former in Bremen, instead, the intriguing nexus of suburban dynamics and the presence of 16.000 émigrés from the Balkan region, makes

4 Interview with Prof. Yasemin Karakaşoğlu, Bremen University, Bremen (Germany), 25 May 2023.

the city an interesting urban space to explore the invisibility of the groups under study vis-à-vis the overwhelming and patronising Turkish diaspora.

### *Italy*

Prior to the 1990s, Italy's migration scenario was described as a turnaround due to the consequence of three main trends: (1) the slow decline in emigration after its peak in the 1960s, (2) the subsequent growth of return migration and then (3) the rapid increase in the number of immigrants, starting in the 1970s and escalating from the 1980s onwards (see King and Andall 1999). In 1987, when Italy passed Law no.984 to regulate the reception and treatment of workers from non-EU countries, it was estimated that around 30,000 Yugoslavs were staying in Italy on "temporary work" (Halilovich et al. 2018:28). As in Germany during the 1950s, public debate on religion and Islam was far from seizing the attention of the wider public.

In the wake of the post-9/11 events, however, Islam began being linked by some political parties, particularly The League (formerly, North League; in Italian, *Lega Nord*), which replaced its political stances against Italy's southerners with the issue of illegal migration from abroad. This phenomenon was labelled as a "Trojan horse" i.e. a gateway to Italy for radical Muslims. Since then, Islam began dominating headlines and newspapers, thereby becoming a subject of controversy in TV shows and radio programmes. The latest reports on Islamophobia note that hate crimes are not marked according to their motivation. Since Italian legislation does not provide a definition of hate crimes, there are no instructions for policy recommendations and guidelines as regards identifying and recording such crimes. Accordingly, data cannot be provided to rightly investigate the category of anti-Muslim hate crimes (Mullol Marin 2023:352). However, Balkan Muslims have managed to integrate well in the northern regions and in smaller urban contexts around Piacenza, Biella, Verona, among others, in spite of the strong identities of Italian regions and cities underpinning the fragmentation of the country on a regional level (Vathi 2015:26). While anti-Islamic feelings run high in these northern regions, there is almost no Muslim presence originating from the Balkans in the southernmost Sicily, Calabria and Apulia, which fell under the control of the Aghlabid Dynasty in the 9th century.

In Milan, the opening of the mosque in Via Padova and the area around it have been described as a continuing Islamisation and perceived as a security issue by residents (Galici 2022). The municipality was also accused of providing "concessions to foreigners" while working to create an almost Islamic ghetto of the city, which is detrimental to the urban fabric and in which the foreign community continues (arguably) to be favoured. This contestation is instructive to understanding the rhetoric of today's leading party of the ruling coalition in the country, Fratelli d'Italia (in English, Brothers of Italy). Along with the mantra of "*Prima gli Italiani*" (in English, Italians first), Giorgia Meloni has gained consensus without directly targeting Muslims and Islam, but subtly warning about a "reverse discrimination" for Italians (Mullol Marin 2023:337). It should be pointed out that Italy has a special relation to the Balkan region in terms of geopolitical proximity and in the contemporary history of immigration. The opening of other smaller mosques in lesser known cities, such as that of Piacenza and Ravenna, have seen the direct contribution of Muslims from Bosnia and North Macedonia, respectively, and not heightened the public political debate.[5] Albanians, who are nowadays one of the largest immigrant groups in the country together with Romanians (Vathi 2015:27), arrived in the early 1990s when Italian society was undergoing a major transformation in order to subscribe to a new discourse of European identity. *L'Unione degli Albanesi Musulmani in Italia* (in English, The Union of Albanian Muslims in Italy) was founded in March 2009 by Albanian citizens originally from North Macedonia, Kosovo and Albania, to encourage and cultivate knowledge, mutual help, coordination and collaboration among Albanian Muslims residing in Italy. Although Italy has not been a typical country of migration for Yugoslavian citizens, the war in Yugoslavia changed that trend rapidly. Between 1992 and 1996, Italy accepted more than 50,000 refugees from the former Yugoslavia. In 1996, the number of Bosnians went beyond 10,000 people, among whom, the so-called "young diaspora" – namely, the second generation, was born (Halilovich et al. 2018:28). On the one hand, Italy continued to remain an unpopular traditional country of migration of Bosnian citizens, making the organisation of the Bosnian diaspora very modest. On the other hand, however, Bosnian Muslims managed to establish their Muslim community in 2019 under the name of "*Comunita' Islamica dei Bosniaci in Italia*" (in Bosnian, Islamska Zajednica Bošnjaka u Italiji). While some young Bosnian Muslim points out the lack of umbrella organisation for Muslims residing in Italy (Voloder 2022), in Val Camonica the Bosnian association Ljiljan is currently trying to unite the different families living around and in Northern Italy[6] to promote initiatives about Bosnian culture and sport, increase visits to Bosnia among the youth and celebrate commemoration such as the seminal event of the 1995 Srebrenica Genocide.

### *Poland*

While Islamophobia in Western Europe outweighs the integration policies, Poland found itself at the centre of the EU political debate for being reluctant to accept Brussels's solidarity plans of redistribution of Syrian and Kurdish refugees in 2015 (Krastev and Holmes 2019).

Although Muslims have never constituted a statistically significant phenomenon within the country, counting only 0,1%, of the whole ethnic makeup, most Poles believe that the number is closer to 10% and growing

5 Interview with Karolina Bielenin Lenczowska, Warsaw (Poland), 12 October 2023.
6 Colloquial conversation with the President of the association (Italy), 14 May 2023.

(see Pędziwiatr 2018). Polish Tatars represent about 5000 members of the historical Muslim community and their religious faith has become, over time, only a matter of folklore and cultural self-understanding of family belonging.[7] Poland's overestimation of the impact of Muslims fuels Islamophobia and this is visible in media headlines.

If religion furthered the construction of civil society in the country (Asad 2003:182), Monika Bobako argues that the Polish example demonstrates that Islamophobia has frequently motivated violence against people who have little to do with Islam (2015:43). Likewise, Konrad Pędziwiatr contends that one of the reasons why Islamophobia has taken deep roots in Poland is because its society has not fully come to terms with its anti-Semitism and never really critically reflected on its relationship with the "ethnic other" (mentioned by Edwards 2018:125). The attack against the Ochota Muslim Central Centre in November 2017, which hosts the largest Islamic community in Warsaw, is telling. Yet, pundits and commentators framed that attack as "resistance to Islamisation", while some politicians of the then-ruling Law and Justice (PiS) contributed explicitly to overwrought anti-Muslim attitudes in the country (Krastev and Holmes 2019:39).

Despite such polarisation, Islam was not seen as an existential threat especially after Russia's full-scale invasion of Ukraine in February 2022. While exploring the few cases of the Balkan Muslim diaspora in Warsaw and other smaller cities such as Toruń and Katowice, Poland's socialist past was recollected during some of the interviews. Between the 1960s and 1970s, the emergence of a "Muslim International" within the socialist and nonaligned world brought the Communist Polish regime to sponsor its Polish Tatar Muslims to deepen contacts with oil rich Arab countries. In return, funds were accepted from Islamic countries to aid in rebuilding mosques. In 1969, the first postwar Polish Muslim congress was also allowed to take place, and two years later the Office for Religious Affairs introduced legislation regarding religious activity among the dwindling Tatar population. Although the situation of the Tatars did not really improve during Communism, the government propagandists highlighted benevolent attitudes toward Polish Muslims. Meanwhile, socialist scholarships were given to students from the socialist-aligned countries of the Global South (Lipska and Talarczyk 2020). A Polish translation of the Qur'an was published in Sarajevo and paid for by the Moroccan government, while at the same time, the Islamic Community of the then-Yugoslav Bosnia was frequently deployed to service Yugoslav ambitions in building non-aligned socialism in the Middle East and North Africa. Tellingly, during those years, Yugoslav Bosnia's Muslim activists were brought to the dock and accused of Islamic fundamentalism. Arrests were made in April 1983, and the accused were members of the "Young Muslims" (in Bosnian, *Mladi muslimani*) in the famous Sarajevo Process (see Chapter 3). The free distribution of that

7 Conversation with a female Polish convert in Warsaw (Poland), 29 November 2022.

Polish-Bosnian publication of the Qur'an in 1981, was followed up with a ceremony staged in Warsaw to impress the several thousand foreign Muslim students studying in Poland in 1983, during the Salat al Fitr-u by days (Broun 1988:1974).

As with the well-established Balkan Muslim communities in Germany and Belgium much earlier in 1989, Poland hosts far smaller groups of Bosnian Muslims who arrived for opportunities related to business and professional development. Both the lack of mosques for Balkan Muslims and the interests of media outlets about their small communities living in Poland brought the groups under study a little step closer to other non-European Muslims. The 1999 Kosovo War brought a few thousand Albanians to seek refuge in Poland (Domachowska 2019). After the number of foreign students dropped in the 1990s, Poland has slowly regained its mantel as an attractive place for European students and scholars from the Balkan region again. An inconspicuous phenomenon of migration has seen Muslim Roma from Bulgaria arrive in Poland and work as street-sellers in local markets across the country.[8] In this regard, the Targowisko Bakalarska open market and the Zacisze neighbourhood, both in Warsaw, have been some of the places fieldwork has been undertaken among other workplaces and religious sites.

## References

Abu-Lughod, L. (1996) 'Writing against Culture', in R. G. Fox (ed.) *Recapturing Anthropology: Working in the Present.* Santa Fe: School of American Research Press, pp. 137–162.

Ahern, K. (2014) Gatekeepers: People Who Can (and Do) Stop Your Research in Its Tracks, *SAGE Research Methods Cases.* Available at: https://doi.org/10.4135/978144627305014536673

Angrosino, M. (2007) *Doing Ethnographic and Observational Research.* London: SAGE Publications. Available at: https://methods.sagepub.com/book/mono/doing-ethnographic-and-observational-research/toc (Accessed: 4 March 2023).

Asad, T. (2003) *Formations of the Secular. Christianity, Islam, Modernity.* Stanford: Stanford University Press.

Azabar, S. and Van Aelst, P. (2023) Religion Works in Different Ways: An Intersectional Approach to Muslims' Noninstitutionalized Participation. *Acta Politica*, 59, pp. 416–438. https://doi.org/10.1057/s41269-023-00300-y

Bakić-Hayden, M. (1995) Nesting Orientalisms: The Case of Former Yugoslavia. *Slavic Review*, 54 (4), pp. 917–931. https://doi.org/10.2307/2501399

Bangel, C. (2019) The Baseball Bat Years, *Zeit Online.* Available at: www.zeit.de/gesellschaft/2019-11/neo-nazis-youth-east-germany-after-berlin-wall-english (Accessed: 18 May 2023).

Bobako, M. (2015) Inventing Muslims in Europe. Religion, Culture and Identity in the Time of Neoliberalism. *Przegląd Religioznawczy – The Religious Studies Review*, 4 (258), pp. 43–55.

8 Conversation with Yelis Erolova, PhD candidate at the Bulgarian Academy of Science – Department IEFSEM-BAS in Sofia (Bulgaria), 3 October 2021; Dr. Kamila Fiałkowska at the Centre of Migration Research at the University of Warsaw (Poland), 30 June 2023.

Bougarel, X. (2008) 'Balkan Muslim Diasporas and the Idea of a "European Islam"', in R. Kostić, T. Dulić, I. Maček, and J. Trtak (eds.) *Balkan Currents. Essays in Honour of Kjell Magnusson*. Uppsala: Uppsala University Press, pp. 147–165.

Bougarel, X. and Clayer, N. (2000) *Le Nouvel Islam Balkanique. Les Musulmans, Acteurs du Post-Communisme* [The New Balkan Islam. Muslims, Actors of Post-Communism]. Paris: Maisonneuve & Larose.

Bougarel, X. and Mihaylova, D. (2005) Diasporas musulmanes balkaniques dans l'Union européenne [Balkan Muslim Diaspora in the European Union]. *Balkanologie – Revue d'études pluridisciplinaires*, IX (1–2), pp. 59–211. https://doi.org/10.4000/balkanologie.577

Broun, J. (1988) *Conscience and Captivity: Religion in Eastern Europe*. Washington: Ethics & Public Policy Center Inc.

Byrd, J. D. (2017) *Islam in a Post-Secular Society. Religion, Secularity and the Antagonism of Recalcitrant Faith*. Boston: Brill.

Canan, C. and Foroutan, N. (2016) The Paradox of Equal Belonging of Muslims. *Islamophobia Studies Journal*, 3 (2), pp. 160–176. http://dx.doi.org/10.18452/22484.

Cesari, J. (2003) 'Muslim Minorities in Europe: The Silent Revolution', in J. Esposito and F. Burgat (eds.) *Modernizing Islam: Religion in the Public Sphere in the Middle East and Europe*. New Brunswick: Rutgers University Press, pp. 251–271.

de la Bellacasa, M. P. (2011) Matters of Care in Technoscience: Assembling Neglected Things. *Social Studies of Science*, 41 (1), pp. 85–106. https://doi.org/10.1177/0306312710380301

Devaux, U. (2017) Ghent as a Second Home for Many Bulgarians Analysis of the City's Policy Regarding Intra-European Migration and the life of Bulgarians, *Ghent University*. Available at: https://lib.ugent.be/en/catalog/rug01:002375913 (Accessed: 14 January 2023).

Didi-Huberman, G. (2016) 'To Render Sensible', in A. Badiou, P. Bourdieu, J. Butler, G. Didi-Huberman, S. Khiari, and J. Rancière (eds.) *What is A People?* New York: Columbia University Press, pp. 65–86.

Domachowska, A. (2019) The Attitude of Poland and Polish Society toward the 1999 Kosovo Refugees. *Slovanský přehled*, 105 (1), pp. 49–63.

Easat-Daas, A. (2020) *Muslim Women's Political Participation in France and Belgium*. Cham: Palgrave Macmillan.

Edwards, M. (2018) Polish Muslims, Polish Fears. A Reflection on Politics and the Fear of the Other. *New Eastern Europe*, 06 (34), pp. 119–127. Available at: https://neweasterneurope.eu/2018/11/05/polish-muslims-polish-fears-reflection-politics-fear/ (Accessed: 3 December 2022).

Finkelstein, K. (2023) *Moderne Muslimas – Kindheit – Karriere – Klischees* [Modern Muslim – Women – Childhood – Carries – Stereotypes]. Berlin: Verlagshaus Jacoby & Stuart.

Fort, E. (2022) Managing Our Personal Traits in the Field: Exploring the Methodological and Analytical Benefits of Mobilizing Field Diaries. *International Journal of Social Research and Methodology*, 25 (3), pp. 349–360. https://doi.org/10.1080/13645579.2021.1883536

Galici, F. (2022) Nuova moschea in via Padova a Milano: "Come un ghetto islamico" [The New Mosque on Padova Street in Milan: "Like an Islamic Ghetto"], *Il Giornale*. Available at: www.ilgiornale.it/news/milano/milano-nuova-moschea-padova-trasformata-ghetto-islamico-2080153.html (Accessed: 8 July 2023).

Gallardo Fernandez, G. (2002) *Communal Land Ownership in Chile: The Agricultural Communities in the Commune of Canela, Norte Chico (1600–1998)*. London and New York: Routledge.

Geertz, C. (1973) *The Interpretation of Cultures: Selected Essays*. New York: Basic Books, Inc., Publishers.

Given, M. L. (2008) *The SAGE Encyclopaedia of Qualitative Research Methods*. London: SAGE Publication.

Grünenberg, K. (2005) Constructing "Sameness" and "Otherness": Bosnian Diasporic Experiences in a Danish Context. *Balkanologie – Revue d'études pluridisciplinaires*, IX (1–2), pp. 173–193. https://doi.org/10.4000/balkanologie.587

Habermas, J. (2009) *Europe: The Faltering Project*. Malden: Polity Press.

Halilovich, H., Hasić, J., Karabegović, D., Karamehić-Muratović, A. and Oruč, N. (2018) *Mapping the Bosnian-Herzegovinian Diaspora (BiH migrants in Australia, Austria, Denmark, Germany, Italy, Netherlands, Slovenia, Sweden, Switzerland, and the United States of America): Utilizing the Socio-Economic Potential of the Diaspora for Development of BiH*. Available at: www.mhrr.gov.ba/PDF/MAPPING%20BIH%20DIASPORA%20REPORT.pdf (Accessed: 10 May 2023).

Harris, S. and Nawaz, M. (2015) *Islam and the Future of Tolerance. A Dialogue*. Cambridge: Harvard Publishing.

Hirsch, M. (2012) *The Generation of Postmemory. Writing and Visual Culture After the Holocaust*. New York: Columbia University Press.

Hoops, J. (2021) Discourses of Integration in Antwerp. *Southern Communication Journal*, 86 (2), pp. 92–106. https://doi.org/10.1080/1041794X.2021.1882544

Hromadžić, A. (2023) On Being Too Close to It. *Genealogy*, 7 (4), pp. 1–10. https://doi.org/10.3390/genealogy7040076

Izetbegović, A. (1990) *Islamic Declaration*. Available at: https://archive.org/details/3IslamicDeclarationEng/mode/2up?view=theater (Accessed: 3 January 2023)

Kamusella, T. (2019) *Ethnic Cleansing during the Cold War. The Forgotten 1989 Expulsion of Turks from Communist Bulgaria*. London and New York: Routledge.

Karabegović, D. (2024) Fixing Things from Outside? Diaspora Politicians and Transnational Political Engagement. *Globalisation*, pp. 1–18. https://doi.org/10.1080/14747731.2024.2336647

King, A. (2004) *Spaces of Global Cultures. Architecture, Urbanism, Identity*. London: Routledge.

King, R. and Andall, J. (1999) The Geography and Economic Sociology of Recent Immigration to Italy. *Modern Italy*, 4 (2), pp. 135–158. https://doi.org/10.1080/13532949908454826

Krastev, I. and Holmes, S. (2019) *The Light that Failed. A Reckoning*. London: Penguin.

Lecoyer, K. (2020) Internormative Family Conflict Mediation within Belgian Muslim Families. *Revue Interdisciplinaire d'Études Juridiques*, 84 (1), pp. 149–177. https://doi.org/10.3917/riej.084.0149

Leiken, R. (2012) *Europe's Angry Muslims: The Revolt of the Second Generation*. Oxford: Oxford University Press.

Lipska, M. and Talarczyk, M. (2020) *Hope Is of a Different Color. From the Global South to the Łódź Film School*. Warsaw: Museum of Modern Art in Warsaw.

Mancheva, M. and Troeva, E. (2011) 'Миграция от и към България: състояние на изследванията' [Migration to and from Bulgaria: The State of Research], in M. Hajdinjak (ed.) *Миграции, пол и междукултурни взаимодействия в България. Проект GeMIC: "Пол, миграции и междукултурни взаимодейс-твия в Средиземноморието и Югоизточна Европа: междудисциплинарна перспектива* [Gender, Migration and Intercultural Interactions in Bulgaria. Project GeMIC: "Gender, Migration and Intercultural Interactions in the Mediterranean and South East Europe: An interdisciplinary perspective"]. Sofia: The International Center for the Study of Minorities and Intercultural Interactions.

Mark, J., Iacob, B., Rupprecht, T. and Spaskovska, L. (2019) *1989. A Global History of Eastern Europe*. Cambridge: Cambridge University Press.

Mayorga-Gallo, S. and Hordge-Freeman, E. (2017) Between Marginality and Privilege: Gaining Access and Navigating the Field in Multiethnic Settings. *Qualitative Research*, 17 (4), pp. 377–394. https://doi.org/10.1177/1468794116672915

McGranahan, C. (2018) Ethnography beyond Method: The Importance of on Ethnographic Sensibility. *Sites: A Journal of Social Anthropology and Cultural Studies,* 15 (1), pp. 1–10. https://doi.org/10.11157/sites-id373

Merdjanova, I. (2013) *Rediscovering the Umma. Muslims in the Balkans between Nationalism and Transnationalism.* Oxford: Oxford University Press.

Millar, G. (2018) Engaging Ethnographic Peace Research: Exploring an Approach. *International Peacekeeping*, 25 (5), pp. 597–609. https://doi.org/10.1080/13533312.2018.1521700

Mullol Marin, A. (2023) 'Islamophobia in Italy: National Report 2022', in E. Bayraklı and F. Hafez (eds.) *European Islamophobia Report 2022.* Vienna: Leopold Weiss Institute, pp. 334–363.

Mushaben, J. M. (2008) Gender, Hip-hop and Pop-Islam: The Urban Identities of Muslim Youth in Germany. *Citizenship Studies*, 12 (5), pp. 507–526. https://doi.org/10.1080/13621020802337931

Özyürek, E. (2015) *Being German, becoming Muslim: Race, Religion, and Conversion in the New Europe.* Princeton: Princeton University Press.

Pader, E. (2006) 'Seeing with an Ethnographic Sensibility', in D. Yanow and P. Schwartz-Shea (eds.) *Interpretation and Method: Empirical Research Methods and the Interpretive Turn.* New York: M. E. Sharpe, pp. 161–175.

Pędziwiatr, K. (2018) The Catholic Church in Poland on Muslims and Islam. *Patterns of Prejudice*, 52 (5), pp. 461–478. https://doi.org/10.1080/0031322X.2018.1495376

Popović, A. (1986) L'Islam Balkanique. Les Musulmans du Sud-Est Européen dans la Période Post-Ottomane. [The Balkan Islam: The Muslims of Southeast Europe in the Post-Ottoman Period]. *Bulletin of the School of Oriental and African Studies*, 52 (1), pp. 134–136. https://doi.org/10.1017/S0041977X00023247

Poulton, H. and Taji-Farouki, S. (1997) *Muslim Identity and the Balkan State.* London: Hurst.

Rexhepi, P. (2023) *White Enclosures. Racial Capitalism & Coloniality along the Balkan Route.* Durham: Duke University Press.

Riniolo, V. and Toivanen, M. (2023) Future Paths in the Study of Migrant Descendants' Citizenship: Engaging with Critical Literature. *Migration Letters*, 20 (2), pp. 301–311. https://doi.org/10.59670/ml.v20i2.2890

Rippin, A. (2001) *Muslims. Their Religious Beliefs and Practices.* London: Routledge.

Roy, O. (2013) Secularism and Islam: The Theological Predicament. *The International Spectator: Italian Journal of International Affairs*, 48 (1), pp. 5–19.

Sander, Å. (2014) 'Negative European Attitudes towards Muslims. Questions, Theories and Possible Explanations', in M. Deland, M. Minkenberg, and C. Mays (eds.) *In the Tracks of Breivik. Far Right Networks in Northen and Eastern Europe.* Vienna and Berlin: LIT Verlag, pp. 127–140.

Sant'Angelo, F. (2004) 'The Council of Europe and the Work Against Islamophobia: Existing Instruments and Standards', in I. Ramberg (ed.) *Islamophobia and Its Consequences on Young People.* Budapest: European Youth Centre Budapest, pp. 29–35. Available at: www.coe.int/en/web/youth/-/islamophobia-and-its-consequences-on-young-people?inheritRedirect=true (Accessed: 12 December 2022).

Schatz, E. (2009) *Political Ethnography: What Immersion Contributes to the Study of Politics.* Chicago: University of Chicago Press.

Simmons, E. and Smith, N. (2017) Comparison with an Ethnographic Sensibility. *American Political Science*, 50 (1), pp. 126–130. http://dx.doi.org/10.1017/S1049096516002286

Simms, B. (2022) *Unfinest Hours. Britan and the Destruction of Bosnia*. London: Penguin. https://www.penguin.co.uk/books/25849/unfinest-hour-by-simms-brendan/9780141937670

Şimşek, A. (2023) German Government Approves Dual Nationality Law, *AA Türkiye*. Available at: www.aa.com.tr/en/europe/german-government-approves-dual-nationality-law/2974563#:~:text=Children%20born%20in%20Germany%20to,the%20citizenship%20of%20their%20parents (Accessed: 24 August 2023).

Smits, A. (2023) 'Islamophobia in Belgium', in E. Bayraklı and F. Hafez (eds.) *European Islamophobia Report 2022*. Vienna: Leopold Weiss Institute.

Sofos, S. and Tsagarousianou, R. (2013) *Islam in Europe. Public Spaces and Civic Networks*. New York: Palgrave Macmillan.

Sürig, I. and Wilmes, M. (2015) *The Integration of the Second Generation in Germany Results of the TIES Survey on the Descendants of Turkish and Yugoslavian Immigrants*. Amsterdam: Amsterdam University Press.

Todd, Z. (2014) Fish Pluralities: Human-Animal Relations and Sites of Engagement in Paulatuuq, Arctic Canada. *Études/Inuit/Studies*, 38 (1–2), pp. 217–238.

Tsagarousianou, R. (2016) European Muslim Diasporic Geographies. Media Use and the Production of Translocality. *Middle East Journal of Culture and Communication*, 9 (1), pp. 62–86. https://doi.org/10.1163/18739865-00901007

Vathi, Z. (2015) Migrating and Settling in a Mobile World Albanian Migrants and Their Children in Europe, *Springer Open*. Available at: https://link.springer.com/book/10.1007/978-3-319-13024-8 (Accessed: 18 July 2023).

Voloder, S. (2022) Nermin Fazlagić: Bošnjaci i Turci imaju odličnu saradnju u Italiji [Nermin Fazlagić: Bosniaks and Turks Have a Tremendous Cooperation in Italy], *AA Türkiye*. Available at: www.aa.com.tr/ba/svijet/nermin-fazlagi%C4%87-bo%C5%A1njaci-i-turci-imaju-odli%C4%8Dnu-saradnju-u-italiji/2713337 (Accessed: 8 August 2023).

Zubair, A. (2023) 'Islamophobia in Germany: National Report 2022', in E. Bayraklı and F. Hafez (eds.) *European Islamophobia Report 2022*. Vienna: Leopold Weiss Institute, pp. 261–284. Available at: https://islamophobiareport.com/islamophobiareport-2022.pdf (Accessed: 19 May 2023).

# 2 The Ummah and the "Balkan Rest"

In the wake of the events of October 7, 2023, the onset of the Israeli-Hamas war within the Gaza Strip overwhelmed millions of Muslims worldwide. The mass mobilisation in favour of a ceasefire and recognition of a Palestinian state shed light on the role of the *ummah*, the global and non-ethnically defined Muslim community. Pro-Palestine protests and public events were held in the major cities of the Balkans. Local Muslims took to the streets with some marginal leftist organisations in solidarity with Gazans, showing how connections to the Middle East are not unique (Sadriu 2017:11).

In a time of increasing connectivity, transformation and absence of an earthly authority (Mahomed 2022:29), this chapter discusses the neat geographical boundaries and historical itineraries between Europe, the Balkans and the Middle East (Sadriu 2019:433) by taking a step back from the events of October 7, 2023, in Israel. It precisely looks at the geographical and confessional interconnections between the young Muslims living outside the Balkans and the rest of the *ummah*. As Islam is a distinctive *dīn* – namely, a way of life for which Muslims will be held accountable and recompensed accordingly – the following sections refer to the *ummah* in the sense of "a people" that can embrace all of humanity (Asad 2003:197), a "community" of coreligionists who (should) live by a set of authoritative texts and practices by accepting moral and institutional boundaries (Haj 2009:36).

Since past studies have shown the analytical limitations in exploring potential pan-religious groupings and generational changes (Spellman Poots 2019:188), the main objective of the fieldwork was not only to conduct in-depth interviews with potential respondents of the groups under study, but also aimed at exploring how the latter subscribe, commit and connect with the *ummah* on religious and eventually political grounds (Mahomed 2022). Hence, two open questions were raised to capture potentially untapped transnational and trans-peripheral entanglements. Respectively, how do young Muslims of Balkan origin juggle the mainstream patterns of Western society secularisation? If at all, do they hold, nurture or care about relationships with the coreligionists in order to counter the tense atmosphere against Islam and Muslims in their places of residence?

DOI: 10.4324/9781003589624-3

Prior to addressing these questions, the chapter takes another step back. It firstly overviews the contribution of Balkan Muslim scholars, the *ulema*, to the *ummah* in order to place their sociocultural and political legacies at the centre of discussion beyond the Balkans and Europe. This part of the chapter showcases the circles of Balkan Muslim intellectuals and how they have been categorised along with the image of the peripheral, impoverished and powerless lands of the Old Continent. The second part draws on the data and knowledge acquired and constructed throughout in-depth interviews. Only first-hand information extracted from the interview material and other related information obtained from second-hand sources are put forward. This is to debunk the idea that potential interactions and encounters of Muslims on political grounds, especially in a confrontational way, constitutes part of a strategy designed to achieve the "takeover" of Europe (Sofos and Tsagarousianou 2013:21). Against this alarmist rhetoric, it is argued that a higher level of religious salience of Muslims does not foster political participation at the city level, nor does it obstruct integration. On the contrary, respondents' opinions, everyday practices and strategic positioning vary on a wealth of g/local dynamics that (may) activate postulates and ideals of transnational solidarity toward their same-age peers and coreligionists in and beyond their places of residence and belonging. In this regard, the "Palestinian cause" and the post-October 7 events are simply instructive.

## In Search of Agency

In Europe, ideologies of the Abrahamic religions date as far back as much earlier traditions of anthropology, history, science and technology (Eze 2007:136). Yet the long history of Islam and Muslim agency has been historically obliterated by the West's exclusively rigid power of radiation (Mbembe 2019:122), thereby silencing ontologies, systems of knowledge and a wealth of practices that "do not fit" into the Western canon (Tlostanova and Mignolo 2012; Bobako 2017:12). Denied by this dominant discourse, Islam's contribution to Europe has been considered nil, with the exception of those Muslim scholars who have translated the works of Aristotle (Khankan 2018:68).

Although concepts of equality, freedom and democracy are not foreign but shared by earlier Islamic reformers, the inaccessibility of information to the latter (Rexhepi 2015:194) inhibits most Western scholars in capturing the relationships that grew fruitfully between Europe and the Islamic world. The spirit of the Enlightenment gradually began to exercise a great influence on Muslims' everyday lives (Hatiboglu 2007) by removing clerical-dominated obscurantism of any sort. The Hegelian legacy came to consider Islam as having vanished from Europe. Even when drawing on the Judeo-Hellenic traditions, which spread geographically and culturally adjacent to Islam (Said 2019:74, Mamdani 2004:18), Muslims were ejected from European imaginaries but not from their territories (Rexhepi 2017b:53; Sofos and Tsagarousianouu 2013:36). Since then, they began facing a spatial and temporal displacement which flies in the face of what equates the Balkans with the idea of "violence" (Bakić-Hayden 1995:917) and a vast fantasy of Orientalism (Hurd 2008:51). This exclusive construction of Europe crucially depends on the silencing of the historical role of its member states and predecessors in creating the main structures of political and economic inequality since the time of the age of colonisation (Boatcă 2022:44). In this respect, Islam has historically been the forward-looking global agency which has anticipated Europe's global expansion well before the Suez Canal, the Franco-Prussian War and the "Scramble for Africa" (Kirchner Reill 2018:25). Yet most multidisciplinary endeavours to rethink the symbolic *universum* of "the West" through the interactions and confrontations with Islam (Bobako 2017) have reduced the latter to some necessarily diminished version of a significant dangerous force for Europe, depicting Muslims as outsiders with a peculiar role *inside* Europe (Said 2019:60, 71).

At times, when Muslims are referred to *as* Europeans or *belonging* to Europe, or even reduced to the status of today's majorities in some Balkan states, all these statements come off as banal and trite, if not meaningless (Karić et al. 2023). This symmetry is not disquieting for relating Muslims to *belong to* Europe, or *come from* within it (Mbembe 2019:122). It is simply deemed necessary to attempt to synchronise the historical, genuine agency of Muslims with(in) Europe, and thereby self-satisfy Western academic discourse about a realignment of Muslims with Europe and the Balkan states (Ferizaj 2023). Thus, this scholarly approach seeks to adjust an historical wrong in the major trends of Western historiography, where a certain logic of reconnecting Muslims from/in the Balkans with contemporary Europe overshadows the much longer historical ties of Islam in al-Andalus in Spain, mediaeval Sicily in Italy, or in the Greek region of Xhanti (Shatanawi et al. 2021).

The genealogy of this comforting amnesia harks back to the Ottoman conquest of the Balkan region, where Muslims receive appraisals and plaudits only when reduced to the role that they had played in and against the Ottoman/Turkish hegemonic position. Among others, an example: Vincent Geisser (2014:37) and Suleiman Mourad (2014:42) contend that the historical expansion of the Ottoman Empire which led to the siege of Vienna (1683) was more a temporal than religious or theological danger. In other words, it was an expedition motivated by the fact that Ottomans themselves came to think of *belonging* to Europe more than to Syria or Egypt. On the one hand, this perspective risks re-proposing a certain asymmetry among Muslims worldwide, and reducing the Ottoman encroachment on the Balkans to a historical event, asserting Balkan Muslims and their Islam into the retelling of Europe's history, political development and cultural canon. On the other hand, it also ascribes, yet again, an image of danger to Muslims from "further east" and posing a threat to "the West" and all of secular (*white*, my emphasis) Europe.[1]

1 For instance, in October 2017, thousands of Poles joined arms to symbolically encircle Poland in a "rosary of the borders" and mark the Fest of the Rosary, a festival celebrating the Christian victory over the Ottoman Turks at the Battle of Lepanto in 1571. The symbolic "defense of the

The fissures and dislocations between Muslims and Europe were caused by the collapse of the Ottoman Empire due to disregard for ethnic, linguistic and tribal ties; these laid the foundations for the tensions we see in this part of the world today (Rahman 2017). The Balkans do not only fall into some historical accounts that equate Europe with Christendom, and later Judeo-Christianity, nor do they align with tropes of "civilisation" evoking a continuing "essence of Europe" embedded in essentially a Christian and simultaneously secular ethos (Gajda 2020:73; Geisser 2014:38). Such a narrative also depicts Islam as a lasting trauma in the so-called "powder keg of Europe", thereby sharpening the demarcation of the historical experiences of Balkan Muslims as categorically different – albeit "European" – from the alleged continuous threat of the Ottoman intruders into a region where whiteness and Christianity had come into contact with non-white and non-Christian populations (Rexhepi 2023:15). This self-stylised image of the protection of the Balkans firstly relates Islam with the anti-democratic, authoritarian, patriarchal and violent features of the Balkan region. It secondly reduces Muslims to the suspicious "European others" (El-Tayeb 2011) – namely, the lurking enemy within (Byrd 2017:5), yet disconnected from Europe's colonial empires and rules (Karić et al. 2023).

Muslims in and from the Balkans barely positioned themselves with the experiences of other coreligionists in the (post-)colonial world, while being aware of having contributed to the history of Europe thanks to the confessional interactions with Muslim world affairs (Sadriu 2017:551). Islam not only provided a national identity against imperialism to the masses outside the imaginary borders of Europe, but also questioned the hegemonic, anti-colonial and post-colonialist discourse of European *demos*. Put simply, Islam reveals how Europe was and still is unable to possess the exclusive (and, in the final analysis, ethnocentric) character of geographical bordering and ideological partitions in light of the fact that the *ummah* has always been real and present (Mahomed 2022:35). Karić et al. (2023) question for effect to what extent the experiences of Muslims in and from the Balkans categorically differ from, say, Muslims in Morocco under French rule or in India under British rule?

The Austro-Hungarian occupation of Bosnia (1878–1918) openly drew on imperialist elements of the then-British occupation of Egypt, the French colonisation of Algeria and the Dutch East Indies (Karić et al. 2023). Bosnia became *de facto* a colony of the Habsburg Empire and a natural frontier for powerful kingdoms, whose rulers quashed local Muslims by overseeing the development of the local Islamic institutions. The establishment of a distinct religious Islamic hierarchy, unknown until then in Bosnia, separated local Muslims not only physically but also spiritually from wider Muslim trends

---

country" from becoming "Eurabia", a colony of Islam, was followed by the then-leader of the Polish Parliament, Stanisław Karczewski, who reminded the Viennese about their historical role in protecting Christian Europe from the Ottomans.

(Khan 2017:208). If Bosnian Muslims had developed their own elites during the permissive environment of the Islamic Ottoman Empire, their interests continued to be expressed into the Austro-Hungarian judicial system thanks to the incorporation of Shari'a courts on a local level. This led to a substantial transformation, particularly through the introduction of an appellate jurisdiction, a new code of civil procedure and the use of the local language in the courtrooms (Kriještorac 2022:44). At the onset of the decolonial struggles of the emerging Balkan nations against the Ottoman Empire, Islamic scholarly elites from the Albanian populace also endured a constant policy of ethnic cleansing, enduring forced separation from Sheik-al Islam, which served as a spiritual legal guide to the *ummah* (Sadriu 2019:438). Across the region, local Muslims were held responsible, in several respects, for the sorry conditions of the countries that had just gained independence. Since then, Muslims have had little or no input into the state of the literature documenting how "indigenous" communities have historically negotiated and promoted their right to heritage as human rights (Grama 2019:2–3). In fact, they contributed to the substantial developments of European countries and institutions (Beribes et al. 2018:76–79), and exercised their agency in powerful ways (Karić et al. 2023) by resisting and boldly contesting forms of coercion and control over their cultural heritage (Trupia 2023a).

Mehmed Handžić (1906–1944), born in Sarajevo and an alumnus of Al-Azhar University in Egypt, was one of the religious leaders[2] keen to improve the social, economic and educational condition of the Muslim community (Khan 2017:303). The subsequent promulgation of "*Islamgesetz*", the Islam Law in 1912, not only offered a unique precedent for the integration of all Muslim communities in a single representational body, but also constituted a model for addressing the challenges of Muslim integration in Europe along with the promotion of an institutionalised "European Islam" (Rexhepi 2019:2; Merdjanova 2013:116). In this respect, Džemaludin Čausević (1870–1938), the *re'is ul-ulema* of the Bosnian Islamic Community from 1914 to 1930, authored "How a Muslim Live a European Cultural Life and Remain a Good Muslim: The Qur'an in Theory and Practice"[3] (my translation) in 1937, advo-

2 With Kasim Dobrača, Mehmed Handžić authored "The Resolution of Sarajevo Muslims" on 4 August 1941. The resolution was delivered after an assembly of el-Hidaje, an association of *ulama* from Bosnia and Herzegovina, then part of the State of Croatia ruled by the ultranationalist movement Ustaše. After Nazi Germany and its allies invaded Yugoslavia in April 1941, Handžić's resolution condemned the persecution of the Serbian population by Croat Ustaše, preventing most Muslims from being associated with SS Handschar's coreligionists who participated in acts of violence. Furthermore, the resolution demanded assistance for victims of all religions and provided information about the persecutions against innocent Muslims conducted by Yugoslav Serb partisans. In fact, the Croatian Ustaše units used to attack Serbian villages by wearing fez and using Muslim names to agitate Serbs against the whole Muslim population (see Sindbaek 2012:207–208).

3 In Bosnian, *Da li moze Musliman zivjeti evropskim kulturnim zivotom i ostati dobar Musliman – Kur'an teoriji i praksi.*

cating a European-type modernisation of the educational and *waqf* institutions, as well as calling for a reform of Muslim dress code (Khan 2017:207).

On the ruins of the Khilafat Movement, the Turkish authority and *sheikh ul-Islam* could not even symbolically represent Muslims across the Balkans. At the same time, other influences arrived from intellectuals promoting the idea of radical reforms after Mustafa Kemal Atatürk came to power in Türkiye (Merdjanova 2013:117). In neighbouring Bulgaria, Yusuf Ziyaeddin Ezheri (1879–1961) was much influenced by Attatürk's secularisation and westernisation (in Turkish, *Attatürk Devrimleri*). Looking at the potential impact of the latter on the post-Ottoman Turkish minority groups, Ezheri praised freedom of thought and expression as a natural human right, and thereby he formulated a new and constructive interpretation of Islam to enable Muslims in Bulgaria to become active citizens within an increasingly secular and multicultural Europe (Khan 2017:248). Yet *orientalistic* deceptions portrayed Balkan Muslims as non-Europeans and as uncivilised people, and definitely, as foreign to the European canon (Müller 2009:66). Across the post-Ottoman Balkan territories, the national assignment of guilt and argumentation against the former colonisers was deployed until the breakup of the Balkan Wars (1912–1913). The Ottoman and its markedly Islamic heritage became a source of insecurity against which a rapid reorder of national and ethnic identities took place (Bougarel 2008:151). To use Samera Esmier's concept of "judicial humanity" in the case of Muslim agency under British colonialism in Egypt (2012), Muslims were not simply dehumanised, but rather supposed to return to their pristine identity after being liberated from the inhuman conditions prescribed by the Ottoman colonisers. Bulgaria's Pomaks – a diverse, complex and stratified Slavic-speaking community, were subjected to the principle of modernity, which aimed at purifying and sanitising the history of nationhood by rectifying a historical wrong (Trupia 2023b:174). On the grounds of saving and converting, Pomaks were treated as "the colonised" to be elevated above their backward status of Muslims. This cultural uplifting (in Bulgarian, *културно издигане*) resonated with Frantz Fanon's explanation of the strict control of a colonised country (1967:142), and masked a de facto eugenic politics that modified the ethnic makeup of Bulgaria (Bjelić 2018:7).

In the wake of the Second World War, the Communist takeover made Balkan Muslims take a defensive stance. Victims of racial policies of discrimination, and often physical persecution, Muslims became more secular and less intellectual. Their Islam was almost completely detached from developments in the broader Muslim world (Sadriu 2017:544) and reduced to a sought-after commodity to exploit under the guise of socialism. When state authorities began to reorder domestic heritage and the institutional landscape, they sought an alternative project of modernisation by eliminating the remnants of domestic ethno-religious diversity (Grama 2019:15; Neuberger 2004:53). In Albania, the brand of strict Marxist-Leninism differed from the type of Communism in Yugoslavia. Hafiz Ali Korca (1873–1956), one of the most influential Muslim scholars and reformers, had foreseen the disruptive role of Bolshevism in his "Bolshevism is a Destruction for Mankind"[4] (my translation) published in March 1925 (Khan 2017:215). In Yugoslavia, competing Serbian and Croatian nationalisms placed Islam beyond their imaginary national borders and labelled Muslims as "improper" Europeans, as the "ultimate orientals" and heirs of the Ottoman Empire (Bakić-Hayden 1995:918). For the Yugoslavian federal census in 1971, Bosniaks were encouraged to declare themselves Muslims in the spirit of Tito's policy of "national equality" (Colic-Peisker 2005:627). Those who made this choice were officially recognised as "people" in the Constitution of the Socialist Republic of Bosnia (Kriještorac 2022:43). Yet the genocidal violence committed against Yugoslav Muslims throughout the 1990s proved that recognition was merely tokenism.

During the decolonisation age, Islamic revolutions were strategically praised by Communist leaders in the former Eastern bloc. Communist Bulgaria marked the high point for Turkish education in the country (Savova-Mahon Borden 2001:66) through the dissemination – in both the Turkish and Bulgarian language – of Nazim Hikmet, a Turkish poet of Polish origin. Meanwhile, Muslim Pomaks' revolts against the assimilation campaign of name-changing and the ban on traditional attire were violently crushed after the deployment of army units and tanks against the disobedient communities in question (Trupia 2023b; Neuberger 2004; Myuhtar-May 2014; Marinov 2009). Hikmet's cultural figure, dubbed "the poet of freedom and peace", was instrumentally exploited by party authorities to depict Turkey as the lackey of the United States of America, casting a dark shadow on the Turkish military operation in northern Cyprus in 1974. By the 1960s, a new direction was taken with the scope of further isolating Bulgaria's Turkish communities from perilous influences emanating from Ankara and "the West". Muslims continued to attend Qur'an reading competitions in Iran. Some could study in Tashkent, Damascus and Cairo to become imams, and student exchange programs were also established with Afghanistan.

This interconnectedness between Eastern bloc and Muslim-majority countries in the Global South (see Mark and Betts 2022 and Mark et al. 2019) was exploited to dismiss the ethnically diverse history of the countries and pivot the geopolitical position of the region vis-à-vis international political turmoil. In 1979, Enver Hoxha had hopes for Iran's Islamic Revolution's anti-imperialist stances and their Marxist potentials. Stefan Andrei, Romanian Minister of Foreign Affairs, openly shared his views with Ceausescu about the revolutionary potential of Islam in the Mediterranean (Mark et al. 2019:156–157). At the grassroots level, the Iranian revolution, the Afghan resistance to Soviet occupation and the continuing Arab-Israeli conflict bolstered a stronger sense of Islamic solidarity and a renewed awareness of being part of the *ummah* (Merdjanova 2013:105). In Yugoslavia, some Muslim activists positioned themselves along these decolonising experiences (Karić et al. 2023) – beyond the

4 In Albanian, *Bolshevizma e Ckaterrimi i Njerezimit.*

non-aligned posture. By seeing themselves as part of a larger revival of decolonial struggles, Smail Balić (1920–2002) presented Islam as a democratic and pluralistic faith which, regardless of its politicisation, was part and parcel of historical and cultural Europe and in harmony with the Western canon (Khan 2017:401). More critically, Melika Salihbegović (1945–2017) and Alija Izetbegović (1925–2003) suggested a different geography of belonging, resistance and liberation from the limits of Yugoslavia's decolonial rhetoric. Salihbegović was a student in Sarajevo, a poet, and a member of the League of Communists and the Union of Writers of Yugoslavia. In the late 1970s, she grew close to a circle of Muslim activists following Alija Izetbegović as she truly believed that decolonisation had to pay more attention to the classed and gendered hierarchies within Muslim communities. In Yugoslavia, Salihbegović argued that particularly Albanian and Roma Muslims were treated not only as second-class citizens but also minoritised within the Muslim context. She spoke about the ongoing violence of indigenous people and people of colour who were frequently rendered invisible in the overall pro-European movements of that time (Rexhepi 2023:22). In fact, the local resistance of Muslim Pomaks in Bulgaria in the early 1960s was barely known at the time, and it was almost unacknowledged by most scholars placing their identities and agency within exclusively rigid national frameworks (Gruev and Kalinovski 2008; Benovska-Sabkova 2015; Kokkas 2004, quoted in Trupia 2023b:161).

Under the influence of European philosophers, Izetbegović's political discourse was influenced by the global "Muslim awakening" (Spellman Poots 2019:192). His key influences were the 1970 Iranian Revolution and its call to pan-Islamism, as well as the exchange of ideas with Sudanese, Lebanese, Saudi, Kuwaiti and Egyptian Muslims studying in Yugoslavia (Mark et al. 2019:162, footnote 143). He argued that the rise of Pan-Slavism and nationalism could be opposed by a great Islamic federation from Morocco to Indonesia, from tropical Africa to Central Asia (Izetbegović 1990:60), across which class distinction would be deemed as equally unjust, and morally and humanly unacceptable, as the national divisions among citizens (ibid. 1990:35). His philosophy was influenced by other Muslim pioneers of Islamic thought in the (post)colonial world, such as in the Indian subcontinent. There, the decolonial struggles were completely ignored as the British colonial gaze perceived Asian political elites along typically ethnic ("Asian') rather than religious ("Muslim") terms (Jones 2021:21). However, Izetbegović's *Islamska Deklaracjia*[5] was influenced by Sayyid Abu'l-A 'la Mawdudi (henceforth Mawdudi) and Muhammad Ali Jinnah (henceforth, Jinnah) in the wake of the Pakistani-Indian efforts to carve a Hindu-majority India and a Muslim-majority Pakistan out of the British Ray.[6] Drawing on Mawdudi's *Jama'at-i Islami* – namely, the "Islamic society"

5 In English, "Islamic Declaration".

6 The blog "Critical Muslims" includes Partition India after the collapse of the British Ray as one of the Top Ten Relationship Break-ups for Muslims worldwide. Available at: https://

(Rippin 2001:213–217), Izetbegović tried to theorise a viable system for Muslims who could live into a state and a democracy, which he himself described as the most desired form of government. The *Jama'at-i Islami* was founded to rival the Muslim League after the Lahore Resolution of 1940 in Pakistan to commit to creating a separate Muslim state (Nasr and Vali 2005:111). Izetbegović argued that Bosnia's Muslims should gather around an Islamic society and acquire the emotional aspects of belonging to Muslim citizenry. He praised a secular state, though, based on modern Western democratic principles where religion has its place on an equal footing with other factors. This perspective produced an instance of ideological difference between Izetbegović and Jinnah. In the 1910s, Jinnah had advocated a Hindu-Muslim unity through the All-India Muslim League, and, between the 1930s and the 1940s, the creation of a Muslim state in British India to counter the possible marginalised status of Muslims after the country gained full independence. Conversely, Izetbegović looked at Bosnia as one of the rare examples where a state is hewn out of three people, three religions, three cultures, maybe even more (Wieland 1999:358); out of such a state, Muslims in Bosnia and Herzegovina could emerge from their marginality (Bougarel 1997:548). Following Mawdudi, Izetbegović's state should not be the enforcer of Shari'a but only implement the will of the people through the modern machinery of government: an elected president, a parliament and an omnipotent judiciary, whose branches would be regulated by checks and balances meted out in a constitution (Nasr and Vali 2005:106), thereby protecting the rule of law and equality, not only among Muslims, but also among all Bosnia's ethnic groups (Delagic and Ushama 2022:48). Unlike Jinnah, who supported a division between Hindus and Muslims (Wieland 1999:360), Izetbegović's position resonated Mawdudi's toward the *zimmis* (non-Muslim minorities), whose extension of rights could not be granted into a "theodemocracy" or a "democratic caliphate" (Nasr and Vali 2005:109) – both deemed unrealistic by Izetbegović himself in a speech from July 1990 (Wieland 1999:353).

Izetbegović was recognised as a theorist of a model of the "European Islam" (Bougarel and Mihaylova 2005:13) only after being accused of conspiring against the Yugoslavian state as the *Mladi Muslimani*.[7] The latter was a movement tolerated by the state at first, but then accused of plotting behind Yugoslavia's back for trying to establish an Islamic state that could link Yugoslavia's Muslims with the *ummah* into a greater Islamic confederation (Rexhepi 2023:21). In March 1983, Izetbegović was arrested along with other Muslim intellectuals: Melika Salihbegović, Omer Behmen, Hasan Čengić, Edhem Bičakčić, Džemaludin Latić, Ismet Kasumagić, Salih Behmen, Derviš Đurđević, Mustafa Spahić, Đula Bičakčić and Rušid Prguda. In what came to

---

criticalmuslim.com/issues/21-relations/top-ten-relationship-break-ups (Accessed: 29 January 2024)

7 In English, "The Young Muslims".

be known and widely publicised as the "Sarajevo Process" (Karić 2021:231), Izetbegović aligned himself with the new pan-Islamism as it was elaborated on in the scholarship of Muhammad Iqbal and Sayid Qutb, among others (Delagic and Ushama 2022:47). By rejecting the opportunities offered to Yugoslav Muslims by the national non-aligned project, he then condemned the instrumentalisation of religion and Islam in particular (Mark et al. 2019:162).

The 1980s was also a tense decade for Muslims in Bulgaria. While Muslims of diverse ethnic backgrounds were never relieved from the decades-long campaigns of name-changing (Gruev and Kalyonski 2008:129), in the summertime of 1984, two bomb explosions at Plovdiv central railway station and Varna airport brought ethnic minorities under accusation of the central authorities. The attacks were soon depicted as the outlaw actions of "Turkish terrorism" and accelerated the assimilation policy on the ground. In a short period of time, precisely between early November 1984 and late January 1985, the campaign of the "Revival Process" was launched.[8] About 800,000 people were forced to change their Muslim- and Arabic-sounding names to new Christian-Slavonic ones (Baeva and Kalinova 2010:68). Those who refused to comply with that imposition faced exile, imprisonment – even death. Some dissidents were imprisoned in the labour camps of Belene and Lovech, while others were also forced to leave to Western Europe (Dobre 2015:308; Baev 2015:164). Yet others began to protest against the government. Although some women-led silent protests in 1984 resulted in the killing of innocents in southernmost Bulgaria (Trupia 2023b:182), hunger strikes and "freedom walks" continued to take place up until to the so-called "events of May 1989" (Atasoy and Soykan 2011). Then, civil disobedience unfolded in the villages and small towns around Varna, Dulovo, Asenovgrad, and Krumovgrad. In the province of Kardzhali, the village of Dzhebel became the centre of public demonstrations where ordinary Turks and Muslims from nearby villages gathered to protest against the regime's assimilation campaign (Karakusheva 2021:66–67). This local resistance, demanding civil rights and free emigration, convinced the Communist authorities to allow "unpatriotic citizens" to flee Bulgaria. About 360,000 Turks and Muslims made their way to Turkey between June and August 1989, while the police continued to operate violently, targeting those who could not escape either to Turkey or to Western Europe. Although the Party's nationalist rhetoric euphemistically depicted the mass-migration as "the great excursion of tourists", that experience culminated in a de facto ethnic cleansing (Kamusella 2019), and it would be a similar precursor to the events that other Muslims had to endure in war-torn

8 In Bulgarian, "Възродителен процес". It should be noted that, in English literature, the term "Revival Process" is used to indicate the name-changing campaign against all Muslims and Turks in the 1980s. Moreover, the Bulgarian term is also used for naming the assimilation campaign of Muslim Pomaks in the 1960s, although English publications refer to the latter as the "Rebirth Process".

Yugoslavia. At the Islamic Conference of May 1988, a resolution openly criticised Communist Bulgaria for its inhuman treatment of the Muslim population, while Iran, Iraq, and Algeria followed suit in their criticism (Stankova 2013:120–304). The Organisation of Islamic Countries sent a delegation to visit Bulgaria, and the United Nations Special Rapporteur on Religious Intolerance for the Human Rights Committee shortlisted the country for systematically preventing the peaceful practice of religion (Savova-Mahon Borden 2001:287). After the events of May 1989, a second wave of public demonstrations took place around the country. In December 1989, hundreds of Turks and Muslims took to the streets of the capital Sofia, heading toward the Parliament under the slogan "we want the names that our mothers gave us back". The protest was also supported by Bulgarians in a unique moment of civic solidarity that occurred in parallel to the dissolution of the socialist regime (Atasoy and Soykan 2011).

The decades-long period of isolation and the turmoil of 1989 had already damaged the accidental connections between Muslims in Bulgaria and the ummah. In Yugoslavia, the war forced thousands of Muslims to navigate the ebbs and flows of decommunisation. In light of the emergence of ethnonational parties in war-torn Yugoslavia, Izetbegović fought to preserve Bosnia until the last moment. He argued that when Yugoslavia began to disintegrate, there was no third choice for Bosnia: either remain in an incomplete Yugoslavia dominated by Serbia and Montenegro or demand independence (Delagic and Ushama 2022:37). Yet again, his ideas were misunderstood in spite of the fact that many connected the would-be first president of independent Bosnia with the renowned personalities of Mahatma Gandhi and Taha Hussein. As he was the founder of a Bosnian Muslim-oriented political organisation in May 1990 – namely the Party of Democratic Action (in Bosnian, *Stranka Demokratske Akcije*) – the latter was considered the continuation of the *Mladi Muslimani* organisation by Serbian nationalists and Slobodan Milošević since 1987. The arrival of mujahideens during the Bosnian war (1992–1995) further jeopardised his intellectual efforts on bridging Balkan Muslims with the *ummah* in a rapidly changing world (Delagic and Ushama 2022:31,37). After quickly replacing the Communist threat after 1989, Islam became Europe's constitutive other (Wintle 2016). If Bulgaria's newly-established democracy saw the constitution of the "Movement for Rights and Freedoms"[9] as a politi-

9 In Bulgarian, „Движение за права и свободи". Since its constitution, this Movement for Rights and Freedoms (herein, MRF) has been de facto the political party of ethnic Turks and Muslims in Bulgaria. After 1989, the Council of Europe pushed the Bulgarian Constitutional Court to allow the MRF to participate in elections to the Constitutional Assembly on 10 June 1990. However, according to the Bulgarian constitutional text (Art. 11 – Section IV), the party was denied its original name – the "Movement for Rights and Freedoms of the Turks and Muslims in Bulgaria". Viewed with controversy and suspicion, the MRF has been dubbed an "enigma-within-an-enigma" in light of the phenomena of radicalisation and radical interpretations of Islam (see Trupia 2019).

cal party that defended the Muslim and Turkish community, the dissolution of Yugoslavia was followed up by a series of genocidal attempts to obliterate the agency of Muslims in their war-torn rising states and suppress their wish for independence. While Croatia and Bosnia fell under the international spotlight, the ethnopolitical conflict in Kosovo received much less attention for a long time, mainly because of its nonviolent character (Leutloff-Grandits 2023:64). The Srebrenica Genocide in 1995 in Bosnia and Milošević's policy in Kosovo, among others, forced Muslims to endure genocidal violence that was misunderstood as civil wars by "the West", and justified by the weight of former Yugoslavia's national rhetoric over the danger of Muslims' intentions to take Vienna, Paris and London after seizing control of the Balkans (Mark et al. 2019:163).

## "We're all Muslims, yet we're Europeans"

At the Bosnian Muslim community in Antwerp, a portrait of Alija Izetbegović stood out above the desk of my interlocutor, even though his political praxis and philosophy were barely mentioned during the interview. Many respondents were particularly knowledgeable about the profound injustice of the Eurocentric approach toward so-called "Balkan Islam" and its historical and scientific contributions to today's European society (Sofos and Tsagarousianou

*Figure 2.1* A portrait of Aljia Izetbegović in the Bosniac cultural centre in Antwerp. Photo by the author.

2013:133). Amina, a female Muslim of Bosnian origin dating a Belgium-born coreligionist with Yemeni origin, shared "the feeling that Balkan Muslims are not even considered seriously by [the *ummah*] because of their loose cultural relations with Islam". Her critical statement resonated in many other in-depth interviews. A large number of examples were in fact made by other respondents (mostly males) when comparing themselves with other same-age Muslims and their families. Amina's words shed light on the untapped experience for young Muslims born outside the Balkans in discovering the *ummah* and strengthening transnational connections with non-Balkan coreligionists. This re-engagement happens at times when "Balkan Islam" is depicted as part and parcel of European Islam, and therefore independent from the Muslim world and foreign to in-group and out-group dynamics (Azabar and Van Aelst 2023) shaped by common histories and experiences of war and genocidal violence.

Among the *generation after*, spontaneous and personal answers debunked, at least in theory, the myth that a higher level of religious salience obstructs integration and widens distance between the core society and so-called "parallel societies" (Mushaben 2008:508). In contested multicultural suburbs of Belgian and German cities, young Muslims of Balkan origin are not found playing a role in the phenomena of "neighbourhood nationalism" (Leiken 2012). If anything, many were found to be outspoken about some other societal issues that are misunderstood by the public. At the open market on Bakalarska street in Warsaw, a young street seller from a Turkish-speaking Roma community originally from Kazanlak, dubbed the "city of roses" in Bulgaria, was upset due to the deep economic uncertainty. Another older Bulgarian Roma who had overheard, jumped in by self-identifying as "*an Arab*" while organising his stall, referring to the high level of Islamophobia widespread throughout Polish society. Likewise, two young Turkish-speaking Roma parents, living in Bremen and originally from Shumen, Bulgaria, were sceptical about their future in Germany in light of the troubles at work with their Turkish boss, the housing crisis in town and the prejudicial police surveillance.

Overall, very few refer to the *ummah* as a benchmark in a global social movement seeking social justice and political actions (Scott 2005:113). To use here Salman Sayyid's concept of imagined *ummah* (2014:103), respondents feel they are members of the latter by proving their assertion of an explicit Muslim subjectivity, belonging to various (post-)migrant communities concentrated in places where a wealth of networks produce, and expose them to, situations in which they (may) encounter different Muslim traditions. The *ummah* is considered neither a nation, nor a common market, nor a global network of labour and capital flows, nor a common way of life or a linguistic community (Sayyid 2014:103). Yet, the spontaneous answers mentioning, referring to and drawing some comparisons with other Muslims revealed a sense of belonging that goes beyond even religious affiliation. As previous studies show in Germany, age and country of origin play a crucial role among those Muslims who feel members of the *ummah*. In terms of age, older respondents are more likely to belong to the global community of coreligionists, while in nationality,

Bosnians, along with Lebanese, Palestinians and Turkish Muslims, all seem more likely to reject such an assumption (Cesari 2013:194). Throughout the fieldwork, most respondents with Bosnian heritage tended to distance themselves from other (racialised) Muslim subjects – be they Moroccans, Pakistanis, Syrians, among others – by making the assumption that "Balkan Islam" is historically "secular" and "it belongs to Europe" (Hurd 2008:58). In everyday life, however, such frictions fade away due to sincere friendships and various personal ties with other Muslims. If compared with other (post-)diasporic forms of Islam, respondents generally reiterate, perhaps unknowingly, the geo-racial distinction between their white, local and European Muslimness from that of black and brown Arabs and Muslims (Rexhepi 2023:65). Often they did so to avoid racialisation and unpleasant encounters in their everyday lives.

> "I feel European. We, Bosnians, are European Muslims. When people here meet us and get to know that we're a Muslim Bosnian family, they cannot believe it. They mostly associate Islam and 'being Muslims' with terrorism; but we all know about such banal and malignant representations. I say to them all the time that we, Bosnians, are not like other Muslims from the rest of the world. Bosnia, and especially Sarajevo, is not like Morocco or Tunisia. In Sarajevo there are churches, and people have lived side by side for centuries".
>
> "For example, Moroccans are very different from us, and to be honest, they do not paint the best picture of Muslims in town. It is about culture, not religion. . . . When Moroccans celebrate [Ramadan, or Bayram], there are always small incidents. There is no way to talk to them about doing some projects together. We feel much closer to Turkish Muslims".
>
> "As European Muslims, we do not have any problems living here in terms of culture, institutions and interreligious respects – we, and those who have lived in the Balkans and especially in Sarajevo, know what it means to live with Jews, Christians and Muslims, so that is something that completely makes us distinct from other Muslim communities such as Turkey and Morocco".

All these interventions suggest that respondents tend to take up an epistemological standpoint from which they position themselves "*inside* Europe" and "*outside* the *ummah*". Covered by a white mask, to allude to Frantz Fanon's historical critique (1967), many reaffirmed the geocultural borders between Europe and *the Oriental*, thereby positioning themselves as different from those arriving from "further east". Simply put, they reified the self-image of "European Muslims" – namely, those who are different from "other Muslims out there" who preach a non-European Islam. What actually motivated respondents to say so, was their unconscious fear of accentuating their Muslimness and align their own critical positions with other coreligionists, lest they might be perceived as the latter (Ferizaj 2019:84) or even accused of "nativism" or "woke gatekeeping" (Ferizaj 2023). As a respondent in Dortmund summarised, "I am Albanian, therefore more European than other Muslim friends of mine whose Islam has little to do with European culture". This statement clearly follows the Eurocentric bent in designing a "European Islam" through a secular and moderate religious identity, entirely disconnected from the distorted image of a Middle Eastern, radical and culturally backward Islam. Among Bosnian Muslim respondents, so-called "Bosnian Islam" is understood as a different kind of Islam preached by "European Muslims" who are "acceptable Muslims" as they themselves are "firstly European and secondly Bosnian or Muslim". As they did not associate their Islam with the Arab world, they attributed quasi-biological and/or cultural characteristics to certain social groups (El-Tayeb 2012). Yet again, this internalised division between "them and the *ummah*" does not prevent most Balkan Muslims identifying with the pleas of the Syrians, the Palestinians, the people of colour, the migrants and Muslims inside the EU or the United States (Rexhepi 2017a:55). Postulates of solidarity are not often enacted as many yearn to present themselves as Europeans in order to ease the burden of belonging to a Muslim-majority country often placed on the periphery of Europe (Ferizaj 2023). However, the triangulation of data analysis and field notes could not ignore how quickly the groups under study and respondents themselves reacted to the Israeli war against Hamas in Gaza in the wake of the events of October 7. Their participation in the ceasefire rallies and social media campaigns for Palestinian civilians debunks the myth of religious distinction and racelessness operating in and beyond the *ummah*. Since October 2023, constant efforts at fitting into Europeanness were replaced by a political and religious call for solidarity with Palestine activated by the lasting legacies of domestic colonisation imposed by the socialist modernisation aspiration in Yugoslavia and other communist regimes.

Hardly surprisingly, respondents seem to have internalised socialism's masked racist-imperialism that their parents passed down behind the cloak of altruism toward "backward" and darker-skinned Muslims who could not benefit from a socialist, classless society (Neuberger 2004; Mark et al. 2019). A Rome-born respondent of Bosnian origin admitted to feeling nostalgic about Yugoslavia after listening to his father's stories of that great country. When he self-identified as a "Yugo Muslim", he likened his everyday lifestyle to the various modes Muslims used to dress up while in Yugoslavia, how they publicly behave and even enjoy listening to rock music from the West before the 1990s. All these instances of "Westernised lookism" did count more than ethnic and religious affiliation before the dissolution of Yugoslavia (see Rigney 2022), but also undoubtedly shaped certain "chameleon-like attitudes" passed down to the generations after. This is why, in the eyes of most respondents, Muslims in and from the Balkans go unnoticed in Europe. The following two interview insights are instructive in this regard:

> "The Muslims from [the Balkans] are seen better by the West, we are the white ones, and Westerners do not really listen more about us, we

are invisible, and it is better to be a Muslim from Bosnia, Sandžak[10] and Kosovo rather than Morocco and Türkiye".

"I think that looking 'white' helped me avoid facing racism. If there is some pre-judgment, it comes from my name, [which] does not sound Belgian, and people do not understand that. My family is modern, but we do not eat pork. It is a balance for me, Muslim Bosnians are the best bridge between the West and the East, and I always thought about this bridge".

Unlike those young Muslims born in Albanian families, most of the efforts of those of Bosnian origin to avoid racialisation revealed the nesting relationship between the emergence of Islamophobia and the contestation of the notion of Europeanness as today uncritically exemplified by white revanchism. More precisely, the persistence of Islamophobia and its entrenchment in public discourses does not simply reinforce a prejudice toward Muslims in and from the Balkans, but also the very acceptance of Eastern Europeans as white Europeans. As introduced previously, whiteness becomes conditional to bypass systemic violence, assimilation and genocidal desire against the Muslim population in and beyond the Balkans. Hence, it does not come as a surprise that most respondents also yearn to present themselves as "good European Muslims" in opposition to "bad Arab Muslims". If Muslims in general identify with a supranational identity, European identity is used to overcome (perceived) barriers of inclusion and exclusion (Driezen 2023:61). Much pressure falls on young Muslims with Albanian heritage who have aligned themselves with Europeanness by reiterating the (peripheral) discourse of Albanian elites in pursuit of Euro-Atlantic integration (Ferizaj 2019:72), thereby adopting the securitised frames of reference in relation to Islam in the Balkans (Sadriu 2017:541). Same-age respondents with Bosnian roots even reiterated, at times, anti-Islam arguments to claim a "true" European identity, revealing once more that internalised Islamophobia has not only been normalised (Ferizaj 2023) but that it also goes unacknowledged and unchallenged within the groups under study. A male interviewee interestingly notes that "some forms of racism toward other cultures have penetrated the Bosnian Muslim diaspora, while 'anti-Semitism' is skyrocketing among Muslims in Bosnia proper".

Having local imams as interlocutors helped change the perspective. As further explained in Chapter 5, an Albanian imam serving the Al-Albani Moskee in the multicultural neighbourhoods of Rabat in Ghent, proudly confirmed to "pray in Arabic, explain the Qur'an in Albanian and try to speak Dutch with the Muslims". A young Dutch convert, who asked and was granted permission

10 Sandžak is a Muslim-majority region extending over the borders of today's Serbia, Montenegro, and the southernmost Bosnia and Herzegovina. Historically, it refers to the Sandjak of Novi Pazar, an Ottoman Bosnia Herzegovina administrative district, later divided between Serbia and Montenegro.

to attend the formal conversation, pointed out that he had discovered Albanian culture through the imam's explanation of the Qur'an. Hence the imam himself added, "God's words are all the same for us [Muslims], and this is the most important factor for a good believer". While visiting the Bosnian mosque in town, the imam admitted that "Bosnian identity can easily fade away from younger generations born in Belgium as their family background can be different and their integration efforts can set them apart from Islam". On the other hand, he adds, "those Belgium-born Muslims encounter other Muslims since childhood at school [and] within the neighbourhood; they soon come to know Islam through such encounters, [thereby understanding] how different our Islam is".

The analysis of qualitative data shows how such a telling division between Albanian and Bosnian Muslim communities is deeply embedded in the privileges and disadvantages of whiteness and "white lookism" in particular. In the Muslim-majority neighbourhoods of Rabat and Gröpelingen in Ghent and Bremen, the order of white proximity does not only arrange subjects in corporal terms but also in sensibilities and practices (Ali et al. 2023:95) that go beyond cultural diversities and a stereotyped image of Muslimness. While the two communities point out that they share very little with other Muslims from Africa or Asia, friendships and family ties were more likely held with other, smaller Balkan communities. Those belonging to smaller groups of Muslims from Sandžak, North Macedonia and Kosovo, respectively, Bosniaks, Pomaks, Gorani and Torberesh, use the former Serbo-Croatian language as a means of communication at the mosque, thereby maintaining community ties also on the basis of the similar political and historical experiences (Kriještorac 2022:87). In Belgium, the Gorani diaspora, a Slavic-speaking Muslim population originally from Kosovo, has maintained good relations with Albanian Muslims on the grounds of faith and lifestyle (Leutloff-Grandits 2023:65). Muslims from Sandžak also attend the praying time and religious celebrations at the Bosnian cultural centre due to the previously established family connections and, more importantly, the shared language used for understanding the sermons of the imam. In Dortmund, the Torberesh Muslims from North Macedonia have also their own mosque to maintain their community traditions and family ties. In Verona, the Bosnian community opened its fourth *džemat* in northern Italy in January 2024, stressing that their community already welcomes all Muslim families from Bosnia, North Macedonia and Turkey who live in the city and the areas nearby.[11] Other young Muslims originally from Bulgaria, mostly with Turkish family heritage, stay closer to the much larger Turkish diaspora. At the same time, almost all young Muslims with Balkan family background

11 The Muslim Bosnian community in Italy arrived between 1992 and 1995 from war-torn Yugoslavia. Since then, they found the "CIBI – Comunità Islamica dei Bosniaci in Italy" (in Bosnian, *Islamska Zajednica Bošnjaka u Italiji*) in the cities of Biella, Piacenza, Vallecamonica, and Verona.

share cultural closeness with the Turkish diaspora. Unlike the second and third generations of Muslims born in Turkish emigre families, Turkey is not seen as a "second homeland" (in Turkish, *Vatan*) for young Muslims of Balkan origin. Yet most respondents express a deep sense of attachment to Turkish friends and coreligionists due to similar family customs and practices of Islam. In Antwerp, Oud-Berchem is the renowned Turkish neighbourhood where a younger generation of highly educated Turkish professionals have played a role in transforming the "ethnic" commerce (Blommaert 2014:4). However, in-depth interviews were mainly set up and held in the multicultural area of Durne and Borgerhout. At the *iftar* evening organised by the youth organisation *Mreža Mladih Antwerpen*, young Muslims from Rotterdam, the Netherlands and Bosnia proper were present along with some Turkish friends from Ghent and Leuven.

Similar to Antwerp, Gröpelingen, the most well-known multicultural neighbourhood in Bremen, shows similar urban dynamics. A few in-depth interviews were facilitated by a young veiled Muslim woman, a student of languages at the university, who used to volunteer for a local NGO helping young Muslims get abreast of challenges in German society. She was willing to help as she herself had many same-age Muslim friends with Balkan family backgrounds. While translating, she opposed the term "fundamentalist" to "moderate", and "extremist" to "secular". Both dichotomies set those Muslims who desire to direct the course of Islam's future from those who are not recognised within the *ummah*. Drita and Antoneta, two sisters whose father escaped right before the 1999 Kosovo War, could not deny that a similar family migration background with the rest of the Muslim community has helped them to have a transnational circuit of friends in Germany – a community which provides a "safety net" against potential exclusion from the core society (Vathi 2015:10). Although they know that the *ummah* cannot be based on the exclusion of another's claim to exclude someone from the *ummah* (Mahomed 2022:36), Drita pointed out that Muslims of Roma and Sinti ethnicity, as well as refugees and asylum seekers from the Middle East, are extremely disadvantaged in town and almost disregarded by the rest of the Muslim community. Slightly in disagreement with her sister, Antoneta laments that certain "backward practices of some Muslims [complicate their] struggling to comply with Germany's gender balances and coming to terms with women's rights". She also added that, in Gröpelingen, unpleasant experiences of catcalling, toxic behaviour related to men and division between generations of male Muslims born in Germany and refugees or asylum seekers, are hiding in plain sight. A similar complaint was also verbalised in Dortmund, where female respondents of Albanian origin associate patriarchy with some forms of religious extremism and low levels of education among the older generations. They are, in other words, two sides of the same coin: a malignant interpretation of Islam that lies in stark opposition to Western values and most cultural views of Islam itself; hence, "extreme Islam" is instrumentally praised to justify gender segregation and efforts to fight the impurity of the West (Cesari 2013:xiv). Although all these claims will receive due attention in Chapter 5, here broader cultural stereotypes of Muslim violence against women illustrate how the corporeal and epistemic experiences of violence against female Muslims themselves (especially if veiled) destroy the illusion that Muslims from/in the Balkans are not subjected to racialisation, blatant Islamophobia and othering. Allusions to gender-based violence essentially reinforce "the West's" predatory, misogynist, and violent rescue rhetoric of the War on Terror. Since then, mainstream anti-Muslim rhetoric has similarly tried to rescue and protect white and European women, as well as Muslim women, especially if they're refugees and immigrants, from the threatening culture and values of Islam (see Spellman Poots 2019).

## Reordering Solidarity

By triangulating interview insights with the discursive characteristics of news media, most respondents seem encouraged to enact postulates of solidarity in light of the predicament of violence and doom of Muslims worldwide. The War on Terror, the aftermaths of the 2003 invasion of Iraq, Syria's post-2011 turmoil, the US withdrawal from Afghanistan in 2022, as well as China's persecution of Uyghurs in Xinjiang and the continuing threats posed by Serb nationalists in Bosnia, Kosovo and Montenegro, were all often mentioned to recollect the troubling predicament of Muslims worldwide, likening the latter with family stories of sorrow and pain.

This condemnation did not completely bridge the groups under study with the pleas of the *ummah*, nor did it condition new forms of religiosity and related expressions within Islamic activist groups (Spellman Poots 2019:194). It should be pointed out that in-depth interviews were conducted a year after Russia's full-scale invasion of Ukraine and right before the October 7, 2023, events in Israel. Both events have undoubtedly taken a toll among the groups under study and respondents in particular. At the time of fieldwork in Antwerp, the Bosnian cultural centre was engaged in a donation campaign for Bosnians and Tatar Muslims fleeing Ukraine. While the powerful earthquake that struck Turkey in early February 2023 mobilised many around solidarity and aid campaigns for people in need, Hamas's gory penetration into Israel and the killing of innocent civilians on October 7, 2023, boosted already-existing Islamophobic hatred and scorn against Muslims in "the West". Scapegoating Hamas and its militias has particularly worsened the political climate in Europe and deepened a sense of distrust toward black and brown Muslims who immediately took to the streets asking for an immediate ceasefire in Gaza. During the fieldwork, the issue of Palestine took a central space in solidarity and support for Palestine. G/local proximity with Muslims and Palestinians, as well as with the Jewish community in Antwerp, is of particular importance as the city has been historically home to an important community of Orthodox Jews who identify themselves as belonging to religious Zionism and maintain a pro-Israel stance in community affairs. Prior to holding in-depth interviews, it was hypothesised that many would have expressed criticism toward Israel in highly emotional terms, perhaps motivating their criticism in light of the mistreatment of Palestinians. Zionism has not only historically led to a strengthening of Islamic identity (Rippin 2001:176), but also exacerbated the discourse over the Israeli-Palestinian dispute since the Six-Day War in 1967 until the expansion of Israeli illegal settlements in East Jerusalem and the so-called West Bank.[12] In this regard, the pitfall of understanding anti-Zionist stances as a camouflaged form of anti-Semitism after October 7 events was a major concern in the midst of the rise of criticism toward Israel among Europe-born generations of Muslims. As Marianne Hirsch pointed out (2024), prominent Jewish survivors and intellectuals like Jean Améry, Primo Levi, Zygmunt Bauman, and, of course, Hannah Arendt, condemned the use of the memory of the Holocaust for the state of Israel's political purposes. Yet confusing anti-Zionism with anti-Semitism, and vice versa, could not only reveal an ideological and political misuse of the Holocaust, but also overlook the fact that anti-Semitism and anti-Muslim xenophobia feed one another in some circumstances. In fact, the imperative to fight both expressions of hate and scorn often include certain elements of Islamophobia and anti-Semitism without taking into consideration the wider historical background (Bobako 2017:2).

Over a Zoom call, Marko confirms that

> "Muslim Bosnians are empathetic toward Palestinians [due to] the similar experiences of suffering in war and the media discourse. [Yet he also states] "while going back home to Sarajevo to participate in an anti-war rally in a time of turmoil between Israel and Palestinians, Bosnian Muslims did not express anti-Israeli sentiment [but they wanted to say] that Sarajevo ought to be on the anti-war map".

In Antwerp, almost all male respondents verbalised their support for Palestine and Palestinians by mixing a sense of piety and care with their solidarity and support for Muslim brothers and sisters. Although the geography of the latter did not become a subject of conversation during the in-depth interviews, this pro-Palestinian attitude is entrenched in Antwerp's history and urban dynamics. As already touched upon, respondents were found to be keen on counteracting with the "very vocal position of local Zionists among the Orthodox Jews in town" by participating in pro-Palestine rallies and engaging in boycott campaigns not simply "against products made in Israel, or even 'Made in Palestine' but produced in specific areas where Israeli settlers have recently

12 On July 19, 2024, the International Court of Justice (herein, ICJ) gave its advisory opinion by responding to the question posed by the General Assembly of the United Nations on the "Legal Consequences arising from the Policies and Practices of Israel in the Occupied Palestinian Territory, including East Jerusalem". ICJ stated that Israel's policies and practices in the Occupied Palestinian Territories are in breach of international law. The maintenance of these policies and practices is an unlawful act of a continuing character entailing Israel's international responsibility, and the continued presence of Israel is therefore illegal.

organised their communities [kibbutz] illegally". One male respondent stated he "disagree[d] with every aspect of the State of Israel [because] every Zionist, or person supporting Zionism, can't be a good person". Less critical opinions were verbalised in Italy, Germany, and Poland, albeit mostly fuelled by annoyance and frustration over "Israeli misconduct against Palestinians in their homeland", and regarding "Muslims [who], in Palestine, are powerless" and "always subjected to the violence of Israeli soldiers at Al-Aqsa Mosque during celebrations and prayer time". A gender perspective is yet again eye-opening. Female respondents are genuinely concerned about other Muslims' fate and "the Third World"; nonetheless, they were less likely than their male peers to participate in any direct political action to translate into practice what they criticise. As they do not generally speak of high politics and political affairs, almost no female interviewees refer to Palestine whatsoever.

If it is true that no hostility against Jews themselves was verbalised during in-depth interviews, the pro-Palestinian position is worth unpacking and further clarifying. To begin with, it should be pointed out that most respondents (especially males) were found to be rather outspoken and critical when touching upon thorny questions and/or taboo issues related to their Muslimness in relation to Islam in the realm of everyday life. The Israeli-Palestinian conflict as a whole was one of the most complicated issues to talk about. Despite the absence of hatred or overt racism toward Jewish people, the local Orthodox Jewish community was at times mentioned to compare Antwerp's historical Jewish neighbourhood with other Muslim-majority areas in town. In this regard, respondents did not imagine Jewishness otherwise (Omer 2022:214). Enabled by a nesting orientalism, they instead drew on "European" and "liberal" values and the practices of their community to show how they comply easily with Antwerp's multicultural urban contexts and disavowing other Muslims' misbehaviour in and beyond town.

> "I often pass by the Jewish quarter, and I was positively surprised by how they celebrate their traditions and ceremonies without problems. Like us, when celebrating Bayram, we ask local authorities to have some public space, to enjoy ourselves and then clean up and go back safely home. Moroccans instead are very different and, to be honest, they do not provide the best picture of Muslims in town. It is about culture, not religion. . . . When Moroccans celebrate [Ramadan, or Bayram], there are always small incidents. There is no way to talk to them about doing some projects together. We definitely feel much closer to Turkish Muslims".
>
> "I try to explain [to my friends] that what they read and listen to in the media is simply untrue . . . about killing and infidels, for instance: our Prophet, Peace be upon Him, never taught us to kill those who think and believe otherwise: when he conquered Jerusalem, he let Jews and Christians live, and only the polytheists, who did not want to coexist, they had to leave the city . . . explaining these things, is very important to me".

To better focus on the potential genealogy of the sense of solidarity toward Palestine, a few interplays cannot but be taken into consideration. At times, the rampant growth of Islamophobia and anti-Semitism stems from the (lack of) recognition of Palestine vis-à-vis the history of the Israeli State, as well as from the polarisation and friction stirred up among the Jewish-Arab diaspora in the West and Middle East, and the reverberations of failed Jewish-Muslim reconciliation in Israel and the Occupied Palestinian Territory proper. Although all these instances remained a multi-faceted knot that was difficult to untie throughout the in-depth interviews, a strong criticism of Israel never became vernacular nor did it reveal traces of anti-Semitic sentiment. To a certain extent, Quranic knowledge helped respondents reject anti-Semitism while supporting Palestinian coreligionists. Overall, cultural and religious differences do not always propose a disquieting binarism between the Muslim *ummah* and the Jewish world. In this regards, respondents do not refer to already-existing actions of solidarities that – at least by a shared sense of outrage – have brought Muslims and Jews together in "the West". In Germany, for example, the decision of a judge in Cologne in June 2012 to outlaw circumcision and define it as an "illegal act of bodily harm" sparked criticism and protests in Jewish and Muslim communities. Because of the amplitude of the complaints, the parliament passed a law a few months later permitting non therapeutic circumcisions to be safeguarded under certain circumstances (Cesari 2013:xiv). Likewise in Belgium, Amine Easat-Daas notes (2018:120) how hypocritical the 2019 legislation banning ritual slaughter in the regions of Wallonia and Flanders was. The hypocrisy behind this "slaughter ban" offended the religious principles of both Jewish and Muslim communities. It firstly shines a light on Europe's double standards which, in theory, legitimise anti-Semitic and Islamophobic religious discrimination while, secondly, setting a precedent that obfuscates the wider public from the much more pressing issues surrounding the broader ethics of the meat industry, i.e. the mass production and consumption of animal products (see also Yuval-Davis 2011:3). In Bosnia, local Jews and Muslims came together on the eve of the yearly anniversary of the Srebrenica massacre via a community forum to talk about the pain of being the victims of the ultimate crime of bigotry, and proposing Sarajevo as the city of a potential peace agreement between Israel and Palestine throughout the Israeli-Hamas war in Gaza.[13]

This important example is instructive to note as family (hi)stories and war traumas were more likely verbalised by respondents to empathise with the pain

13 After the escalation of the war against Hamas in Gaza, many Bosnians drew a parallel to the siege of Sarajevo. The violence endured by Palestinian civilians in besieged Gaza was considered in many ways identical to the one that Bosnian Muslims endured in the 1990s. While Emir Suljagić, a Srebrenica survivor himself, was accused of legitimising Hamas after refusing to comment on the war, the launch of the Srebrenica Muslim-Jewish Peace and Remembrance Initiative officialised a Jewish-Muslim call for peace from Bosnia amidst the Israeli-Palestinian dispute in the Middle East.

and sorrow of Gazans rather than employing anti-Semitic sentiments toward the Jewish State of Israel. Postulates of solidarities do not resemble what Atalia Omer refers to as "prophetic pastiche" – namely, a Jewish Palestine solidarity activism that produces, through the social movement's dynamics, a movement in generic human rights terms (2022:217). Nor do they essentialise a certain Jewish/Muslim binarism (Bobako 2017:12). In contrast, respondents failed to realise that the particular vision of the Jewish-Muslim diatribe, in and beyond Palestine, is deeply interlinked with the history of most Western societies. The latter also often overlook Europe's tragic relationship with the Holocaust and the Nakba as both historical events resulted from centuries-long colonial expansion, racialised capitalism, colonial genocide and exclusionary logics of nationalism, which date back to blood purity laws during the Inquisition (Omer 2022:216). At the same time, there is little doubt that respondents do not self-reiterate a "new anti-Semitism", one which is based on the grounds of cloaking their anti-Semitism. This potential camouflage technique is not only today's exclusive domain of right-wing political groups using the idea of pure national identity and white Christian or European supremacy to hide their hatred against Jews (Barna et al. 2018). It similarly represents the overlapping positioning of Muslim minorities and certain Western left-wing groups (Bobako 2017:6) often concealing anti-Semitism under the guise of decolonisation, self-determination and the people's will. Uncritical accusations of "new anti-Semitism" may gloss over the anti-Muslim rhetoric that is neutralising, silencing and delegitimizing any critical stance at the politics of Israel, but also the heterogenous stances that young Muslims themselves hold and nurture with regard to the Palestine cause.

> "Please keep this off the record [a male respondent asked, as] anti-Semitism is definitely on the rise in the Bosniak region more than [anonymised place], but people do not know that Jews were the main ally of the Bosnian question during the [Yugoslavian] war . . . the wife [anonymised name], a Jewish woman . . . did so much to connect both communities over the Bosnian question, and now you have such anti-Semitic sentiment? I have Palestinian and Jewish friends [anonymised place], and when we discuss, you can't really compare Bosnia with Palestine because when Bosnians were on the edge of disappearance, we Bosnians took arms and raised up, while for the Palestinians it was not the case . . . Palestinians historically waited for someone to fight for them".

This intervention can be unpacked as follows: first, he rightly warned about the rise of some anti-Semitic *topoi* in and beyond the Balkans, correctly assessing the danger of anti-Semitism across Europe. Second, his refusal to align with most Bosnian Muslims' critical voices at the politics of Israel constitutes a reason to not consider anti-Zionism and anti-Semitism as two faces of the same coin. As Bobako points out (2017:8), such a potential equation constitutes a gesture that entails a certain form of collective de-subjectification of Muslims, and it may be classified as a manifestation of anti-Muslim racism instead. The anti-Zionist opponents of Israeli politics are too often disqualified as *political* subjects (my emphasis), and the values of their criticism against Israel are considered to be devoid of both political and moral legitimacy. This disqualification not only takes on the particular form of the "Palestinian knot", but it also renders any political stance nil. In this regard, g/local perspectives are taken into account for comparing political affairs between young Muslim of Balkan origin and other subaltern groups, as well as between Muslims in the Balkans proper and other Muslim-majority areas across the world.

Some respondents admitted to having participated in "Black History Month" and asserted their personal solidarity with whoever may be a victim of police brutality, racial profiling, and racism in general. As discussed in Chapter 3, what activates this form of political sensitivity toward other Muslims or racialised communities is the recollection of their family (hi)stories and ongoing marginalisation and discrimination. For many, the killing of George Floyd was a seminal event and plunged respondents with a conscience into a deeply pensive mood toward Black Muslims and Roma, brown Muslims or otherwise.[14] In fact, respondents spontaneously made comparisons between certain global dynamics of racism and genocidal violence with events taking place in the place of residence or having an impact on a global scale. A young respondent of Bosnian origin warned about the stale aftertaste of orientalist and Islamophobic stereotypes used by the media during the 2022 FIFA World Cup in Qatar. In this regard, he explained that

> "when we discuss[ed] about Qatar [in Germany], I see the bias behind all the TV special programs about human rights and violations of women's rights, and when you have tough rhetoric against a Muslim-majority country I feel attacked in a certain way . . . also, I do not remember all of these special programs for the 2018 Russia world championship, somehow Russia was understood as part of Europe and Orthodox Christian . . . no one talked about homophobia and the totalitarian aspects of Russian society".

What the respondent referred to was nothing new. The renowned scientist Khaled al-Hroub noticed the embedded racism shown against Morocco for its wrongdoings – namely, for supporting Palestine through its display of the Palestinian flag. Disparaging cultural statements and stereotypes were also

14 An informal group of young, brown Muslims composed of activists and community leaders came to support the rally held at the Toronto Police Headquarters, holding their first iteration of a sign that read: "Muslims in Solidarity with Black Lives Matter" (See Ali et al. 2023). Also, the Czech Roma community's reactions to the death of Stanislav Tomáš, a Roma who died after a police intervention, analogous to the death of George Floyd in the United States, sparked anger and street demonstrations in Prague and across the country (see Kola et al. 2022:1413–1415).

employed to allude to Moroccans' anti-Semitic offences and connections with the Islamic State (Zubair 2023:276). In the 2010 World Cup in South Africa, similar accusations were raised by Marine Le Pen against the same French football team for displaying non-French symbols and flags of France's former African colonies (Amara 2013:651). Also in Germany, Shkodran Mustafi, born in an Albanian family from North Macedonia and who played for Germany in the international football arena, was not perceived German enough, nor "really German", in the media landscape (Ferizaj 2019:78). A similar situation happened to Mesut Özil, whose Turkish heritage was emphasised in terms of foreignness to Germany after he took a picture with the Turkish President, Recep Tayyip Erdoğan. As Tawseef Khan argues (2022:53), nothing similar happened as regards Lukas Podolsk and Miroslav Klose's Polish heritage, nor were there repercussions when Lothar Matthaus met Vladimir Putin.

## References

Ali, N., El-Sherif, L. and Mire, H. (2023) Islamophobia and Proximities to Whiteness: Organising Outside of the Brown Muslim Subject. *ReOrient*, 8 (1), pp. 78–100. https://doi.org/10.13169/reorient.8.1.0078

Amara, M. (2013) Sport, Islam, and Muslims in Europe: In between or on the Margin? *Religions*, 4 (4), pp. 644–656. https://doi.org/10.3390/rel4040644

Asad, T. (2003) *Formations of the Secular. Christianity, Islam, Modernity*. Stanford: Stanford University Press.

Atasoy, E. and Soykan, A. (2011) Freedom Walk of the Turks in Bulgaria: The Events of May in 1989 and their Reflections. *Procedia Social and Behavioural Science*, 19, pp. 112–120. https://doi.org/10.1016/j.sbspro.2011.05.113

Azabar, S. and Van Aelst, P. (2023) Religion Works in Different Ways: An Intersectional Approach to Muslims' Noninstitutionalized Participation. *Acta Politica*, 59, pp. 416–438. https://doi.org/10.1057/s41269-023-00300-y

Baev, J. (2015) 'De-Stalinisation and Political Rehabilitations in Bulgaria', in K. McDermott and M. Stibbe (eds.) *De-Stalinising Eastern Europe. The Rehabilitation of Stalin's Victims after 1953*. London: Palgrave Macmillan, pp. 150–169.

Baeva, I. and Kalinova, E. (2010) 'Bulgarian Transition and the Memory of the Socialist Past', in M. Todorova (ed.) *Remembering Communism: Genres of Representation*. New York: Science Research Council, pp. 57–94.

Bakić-Hayden, M. (1995) Nesting Orientalisms: The Case of Former Yugoslavia. *Slavic Review*, 54 (4), pp. 917–931. https://doi.org/10.2307/2501399

Barna, I., Félix, A., Mesežnikov, G., Pankowski, R. and Šternová, V. (2018) 'Contemporary Forms of the Oldest Hatred: Modern Antisemitism in the Visegrád Countries', in A. Bíró and K. Lantos Swett (eds.) *The Noble Banner of Human Rights. Essays in Memory of Tom Lantos*. Leiden: Brill Nijhoff, pp. 303–338. https://doi.org/10.1163/9789004376960_009

Benovska-Sabkova, M. (2015) Urban Culture, Religious Conversion, and Crossing Ethnic Fluidity among the Bulgarian Muslims ("Pomaks"). *Etnografiski Institut SANU*, 1, pp. 49–71.

Beribes, A., Mausbach, L. and Jungeblut, J. (2018) Is Islam a Part of Eastern Europe? Thoughts on History, Religion, and National Identity in the Eastern EU Countries, *Konrad Adenauer Stiftung*. Available at: www.kas.de/en/web/auslandsinformationen/artikel/detail/-/content/gehoert-der-islam-zum-oestlichen-europa- (Accessed: 22 October 2021).

Bjelić, D. (2018) Toward a Genealogy of the Balkan Discourses on Race. *Interventions – International Journal of Postcolonial Studies*, 20 (6), pp. 906–929. https://doi.org/10.1080/1369801X.2018.1492955

Blommaert, J. (2014) Infrastructures of Superdiversity: Conviviality and Language in an Antwerp Neighbourhood. *European Journal of Cultural Studies*, 17 (4), pp. 431–451. https://doi.org/10.1177/1367549413510421

Boatcă, M. (2022) 'Race and Politics', in T. Golash-Boza (ed.) *A Cultural History of Race in the Modern and Genomic Age*, Vol. 6. London: Bloomsbury Academic, pp. 87–105.

Bobako, M. (2017) The Palestinian Knot: The 'New Anti-Semitism', Islamophobia and the Question of Postcolonial Europe. *Theory, Culture and Society*, 35 (3), pp. 99–120. https://doi.org/10.1177/0263276417708859

Bougarel, X. (1997) From Young Muslims to Party of Democratic Action: The Emergence of a Pan-Islamic Trend in Bosnia and Herzegovina. *Islamic Studies*, 36 (2–3), pp. 533–549.

Bougarel, X. (2008) 'Balkan Muslim Diasporas and the Idea of a European Islam', in T. Dulić, R. Kostić, R., I. Maček, and J. Trtak (eds.) *Balkan Currents. Essays in Honour of Kjell Magnusson*, Uppsala: Uppsala University Press, pp. 147–165.

Bougarel, X. and Mihaylova, D. (2005) Diasporas musulmanes balkaniques dans l'Union européenne [Balkan Muslim Diaspora in the European Union]. *Balkanologie – Revue d'études pluridisciplinaires*, IX (1–2), pp. 59–211.

Byrd, J. D. (2017) *Islam in a Post-Secular Society. Religion, Secularity and the Antagonism of Recalcitrant Faith*. Leiden and Boston: Brill.

Cesari, J. (2013) *Why the West Fears Islam. An Exploration of Muslims in Liberal Democracies*. New York: Palgrave Macmillan.

Colic-Peisker, V. (2005) At Least you are the Right Colour: Identity and Social Inclusion of Bosnian Refugees in Australia. *Journal of Ethnic and Migration Studies*, 31 (4), pp. 615–638. https://doi.org/10.1080/13691830500109720

Delagic, L. and Ushama, T. (2022) Alija Izetbegović's Contribution to Socio-Political and Religious Thought. *Hamdard Islamicus*, 45 (4), pp. 29–52. https://doi.org/10.57144/hi.v45i4.501

Dobre, C. (2015) 'Use and Misuse of Memory. Dealing with the Communist Past in Postcommunist Bulgaria and Romania', in M. Pakier and J. Wawrzyniak (eds.) *European Memory: Eastern Perspectives*. New York and Oxford: Berghahn Books, pp. 299–315.

Driezen, A. (2023) Youth Navigating the Superdiverse City of Antwerp: Constructing and Negotiating Ethnic and Religious Symbolic Boundaries, *University of Antwerp*. Available at: https://repository.uantwerpen.be/docman/irua/986f79motoM53 (Accessed: 2 March 2024)

Easat-Daas, A. (2018) 'Islamophobia in Belgium', in E. Bayraklı and F. Hafez (eds.) *European Islamophobia Report 2018*. Istanbul: SETA, pp. 141–166. Available at: www.setav.org/en/european-studies/european-islamophobia-report-2018-eir2018 (Accessed: 2 February 2021)

El-Tayeb, F. (2011) *European Others: Queering Ethnicity in Postnational Europe*. Minneapolis: University of Minnesota Press.

El-Tayeb, F. (2012) 'Gays Who Cannot Properly Be Gay': Queer Muslims in the Neoliberal European City. *European Journal of Women's Studies*, 19 (1), pp. 79–95. https://psycnet.apa.org/doi/10.1177/1350506811426388

Esmier, S. (2012) *Judicial Humanity. A Colonial History*. Redwood City: Stanford University Press.

Eze, E. C. (2007) *On Reason. Rationality in a World of Cultural Conflict and Racism*. Durham: Duke University Press.

Fanon, F. (1967) *The Wretched of the Earth*. New Work: Grove Press.

Ferizaj, A. (2019) Othering Albanian Muslim Masculinities: A Case Study of Albanian Football Players. *OCCHIALÌ – Rivista sul Mediterraneo Islamico*, 5, pp. 71–93.

Ferizaj, A. (2023) The Desperate Desire to be 'European', *Kosovo 2.0*. Available at: https://kosovotwopointzero.com/en/the-desperate-desire-to-be-european/ (Accessed: 3 December 2023)

Gajda, K. A. (2020) 'Eastern Europe's Orientalised Identity', in A. Balazs and C. Griessler (eds.) *The Visegrad Four and the Western Balkans*. Baden-Baden: Nomos Verlag, pp. 63–83.

Geisser, V. (2014) 'Islamophobia in Europe: From the Christian Anti-Muslim Prejudice to a Modern Form of Racism', in I. Ramberg (ed.) *Islamophobia and Its Consequences on Young People*. Budapest: European Youth Centre Budapest, pp. 36–46. Available at: www.coe.int/en/web/youth/-/islamophobia-and-its-consequences-on-young-people?inheritRedirect=true (Accessed: 8 December 2022).

Grama, E. (2019) *Socialist Heritage: The Politics of Past and Place in Romania*. Bloomington: Indiana University Press.

Gruev, M. and Kalyonski, A. (2008) *Vazroditelniat Protses: Komunisticheskiat Rezhim i Myusyulmanskite Obshtnosti* [The Revival Process: The Communist Regime and the Muslim Communities]. Sofia: CIELA.

Haj, S. (2009) *Reconfiguring Islamic Tradition: Reform, Rationality and Modernity*. Stanford: Stanford University Press.

Hatiboglu, I. (2007) Religio-Intellectual Relations between Bulgarian and Non-Bulgarian Muslims in the First Half of the 20th Century. *Journal of Islamic Studies*, 46 (1), pp. 73–86.

Hirsch, M. (2024) Rethinking Holocaust Memory after October 7, *Public Books*. Available at: www.publicbooks.org/rethinking-holocaust-memory-after-october-7/ (Accessed: 1 August 2024)

Hurd, S. (2008) *The Politics of Secularism in International Relations*. Princeton: Princeton University Press.

Izetbegović, A. (1990) *Islamic Declaration*. Available at: https://archive.org/details/3IslamicDeclarationEng/mode/2up?view=theater (Accessed: 3 January 2023).

Jones, S. H. (2021) *Islam and the Liberal State. National Identity and the Future of Muslim Britain*. London: I.B. Tauris.

Kamusella, T. (2019) *Ethnic Cleansing during the Cold War: The Forgotten 1989 Expulsion of Turks from Communist Bulgaria*. London and New York: Routledge.

Karakusheva, S. (2021) Memory Practices and Memory Politics in the Town Fest of Dzhebel, *Ethnologia Bulgarica. Yearbook of Bulgarian Ethnology and Folklore*, VII (1), pp. 62–76.

Karić, D., Buljina, H. and Rexhepi, P. (2023) Feel-good Orientalism and the Question of Dignity, *Maydan. Islamic Thought*. Available at: https://themaydan.com/2023/02/feel-good-orientalism-and-the-question-of-dignity/ (Accessed: 2 January 2024).

Karić, E. (2021) Confessions of a Muslim Humanist. *İnsan ve Toplum Dergisi*, 11 (4), pp. 229–239. dx.doi.org/10.12658/R0026

Khan, M. M. (2017) *Great Muslims of the West: Makers of Western Islam*. Leicester: Kube Publishing Ltd.

Khan, T. (2022) *Muslim, Actually. How Islam is Misunderstood and Why It Matters*. London: Atlantic Books.

Khankan, S. (2018) *Women Are the Future of Islam. A Memoir of Hope*. London: Penguin.

Kirchner Reill, D. (2018) 'Balkan Initiatives to Make Europe: Two Cases from Mid-Nineteenth-Century Dalmatia', in T. Snyder and K. Younger (eds.) *The Balkans as Europe. 1821–1914*. Rochester: University of Rochester Press, pp. 11–30.

Kokkas, N. (2004) The Incorporation of Traditional Values in Pomak Folk Tales. *Περί Θράκης*, 4, pp. 1–19.
Kola, A., Domachowska, A., Gemziak, Ł. and Trupia, F. (2022) Mnemonic Wars and Parallel Polis: The Anti-Politics of Memory in Central and Southeast Europe: Kosovar Women and Black/Roma Lives Matter. *Memory Studies*, 15 (6), pp. 1406–1419. https://doi.org/10.1177/17506980221134936
Kriještorac, M. (2022) *First Nationalism Then Identity. On Bosnian Muslims and Their Bosniak Identity.* Ann Arbor: University of Michigan Press.
Leiken, R. (2012) *Europe's Angry Muslims: The Revolt of The Second Generation.* Oxford: Oxford University Press.
Leutloff-Grandits, C. (2023) *Translocal Care Across Kosovo's Borders. Reconfiguring Kinship along Gender and Generational Lines.* New York and Oxford: Berghahn.
Mahomed, N. (2022) The Elusive Ummah: Between the Political, Sectarianism, and Authority. *ReOrient*, 7 (1), pp. 27–45. https://doi.org/10.13169/reorient.7.1.0027
Mamdani, M. (2004) *Good Muslim, Bad Muslim.* New York: Pantheon Books.
Mark, J. and Betts, P. (2022) *Socialism Goes Global: The Soviet Union and Eastern Europe in the Age of Decolonization.* Oxford: Oxford University Press.
Mark, J., Iacob, B., Rupprecht, T. and Spaskovska, L. (2019) *1989. A Global History of Eastern Europe.* Cambridge: Cambridge University Press.
Marinov, T. (2009) Ot "Internatsionalizŭm" kŭm Natsionalizŭm. Komunisticheskiat rezhim, Makedonskiat vŭpros i politikata kŭm etnicheskite I religioznite obshtnosti" [From Internationalism to Nationalism. The Communist Regime, the Macedonian Question and the Politics of Ethnic and Religious Minorities], in *Istoria na Narodna Republika Bŭlgariia. Rezhim i Obshtestvoto* [History of People's Republic of Bulgaria. Regime and Society]. Ciela: Sofia, pp. 481–516.
Mbembe, A. (2019) *Necropolitics.* Durham and London: Duke University Press.
Merdjanova, I. (2013) *Rediscovering the Umma. Muslims in the Balkans between Nationalism and Transnationalism.* Oxford: Oxford University Press.
Mourad, S. (2014) Riddles of the Book. *New Left Reviews*, 68, pp. 15–52.
Müller, D. (2009) Orientalism and Nation: Jews and Muslims as Alterity in Southeastern Europe in the Age of Nation-States, 1878–1941. *East Central Europe*, 36 (1), pp. 63–99. https://doi.org/10.1163/187633009X411485
Mushaben, J. M. (2008) Gender, HipHop and Pop-Islam: The Urban Identities of Muslim Youth in Germany. *Citizenship Studies*, 12 (5), pp. 507–526. https://doi.org/10.1080/13621020802337931
Myuhtar-May, F. (2014) *Identity, Nationalism, and Cultural Heritage under Siege.* Leiden: Brill, Leiden.
Nasr, S. and Vali, R. (2005) 'Mawdudi and the Jama'at-i Islami: The Origins, Theory and Practice of Islamic Revitalism', in A. Rahnema (ed.) *Pioneers of Islamic Revival.* London: Zed Books Ltd., pp. 98–124.
Neuberger, M. (2004) *The Orient Within: Muslim Minorities and the Negotiation of Nationhood in Bulgaria.* Ithaca and London: Cornell University Press.
Omer, A. (2022) Reorienting Jewishness, Palestine Solidarity, and Prophetic Pastiche. *ReOrient,* 7 (2), pp. 214–221. https://doi.org/10.13169/reorient.7.2.0214
Rahman, S. (2017) Top Ten Relationship Break-Ups, *Critical Muslims.* Available at: https://criticalmuslim.com/search/node/Top%20Ten%20Relationship%20Break-ups (Accessed: 29 January 2024).
Rexhepi, P. (2015) Mainstreaming Islamophobia: The Politics of European Enlargement and the Balkan Crime-Terror Nexus, *East European Quarterly*, 43 (2–3), pp. 189–214. Available at SSRN: https://ssrn.com/abstract=2706058
Rexhepi, P. (2017a) 'Unmapping Islam in Eastern Europe Periodization and Muslim Subjectivities in the Balkans', in I. Kacandes and Y. Komska (eds.) *Eastern Europe*

*Unmapped. Beyond Borders and Peripheries*, New York and Oxford: Berghahn, pp. 53–77.
Rexhepi, P. (2017b) Borders. *Critical Muslim*, 21, pp. 45–56.
Rexhepi, P. (2019) Imperial Inventories, "Illegal Mosques" and Institutionalised Islam: Coloniality and the Islamic Community of Bosnia and Herzegovina. *History and Anthropology*, 30 (4), pp. 1–13.
Rexhepi, P. (2023) *White Enclosures. Racial Capitalism & Coloniality along the Balkan Route*. Durham: Duke University Press.
Rigney, R. (2022) Sergej Kreso: 'Religious Identity Didn't Mean Much to My Generation'. *Balkan Insights*. Available at: https://balkaninsight.com/2022/10/20/sergej-kreso-religious-identity-didnt-mean-much-to-my-generation/ (Accessed: 2 December 2022).
Rippin, A. (2001) *Muslims. Their Religious Beliefs and Practices*. London: Routledge.
Sadriu, B. (2017) Grasping the Syrian War, a View from Albanians in the Balkans. *The Journal of Nationalism and Ethnicity*, 45 (4), pp. 540–559. https://doi.org/10.1080/00905992.2017.1292498
Sadriu, B. (2019) Rebranding the War on Terror and Remaking Muslim Subjectivities. *East European Politics*, 35 (4), pp. 433–456. https://doi.org/10.1080/21599165.2019.1662399
Said, E. (2019) *Orientalism*. London: Penguin Classics.
Savova-Mahon Borden, M. (2001) The Politics of Nationalism under Communism in Bulgaria. Myths, Memories and Minorities, *The School of Slavonic and East European Studies*. Available at: https://discovery.ucl.ac.uk/id/eprint/1317549/ (Accessed: 20 January 2022).
Sayyid, S. (2014) *Recalling the Caliphate: Decolonisation and World Order*. London: Hurst & Company.
Scott, T. (2005) *The Global Resurgence of Religion and the Transformation of International Relations. The Struggle for the Soul of the Twenty-First Century*. New York: Palgrave Macmillan.
Shatanawi, M., Macdonald, S. and Puzon, K. (2021) *Islam and Heritage in Europe*. London: Routledge.
Sindbaek, T. (2012) *Usable History? Representations of Yugoslavia's Difficult Past from 1945 to 2022*. Aarhus: Aarhus University Press.
Sofos, S. A. and Tsagarousianou, R. (2013) *Islam in Europe. Public Spaces and Civic Networks*. New York: Palgrave Macmillian.
Spellman Poots, K. (2019) 'Muslim Diasporas in Transition: Islam, Gender and New Regimes of Governance', in D. Kandiyoti, N. Al-Ali, and K. Spellman Poots (eds.) *Gender Governance in Islam*. Edinburgh: Edinburgh University Press, pp. 186–215.
Stankova, M. (2013) A Socialist Foreign Policy. Bulgaria's Relations with the Mediterranean Arab States in the 1970s and 1980s. *Dans Les Cahiers Irice*, 1 (10), pp. 107–121. https://doi.org/10.3917/lci.010.0107.
Tlostanova, M. and Mignolo, W. (2012) *Learning to Unlearn: Decolonial Reflections From Eurasia and the Americas*. Columbus: Ohio State University Press.
Trupia, F. (2019) 'Idiosyncratic Identity of Muslim Turks and the Romani of Bulgaria: Rethinking Human Security through the Prism of Self-Governing Rights', in E. Doğan (ed.) *Reimagining Eastern Europe – Imaginaries, Identities and Transformation*. London: Transnational Press London, pp. 115–130.
Trupia, F. (2023a) 'Between State Violence and Resistance: The Co-Belonging and Non-Exclusivity of the Pomak Heritage', in A. K. Kinga (ed.) *The Heritage of Central and Eastern Europe*. Berlin: Peter Lang, pp. 159–177.
Trupia, F. (2023b) 'Decolonising Bulgaria's Official Amnesia of the Communist Past: A Pericentric Approach to Minority Memories of Anti-Communist Resistance', in

C. Voß, K. Kralova, and S. Ferhadbegović (eds.) Mem*ory Cultures in Southeast Europe since 1945*. Berlin: Südosteuropa-Jahrbuch, pp. 169–186.

Vathi, Z. (2015) *Migrating and Settling in a Mobile World Albanian Migrants and Their Children in Europe*. Springer Open. Available at: https://link.springer.com/book/10.1007/978-3-319-13024-8 (Accessed: 18 July 2023).

Wieland, C. (1999) Izetbegović und Jinnah – Die Selektive Vereinnahmung Zweier "Muslim-Führer" [Izetbegović and Jinnah – The Selective Appropriation of Two "Muslim Leaders"]. *Südosteropa Mitteilungen*, 4 (39), pp. 351–368.

Wintle, M. (2016) Islam as Europe's "Other" in the Long Term: Some Discontinuities. *History*, 101 (344), pp. 186–224.

Yuval-Davis, N. (2011) 'Power, Intersectionality and the Politics of Belonging', in W. Harcourt (ed.) *The Palgrave Handbook of Gender and Development*. London: Palgrave Macmillan, pp. 367–381. https://doi.org/10.1007/978-1-137-38273-3_25

Zubair, A. (2023) 'Islamophobia in Germany', in E. Bayraklı and F. Hafez (eds.) *European Islamophobia Report 2022*. Vienna: Leopold Weiss Institute, pp. 261–284.

# 3 Echoes of War

After the fall of the Berlin Wall in 1989, ancient hostilities and ubiquitous nationalisms re-emerged from the depths of former socialist societies. In the Balkans, communist Bulgaria's decades-long assimilation policies ended in the ethnic cleansing of most Turkish and Muslim nationals right before 1989 (Kamusella 2019; Marinov 2009; Gruev and Kalyonski 2008). The war crimes committed in war-torn Yugoslavia brought Douglas Hogg, the British Minister of State in the Foreign Office, to liken, in moral terms, what happened in Bosnia to what had happened in Europe as a result of Nazism (Simms 2002:4). Žarko Korać, academic and later deputy prime minister of Serbia, likewise compared the position of Jews in Nazi-occupied Europe to that of Albanians and Muslims in Bosnia and Kosovo (Kola et al. 2022:1412). Miloš Minić (2000), former Yugoslav Minister of Foreign Affairs (1972–1978), labelled Slobodan Milosević's police and military offensive in Kosovo as ethnic cleansing, the goal of which was to alter the ethnic makeup of the Albanian-majority region. The punitive justice measures developed through trials of war criminals at the International Criminal Tribunal for the Former Yugoslavia (ICTY), ruling that the Yugoslav Army and the Serbian Ministry of Interior committed war crimes in Kosovo (Krstić 2019). In August 2001, a trial chamber of the ICTY handed down the tribunal's first genocide conviction for the killing of 7000–8000 Bosnian men in Srebrenica by Serbian forces in 1995. The trial chamber acknowledged the need for a dramatic expression of moral outrage at the most morally reprehensible massacre in Europe since 1945 (Southwick 2014). The fate of Muslims in Bosnia resembled Rwanda's genocidal events (Koinova and Karabegović 2016:4).

When Russia's full-scale invasion of Ukraine in 2022 was touted as an unprecedented crisis, the phrase "not since World War II", or variations of it, sparked angry outbursts among thousands of former socialist citizens in Europe. Questions arose instantly: what about the commemorations of the merciless assimilation of the "Revival Process" orchestrated by Todor Zhivkov's regime in Bulgaria? How do they come to terms, if at all, with the genocidal campaigns against Muslims and Albanians in Bosnia and Kosovo during the dissolution of Yugoslavia? How do cases of genocide and violent events

DOI: 10.4324/9781003589624-4

involving Southeast European civilians resemble the current violence in Ukraine, Palestine and Israel, and Sudan?

These questions are not simply rhetorical. They rather motivate scholars to delve deeper into (geo)political events and spontaneous practices of commemoration to further explore the history of reconciliation and recognition. They also confer meaning to the unspeakable and proper words for discussing historical events of violence. While literature on trauma and memory produced in the Balkans is countless,[1] a less concrete analysis has been initiated among the generations born and living outside the region as a byproduct of the genocidal politics of the 1990s. In a time of crisis for liberal democracy, coupled with necropolitical migration policies and geopolitical turmoil, who could tell this story better than the survivors themselves or their children (Dupuis-Tordjenab 2024)?

This chapter explores how the groups under study recollect the violent events of the past that their families and communities endured during the 1990s. This angle of investigation was employed to shed light on the different modes used by the *generation after* to verbalise family experiences of war, dislocation and persecution during the in-depth interviews. This web of post-memories, as Marianne Hirsch (2012) refers to it, not only took a central space at the time of the fieldwork, but also opened the doors to intimate milieus where Islam is deeply connected with families' tragedies and traumas. This linkage was particularly noticed while observing the ways human relations with older generations were nurtured and cherished to safeguard a culture of remembrance that allows the *generation after* to learn, discover and interpret the past as a means to referentially connect it with present-day issues.

The following sections discuss respondents' personal experiences of coming to terms with family traumas, and how the latter reverberate through an unsettling long durée of violence that continues, at times, to besiege the groups

1 Among others, Todorova, M. (2010) *Remembering Communism: Genres of Representation.* New York: Social Science Research Council; Todorova, M., Dimou, A. and Troebst, S. (2014) *Remembering Communism. Private and Public Recollections of Lived Experience in Southeast Europe.* Budapest: Central European University; Pakier, M. and Wawrzyniak, J. (2015) *European Memory: Eastern Perspectives.* New York and Oxford: Berghahn Books; Ognjenovic, G. and Jozelic, J. (2021) *Nationalization and Politicization of History in the Former Yugoslavia.* London: Palgrave Macmillan; Palmberger, M. (2016) *How Generations Remember: Conflicting Histories and Shared Memories in Post-war Bosnia and Herzegovina.* Singapore: Palgrave Macmillan; Kolind, T. (2008) *Post-war Identification: Everyday Muslim Counterdiscourse in Bosnia Herzegovina.* Aarhus: Aarhus University Press; Trajanovski, N., Todorov, P., Volchevska, B., and Risteski, L. (2021) *Cultures and Politics of Remembrance: Southeast European and Balkan Perspectives.* Skopje: forumZFD; Trajanovski, N. (2022) *Remembering the 2001 Armed Conflict in Macedonia: Modes of Commemoration and Memorialization.* Belgrade: Humanitarian Law Center; Gruev, M. and Kalyonski, A. (2008) *Vazroditelniat Protses: Komunisticheskiat Rezhim i Myusyulmanskite Obshtnosti* [The Revival Process: The Communist Regime and the Muslim Communities]. Sofia: CIELA; Kamusella, T. (2019) *Ethnic Cleansing during the Cold War. The Forgotten 1989 Expulsion of Turks from Communist Bulgaria.* London and New York: Routledge.

under study decades after the end of socialism and wartime. Mainly in Antwerp, most respondents recollected being born in former refugee Bosnian families originally from Prijedor and other small towns in Northwestern Bosnia, such as Sanski Most, Bihać and Ključ. Some recalled their parents experiencing concentration camps in the Keraten factory, the Omarska mines complex and the Trnopolje camp. Others were heavily wounded and arrived in "the West" through UN-sponsored programs for war refugees and displaced people. Similar traumas circulate among many young Muslims with Albanian family heritage from Kosovo and North Macedonia. Both groups pointed out how their families could not travel back home as private property fell under Serbian control in Bosnia or was heavily damaged in the already economically underdeveloped towns of Kosovo. These localities are not only important to create stronger links and encourage peacebuilding in the post-conflict period (Karabegović 2024:4), but also echo the fate of war refugees and unarmed civilians in Ukraine and Palestine, among others. Also, certain events reactivate memories that connect related traumas from the past to present-day upheavals.

After the barbarism of the Second World War and, by extension, the horror of Auschwitz, Marianne Hirsch no longer refers to the Holocaust as a conceptual limit case in the discussion on the transmission of historical trauma and related thorny questions of healing and forgetting (2012:18). Hirsch's pronouncement (2024) does not undermine by any means the horrific and daunting post-memory of the Holocaust, but rather includes the latter along with the brutal dictatorships in Latina America, the genocides in Bosnia, Rwanda and Darfur, the unsolved decades-long conflicts in the Middle East and Africa, the events of October 7 and the genocidal violence in the Gaza strip. Hence, this chapter's analysis delves into the troubling nexus of family traumas and their afterlives on individual, societal and institutional grounds. In simpler words, how does the violence of the present and past converge and resurface among the *generation after*? How does Islamophobia and geopolitical upheavals reopen old wounds and perpetuate the traumatic scars of violence among young Muslims of Balkan origin born and raised in "the West"?

## Epistemes after Socialism

Two lines of thought are brought together in the following sections. The first considers the scholarship of epistemic community, which was proposed in sociology at the end of the 1970s and gained scholarly credibility at the beginning of the 1990s (Haas 1992; Henderson 2021, among others). The second refers to Marianne Hirsch's concept of post-memory (2012), which has recently been at the centre of scholarly interest in the Balkan region (Trupia 2022; Trajanovski 2022, among others). This tandem was thought of throughout the fieldwork and later justified in the data triangulation.

The notion of "epistemic community" has so far largely been used to theorise a procedural knowledge, which, following Max Weber's formal rationality approach, shows a kind of goal-oriented and rational calculation, and provides policy guidance for communities of experts. In turn, research on epistemic communities looks at the overlap between experts and policymakers, both categories contributing to organise the patterns of state behaviour in an uncertain and complex global context (Ahmadzai 2022; Sandal 2011; Scott 2005:109, among others). Although the groups under study neither belong to a mere community of professionals, nor do they possess recognised expertise and particular competence within that domain or issue area (Haas 1992), they have nonetheless a sense of "epistemic gate-keeping" in a personal and collective dimension of belonging and engagement (Henderson 2021). Similar to other transnational anti-racist movements, such as Black Lives Matter, MeToo#, the Indigenous Rights Movement, and other activist groups, they yearn to seek social justice and shape densely packed cross-cutting world politics and the global public arena (Zanoni et al. 2023:1184). The narrow definition of epistemic community omits some groups and communities from official and institutionalised hubs of knowledge production and distribution (Kofman 2020:2; Scott 2005:110). To lump young Muslims with Balkan family heritage with epistemic communities not only grants them better position and agency in and beyond their community, but it also means acknowledging their opinions, worries and practices within a broader web of data and knowledge that may contribute to the development of transnational theories of order and change beyond conventional theories of war and peace (Sandal 2011:932). In this study, qualitative data and knowledge suggest that the Islamic episteme plays a pivotal role in transmitting a value system which is translated into a stock of practices and untapped remedies for healing and transforming. Although not of logo-centred formal rationality, Islamic faith can here be categorised as moral or ethical knowledge (Scott 2005:109), which illuminates the nature of the latter and provides practical means of remembering the past and healing from it. In a Foucauldian sense, this form of religious episteme also clarifies what a potential recollection implies and how it makes possible an understanding of what is true and false, thereby showing the values of what can be characterised as science proper from what is not properly scientific – such as rituals, practices, modes of living and so on (Spivak 1999:288, Sandal 2011:934).

When respondents recollect violent experiences that their families and communities endured by referentially connecting them with the present-day war in Ukraine and Palestine, this comparison does not coherently reconstruct historical events as they *really* occurred. In this regard, it should not be forgotten that the term "post-memory" was coined to question exactly what the transmission of past experiences, traumas and syndromes of survivors evokes in their children. The same term shows how prominently the spectre of the past has loomed in the aftermaths of the experiences of surviving, hiding, fleeing their countries with false papers or with special waivers, and so forth. Delving into this generation of postmemory as a person born in a Jewish family who fled Europe because of Nazism, Hirsch herself questions how the past can be appropriated by "those who come after" – namely, by a post-memory generation that can over-identify itself with the envious stories and dramas of the past but barely associated with present experiences (2012:15).

Viewed from this perspective, the genuine grievance of some respondents signals the long-lasting burden of belonging. As further discussed in Chapter 4, belonging needs to be properly addressed (Harris and Nawaz 2015:58) in relation to Europe's grim and racist reality that harks back to the historical turmoil when the Balkans were carved out of Ottoman provinces and generations of Muslims survived the state-run violence and other atrocities (Amzi-Erdğdular 2024; Rexhepi 2019:8). Keeping this perspective in mind would expand the horizon of the formation and configuration of the notion of epistemic community, whose knowledge is produced and circulated by reinforcing older colonial, hegemonic hierarchies outside *other* hubs of knowledge and their holders (Kofman 2020:2, Zanoni et al. 2023:1183).

As remembering is not simply a means of reproducing a record of what one has experienced (Frise 2024), new meanings and significance given to the past shine a spotlight on the nature of memory and the conditions through which to know the past. Respectively, interview insights show inter- and trans-generational knowledge and a sense of "guardianship" built upon family heritage and (hi)stories of Muslims *from* and *in* the Balkans. In this challenging process, the *episteme* of the war often proliferates in a condition of "postness", thereby indelibly stamping itself on the constant practices of negotiation and renegotiation of identity and positionality (Hirsch 2012:6). In other words, respondents were born in a post-socialist predicament and grew up in a post-migrant context, grappling with post-modern dilemmas while living in a post-secular society. Although both the structure and organisation of families have undergone profound changes, their grand/parents had to somehow reinvent, rediscover or even redefine what still belongs to their religious world in a new country (Roy 2013; Merdjanova 2013:105; Grünenberg 2005:190). With their parents originally from places that still resonate with violence and injustice (see Chapter 4), respondents are no longer burdened by the question of staying or leaving. Yet long-lasting trauma and sorrow recognise them as being the progeny of their families' identity categories and boundary markers (Mushaben 2008:509, Hirsch 2012:5).[2]

2 In the online class on 'A Virtual Tour of Bosnia. Bosnian Diaspora in Ghent' (2 April 2021), Maja Sahadžić, Visiting Professor at Antwerp University in 2022, pointed out how Bosnian generations who escaped from war and settled down in Western Europe have kept the same mentality of those who instead managed to remain in their places of residence in the Balkans. During the Q&A session, many attendees from the Balkan diaspora in Belgium went into details. In public offices, for instance, like in Bosnia, older generations look for "someone they know to sort out paperwork and make it easier and faster". During summertime, "they prefer travelling either by car or bus, almost ignoring flight connections, to carry more stuff to travel with", e.g. traditional food, personal belongings and house items. Most of them, unlike the new generations, "have built their houses in villages and small towns to keep a stronger connection with the homeland". In this regard, an important issue is given by the socio-spatial

To add another epistemic layer, critical viewpoints echoed what Hans Kundnani (2023) aptly terms "Eurowhiteness". By definition, "Eurowhiteness" brings together liberal and illiberal regimes in today's refugee crisis – from the Mediterranean Sea to the Polish-Belarus and the EU/non-EU borders. According to some respondents, Eurowhiteness was already visible in Yugoslavia's successor states' desire to build ethnically pure (white) nations, and how today the latter inspires Western Europe's far-right actors in "guarding the national frontiers" against Islam and Muslims. Throughout the 1990s, "white" immigration biases drove proactive responses to the plight of Muslims in Bosnia and Kosovo in 1990s, in striking contrast to other waves of refugees. That proactiveness, once supported by state institutions and officials, revealed most Europeans' misconception of the former Yugoslavian populations who were considered white as in "the West" and were bearers of a similar history (Colic-Peisker 2005; Domachowska 2019; Hromadžic 2023, among others). After February 2022, the West's geopolitical awakening over the Russian war against Ukrainians came to prove yet again Europe's selectively positive attitudes toward *some* refugees. In fact, speculation arose over the peculiar form of "Eurowhiteness solidarity" activated by geographical proximity, the gender makeup of refugees, and the (white) ethnicity and Christian (rather than, especially Muslim) background of the people in need (Moise et al. 2024). Most scholars and pundits accused Russia of provoking Europe's fastest-growing refugee influx since the Second World War, arguing that the large surge of refugees entering the European Union is, in sheer numbers, comparable with the refugee crisis of 2015–2018 (Pita and Cost 2022; Iddon 2022, among others).

As discussed further in this chapter, most respondents openly criticised the West's selective indignation and hypocritical "responsibility to protect" when reflecting on what their families had gone through prior to arriving in "the West" as war refugees. In some cases, frustration runs high in light of the West's cold calculation to intervene in some countries' internal affairs rather than others, while avoiding openly admitting their vested interests. What also hits a nerve is the continuous politicisation and securitisation of the EU's "welcome shift" along its external borders eastward (as defined by Cantat 2022). While the latter provides a rather misleading idea of both Europe and Europeans (Grzymski 2019:137, Shatanawi et al. 2021:7), the former glosses over a series of proxy political factors, on national and international grounds, that drive different states to welcome different groups facing the persecution or war (Costello and Foster 2022:246). However, both hide the inconspicuous yet present desire of "walling whiteness" to use Piro Rexhepi's work (2023, 2017), which officialises the markers of extremist, suspect and fundamentalist fellows by clearly defining who can be integrated into the EU from those who must remain outside.

---

characteristics of cities, making them distinct from rural areas and playing an important role in the development of "cosmopolitan" and "urban identity" (Domaradzka and Hamel 2024:5).

After the borders of Muslim-majority countries in the Balkans began merging with those of the EU – such as the Bosnian-Croatian borders – "Eurowhiteness" has considerably deteriorated the constitutional mechanisms and procedures of protection that safeguard the rule of law and basic human rights within the respective institutions (Basheska and Kochenov 2024:20). Yet, it has also deployed colonial legacies (Rexhepi 2019:5) by strengthening a security-oriented approach based on a "crime-terror nexus" enacted under the complex rubric of the "quasi-criminal connotation" of *all* Muslims.

## Dark Past, Murkier Present?

A web of deeply pervasive memories was intercepted during many in-depth interviews. Relatedly, the way respondents recollected "chosen traumas" and selected seminal events was also eye-opening. Three tropes of post-memories were recollected, respectively, in chronological order: the expulsion of Turks and Muslims from communist Bulgaria throughout the "Revival Process" (1984–85); the war in Bosnia, particularly stressing the ethnic cleansing in Prijedor (1992–93) and the Genocide in Srebrenica in 1995; the troubling predicament of ethnic Albanians under Slobodan Milosević's genocidal violence in then-Yugoslav Kosovo prior to the 1999 NATO bombing.

The first trope of post-memories referred to the expulsion of about 360,000 Muslims and ethnic Turks from communist Bulgaria after the state-run name-changing campaign and parallel restrictions on speaking Turkish, worshipping at the mosque, celebrating Islamic festivities, performing Muslim rituals and so forth (Kamusella 2019; Gruev and Kalyonski 2008; Stoyan 1992, among others). A Turkish woman from Shumen, northeast Bulgaria, recalled her arrival in Bremen after a short stay in Turkey. Once on German soil, the "police could not figure out why [her family members] had two names – one Bulgarian, one Turkish and two IDs". In Warsaw, a young Roma Muslim street vendor explained his life in Poland "as a Bulgaria-passport holder since [the time of] war with Turkey". In truth, there was no war between the two countries; however, what he was referring to was the tense diplomatic stand-off between Bulgaria and Turkey from the mid-1980s onward.

The second trope of post-memories recollected the war crimes committed against the Muslim population during the collapse of Yugoslavia. Often, respondents of Bosnian origin described that genocidal violence as the worst human rights violation that occurred in Europe since the Second World War. More precisely, some referred to the acts of dislocation, sexual assault, murder, rape and torture of civilians waged by the Bosnian Serb forces against Muslims and Croats from Bosnia and Herzegovina. This selective recollection of historical events is embedded in respondents' family heritage and traumas. The Siege of Sarajevo (1992–96) was less likely verbalised in comparison with the experiences of family members being detained temporarily in one of the concentration camps set up in Northwest Bosnia. The brutal execution of more than 8,000 Muslim men and boys in Srebrenica in July 1995 is a seminal event, and, as dubbed by respondents, a self-fulling prophecy that came true after the blackmailing of Serbian neighbours before the breakup of the war and the echoes of violence arriving from nearby Croatia. Many respondents *remember* their "parents attempt[ed] to go back home", but eventually "stay[ed] in Belgium to provide a better future for their children" and avoid "the climate of civil war that still divides people" and "the outburst of corruption and nepotism" across Bosnia.

The third trope of post-memory was verbalised by young Muslims (mostly males) born in Albanian families in Bremen and Dortmund recounting the (hi)story of their family members joining the Kosovo Liberation Army (KLA). The plight of Albanians was associated with the fate of other "Muslim-majority countries still suffering after decades" along with that of "the Albanian diaspora residing more in Europe and overseas than Albania and Kosovo combined together". This constellation of post-memories turns out to be of particular concern for two reasons: first, respondents do not avoid associating their parents with the KLA, in spite of the latter going under international pressure at the time of the interview.[3] Second, they yearn to liken family traumas to the present-day predicament of sorrow and suffering that most Muslims live through worldwide, thereby pointing to the constant phenomenon of stigmatisation and racialisation that ascribe Albanians to the stereotypical image of drug dealers, petty criminals and migrants in general. Likewise, young Bosnian Muslims also associated the war-like atmosphere in the 1990s with the contemporary atmosphere of hate and hostility against Muslims in "the West". After sharing his pro-Palestinian stance, a male respondent went further: "I have no doubt that what Zionists do against Palestinians is just like what Serbs did to us in Bosnia".

All these instances of war-related traumas circulate in different yet equally intimate contexts: in the family context, in community events at the local mosques and during public events concerning anniversaries and religious festivities. These are more than simple occasions of cultural performance and rites of family and community communication (Assmann and Czaplicka 1995:126). For the *generation after*, these events are about the family members and the people they trust the most, while listening to and acquiring knowledge from the past (Lesschaeve and Glaurdić 2023:9). Even though the transmission of the latter does not pass down historical knowledge correctly, most respondents

3 The KLA was depicted by the Yugoslav Serbian authorities as a terrorist group. Many reports described the war crimes committed by the KLA members during and after the 1999 Kosovo war. Violence was directed not only against ethnic Serbs, but also against other ethnic minorities (primarily the Roma) and ethnic Albanians themselves. The latter were accused of collaborating with Serb authorities or simply holding a critical position against KLA commanders and officials who made inroads into politics and Kosovo's political and institutional landscape. Since 2005, KLA commanders and officials have been brought to the dock. The ICTY handed down conviction of war crimes against former KLA members, sparking anger in Kosovo and Albanian diaspora against the betrayal of "the West" toward its allies in war-torn Yugoslavia.

firmly rely on their post-memories to assess the history and culture of Balkan Muslims as the last remaining thorn to be torn and ripped. This is why they feel themselves to be the byproduct of war, and their words do not sound apologetic at all – even when they recollect the engagement of their fathers and other family members in the war. As already introduced, they do not care a jot about the ubiquitous vilification of Muslim jihadism and Islamic terrorism being the cause of the collapse of Yugoslavia, an accusation that came to justify the collective violence against Muslims in Bosnia, Kosovo and North Macedonia (Rexhepi 2017:52). On the contrary, they were often found looking for the right words to value their everyday efforts towards remembering while healing, as well as forgiving in order to reconcile. Even when recollection of the past stemmed from rather poignant reminders of family history, respondents did not tokenise the post-war generations but simply searched for justice against the fear of oblivion and people's ignorance.

> "I really care about my family heritage and Islam because of our history. . . . I have to thank my parents for teaching me how to speak Bosnian fluently and worship Islam. Both keep me close to my history and Bosnia".
>
> "Every July 20th, I participate at "White Armband Day" to commemorate the ethnic cleansing committed in 1992 in the town of Prijedor. . . . There, just five years ago, my father's brother, an uncle I never knew, was found. I usually say that his body was found, but in reality, only a few body parts were actually found and used for identification."[4]

At times, painful recollection helps respondents feel closer to the Balkans, ensuring their contribution in seeking recognition for the traumas that their families endured. In fact, recollection here takes the shape of a political form of participation in the public sphere, one which assigns an active role to the *generation after*, and allows the latter to name and shame perpetrators, secure ethical or material compensation, or simply raise awareness about immoral and illegal actions. For instance, a female respondent pointed out that "the village where [her] mum is from, nearby Prjiedor, where Serbs set up concentration camps, refugees today live in 'jungle camps'". While some complained about the current Serb administration obstructing commemoration events (Paul 2023) and rejecting the recognition of the 1995 genocide in Srebrenica, the Bosnian community in Val Camonica, northern Italy, managed to inaugurate the "Garden of Friendship" and build a small commemoration monument in memory of the victims. In Dortmund, while attending the annual Silent March commemoration for the Srebrenica Genocide, I could not but

4 White Armband Day (in Bosnian, *Dan bijelih traka*) is a day of commemoration which takes place on May 31st in memory of the 3,176 Croats and Muslims who were ethnically cleansed by Serbian forces in the city of Prijedor.

notice the significant participation of young Muslims along with their parents, older generations of eyewitnesses and politicians who took to the streets of the city centre to foster a culture of commemoration and counteract the rise of nationalism.

According to some respondents, awareness of "what happened to Muslims in the Balkans" contributes positively to counteracting anti-Muslim rhetoric and Islamophobia in "the West". Recollecting family traumas and experiences during wartime activates a certain desire for justice and truth among those who were born afterward. Two male respondents and one female who were born and grew up in Italy and Belgium, respectively, admitted having begun their careers in the music sector and journalism after learning the history of their families. Since then, they have never stopped participating in solidarity campaigns of the "Mothers of Srebrenica" and speaking up at all possible events and spaces:

> "[T]he professor mentioned the Srebrenica genocide in class. . . . Most Italian students started to question the use of the term 'genocide'. During the discussion, they came to compare what happened in Srebrenica with the 'Armenian genocide', defining the latter as such while sceptically

*Figure 3.1* Young Bosnians marching through Dortmund during the Silent March for the commemoration of the Srebrenica Genocide. Photo by the author.

mulling over the former. Of course, the 'genocide against Armenians' was carried out by Turks, Muslims, so it immediately rings a bell. . . . I openly said that a genocide did happen in Srebrenica! 9000 men were killed, meaning that they wanted to eliminate an entire ethnic group so future kids from different fathers would not be Bosniaks".

> "I organised the public event about Srebrenica at [anonymised place]. Besides, I ask myself everyday 'Can I do something?', and now I've found my way: I started a journalism career and I wrote an article about the Mothers of Srebrenica. People's ignorance [about Srebrenica] really frustrates me . . . how the media depict Bosnia, as a [country where a war is still ongoing], and how they do not frame the war in Bosnia correctly: it was Serbian aggression against Bosnian Muslims, in the same way everyone is now referring to the Russian aggression of Ukraine. I felt like writing about the Mother of Srebrenica, combining their stories with that of my family, it was my way to highlight the event on the commemoration of Srebrenica".

In Bremen, Adin recollects a "funny story", as he himself defined it. He says with a bitter sense of humour that his family

> "firstly went from Sarajevo to Mostar to avoid the siege by Serbian forces, pretending to be a Croatian refuge family. Despite trying to hide in Dubrovnik, it did not work out, so [they] quickly left the city undercover, traveling up to Austria. . . . My family was shot by anyone in that war".

Adin's trope of post-memory was quite common throughout the fieldwork, since most of their parents still struggle with their own trauma long after the conflict ended (Lesschaeve and Glaurdić 2023:5). Spontaneous recollection of the past was more likely verbalised in bits and pieces, often hidden under the guise of reconciliation understood in terms of "moving on" and leaving the pain behind. Unlike Adin, a certain culture of silence was also noticed due to the unspeakable nature and incommensurability of certain traumas (Müller-Suleymanova 2023:265). The following interview insights are instructive:

> "My father was a kind of paramilitary guy and [together with other neighbours] they had weapons. I do not know from whom they got them . . . when they started to tell him to shoot at people who used to live on the other side of the street, and he saw a person he knew getting shot. He became traumatised and was never the same again. . . . My father is still traumatised and he is still going through therapy. Often he seems really good and happy, but sometimes he goes antisocial, crying in despair, saying that the 'world is harming [him], hates [him]', and he is still thinks he is a refugee in Germany".

> "My mum is not capable of visiting her birthplace in Bosnia. She left because of the war, and once she suffered serious panic attacks while being [anonymised place] with us. It was summertime, and she could not stay anymore there, the village of her parents, my grandparents. Since then, we decided to stop spending holydays there, but instead began travelling to Sarajevo to meet up with some family and old friends".

To conclude partially here, family and community spaces are where these traumas still linger. In all the countries where interviews took place, respondents (primarily females) were found studying or pursuing professional careers in security studies, working in the civil society and NGO sector, and cultural diplomacy. Males were instead mostly IT experts and hoping to avoid economic insecurity in the future. They were also found to be engaged with other young Muslims in volunteering for local career centres and establishing networks in the field of digital market and STEM industry. When information allowed one to compare the family background with the respondent's identity, it seems that the past is yet again guiding their day-present course of actions.

## "It was different for us, wasn't it?"

If the violence of the 1990s in the Balkans was associated with day-present nesting phenomena of racism in "the West", the geopolitical turmoil on Europe's eastern borderlands has made space for the past traumas to resurface. At the time of the fieldwork, Russia's full-scale invasion of Ukraine and the merciless military attacks against civilians had already taken a heavy toll on respondents and their families. Qualitative data show that the younger the respondents were, the more they were inclined to speak up about the West's "double standards", and the heavier the burden to carry. While same-community peers born or raised after 1989 hold more reflective and cautious attitudes toward the echoes of war, younger respondents (19 to 25 years old) quickly associated today's Islamophobia with the genocidal politics that their parents survived in and before the 1990s. Although the former group of respondents grew up throughout the violent years of the 1990s, the latter gave a new meaning and significance to what happened to their families in light of the geopolitical turmoil in Ukraine. Hence, younger respondents recollected the political atmosphere of war-torn Yugoslav Bosnia in order to point out the similar features in Belgium's harsh debate over Flemish regional nationalism.

When respondents thought of what their parents went through, many felt transported back to the early 1990s. Viral images of suffering women holding their small children, soldiers and tanks leaving destruction behind, and painful stories gone viral on social media all quickly fuelled existential fears and ruptured unhealed wounds (Lesschaeve and Glaurdić 2023). Emotions ran high when pundits and commentators drew parallels between the siege of Sarajevo during the 1990s with that of Mariupol in 2022 (Karabegović 2024:11). The Bucha massacre committed by Russian forces near Kyiv echoed the ethnic cleansing in Prijedor and the genocide in Srebrenica; the climate of Islamophobia amplified younger respondents' feelings of danger and insecurity even more. With Russia invading Ukraine, Bosnia was also further depicted as a living example of how not to reorganise post-war life (Džidić 2024), and how those who were fleeing Ukraine on the border with Poland, sometimes wearing nothing but slippers, were reminiscent of those escaping the war in Bosnia.

In the meantime, a great resentment was born out of the close ties between the Serbian political elite and the Russian regime of Putin (Haye 2022:65). Of particular interest here is the frustration and outrage shared by some respondents, who accused the West's values-based idea of peace of being deeply rooted in racism and hypocrisy. Some pointed out that it was much harder for their (grand)parents to flee the war-torn and economically exploited Balkans, seek refuge somewhere else, settle down in a "host country", or eventually return home. Others went even further, hypothesising Europe's (racial) biases to explain the West's lack of vested interests in helping Muslims in Yugoslavia, a country in the very heart of Europe. According to this group of respondents, the West's "double standards" also resonated in the media landscape, repeatedly highlighting the hypocrisy of Western support for Ukrainians rather than other refugees. This debunking campaign lends further support to the hypothesis of the West's double standards (Moise et al. 2024:371). In Antwerp and Bremen, three young women with Bosnian and Kosovo family heritage, respectively, say that

> "The media do not portray the past and present situation properly: there was no longer war in Bosnia, but simply the merciless aggression of Serbian forces against Muslims and Croats in the same way it is right now with Russia's merciless aggression against Ukrainians".
>
> "When the war broke out, and Ukrainians began arriving in Germany, the country was ready: the educational system accepted new students who do not speak German, their diplomas were not [a subject of controversy] for university admission, they got houses and jobs by simply having their Ukrainian documents. My father and the rest of my family escaped from Kosovo, and once here they had to struggle a lot before integrating. My father was an educated person: he had a degree in music but he could only work as a doorman for the first couples of years".
>
> "Ukrainians just arrived and were able to move into an apartment, find a job, attend German courses for free . . . everywhere they see their flags displayed on institutional buildings, people they do not even know, chant *Slava Ukraina!* when they meet them".

If knowing requires truth, so does remembering. What many respondents alluded to was not raised against Ukraine, nor did they otherise Ukrainian war refugees. Differences between "real refugees" and "war refugees", as well as between "deserving and/or underserving" people (Zogata-Kusz et al. 2023), were not made, nor did their critical views delegitimise protection and aid programs. For instance, the Bosnian mosque in Antwerp had been collecting donations for war refugees and some Bosnian expats residing in Ukraine before February 2022. If anything, their critical views were directed against the EU's largest sanctions package against Russia, the military support to a third country under the European Peace Facility (EPF), the absence of lengthy asylum procedures for Ukrainians. In particular, the fact that those political parties that unfairly mulled over security issues or socio-economic implications for helping refugees from Africa and Asia during the 2015 refugee crisis were suddenly keen on welcoming Ukrainians hit a nerve with the groups under study. What was at stake was not the feeling of empathy and solidarity toward Ukrainian newcomers, as their experiences and stories were promptly associated with those of the families of the respondents. Undoubtedly, the latter largely criticised the West's "civilisational" response that both geographically and psychologically came to quickly and actively support a group of war refugees who do not challenge the Christian identity of European countries (Farrell-Banks 2022:209; Ramberg 2004:5), unlike those who arrive from countries perceived as far from Europe (Politi et al. 2023:949, Costello and Foster 2022:245, Moise et al. 2024:357). Simply put, respondents openly argued that the Western European public prefer migrants "with the same [white] colour" in great contrast to other war refugees from Arab and African countries (mostly Muslims) whose ethnic and/or religious background do not resemble the European identity.

In bringing attention to this unequal treatment and response, it should be pointed out that the respondents' allusion did not come out of the blue. Studies regarding perceptual "closeness," dispositional prosociality, and "identity fusion" with Ukrainians confirmed that the vast mobilisation of European (white) societies in support of Ukraine was somewhat unprecedented (Politi et al. 2023:948). In contrast, when Afghans tried to evacuate *en mass* a few weeks after the US withdrew from the country, political actors began warning about the growing number of additional refugees entering Europe. In spite of being unaware of this emerging literature at the time of the fieldwork, respondents perceived how the "identity card" in favour of "Ukraine as a member of Europe" and "Ukrainians as Europeans" was instrumentally played by the same conservative governments and illiberal regimes that had previously refused to deploy the same "welcome package" to Afghani and Somali refugees, among others (Moise et al. 2024:368). This widespread perception also spilled over into another similar form of criticism that pointed to the politics of "Eurowhiteness solidarity" (as quoted in Basheska and Kochenov 2024:4). The bitter reference of a Bosnian father in Toruń, Poland, was telling:

> PiS's positive attitude and migration policy toward white, Christian Ukrainians entering the country while turning a blind eye to the Polish-Belarus border where hundreds of darker and most

probably Muslim refugees continued to suffer push-backs and die during frosty days.

Having said that, all these well-grounded critical opinions deserve a final contextualisation. In theory, according to most respondents, the recollection of the violent past shines a light on a murky present due to a high level of Islamophobia in and outside the Balkans. However, such a recollection fundamentally contradicts historical information and also misleads those who rely on their post-memory to judge the past in relation to today's events. In practice, there is little doubt that post-memory lies in the retrospection of the past and may indeed show incongruities and contradictions, as well as reparative reading and paranoid scrutiny (Hirsch 2012:75).

With this in mind, it should be pointed out that the plight of former Yugoslavian war refugees also inspired compassion and sympathy in the West in the 1990s. In Australia, for instance, if compared with other war-affected nations and minorities around the globe, Bosnian Muslims benefited from the apparent "entry advantage" on the basis of their perceived whiteness (Colic-Peisker 2005:616). In Belgium, Yugoslavian refugees were also accommodated with a changing asylum regime that allowed them to exit the country and return to it. In Germany, a country which accepted nearly 320,000 refugees from Bosnia and Herzegovina and, along with Austria and Sweden, was one of the main countries that provided a haven for those fleeing war, a second-generation identity turned out to be an advantage in political life (Karabegović 2024:10). Azra Hromadžic, a professor at Syracuse University in the US, recollects her memory about "spaces of privilege" and the friendly atmosphere in the US. She adds that Bosnians often felt special when invited to events where their stories were told and repeated, often interviewed by local and regional newspapers where their experiences were listened to and consumed with interest, amazement, shock, care and concern. They had, in other words, a special voice that demanded and received respect (2023:4). Hromadžic's analysis resonates with a few older respondents who, after arriving in Germany with their families, reflected on why a great sense of frustration over Europe's "double standards" arose among younger Muslims from and in the Balkans. Among others, Jonas looked at "the different ways Ukrainians and Bosnians could and can express their traumas: the latter have entered the sphere of art, literature and theatre, while the former is still grappling with fresh wounds and traumas". By the same token, Jasmine pointed out that

> "the West's lack of intervention in Bosnia probably stemmed from the same Western misinterpretation of Yugoslavia, a country which, after Tito's death, was still seen as a big power in a time when Germany was going through the troubling post-unification period. . . . Now, the whole geopolitical context is different: Ukraine is a very weak country in comparison to Russia, and Germany is able to respond properly and handle refugees and war-related consequences".

## References

Ahmadzai, A. (2022) The Challenges of Epistemic Communities in Shaping Policy in the Age of Post-Truth, *E-International Relations*. Available at: www.e-ir.info/2022/10/06/the-challenges-of-epistemic-communities-in-shaping-policy-in-the-age-of-post-truth/ (Accessed: 28 March 2023)

Amzi-Erdğdular, L. (2024) The Post-WWI Migrations That Built Yugoslavia and Turkey Have Left a Painful Legacy, *New Lines Magazine*. Available at: https://newlinesmag.com/essays/the-post-wwi-migrations-that-built-yugoslavia-and-turkey-have-left-a-painful-legacy/ (Accessed: 1 August 2023)

Assmann, J. and Czaplicka, J. (1995) Collective Memory and Cultural Identity. *New German Critique*, (65), pp. 125–133. https://doi.org/10.2307/488538.

Basheska, E. and Kochenov, D. (2024) Migration and Citizenship in Europe – Does 'Illiberalism' Matter? Eurowhiteness Solidarity from the EU and Hungary to the UK, *The Centre on Migration, Policy & Society*. Available at: https://papers.ssrn.com/sol3/papers.cfm?abstract_id=4742900 (Accessed: 12 April 2024)

Cantat, C. (2022) The Reception Spectacle: On Ukrainian Displacement and Selective Empathy at Europe's Borders, *Focaal Blog*. Available at: www.focaalblog.com/2022/06/28/celine-cantat-the-reception-spectacle-on-ukrainian-displacement-and-selective-empathy-at-europes-borders/ (Accessed: 19 March 2023)

Colic-Peisker, V. (2005) At Least You Are the Right Colour: Identity and Social Inclusion of Bosnian Refugees in Australia. *Journal of Ethnic and Migration Studies*, 31 (4), pp. 615–638. https://doi.org/10.1080/13691830500109720

Costello, C. and Foster, M. (2022) (Some) Refugees Welcome: When Is Differentiating between Refugees Unlawful Discrimination? *International Journal of Discrimination and the Law*, 22 (3), pp. 244–280. https://doi.org/10.1177/13582291221116476

Domachowska, A. (2019) The Attitude of Poland and Polish Society toward the 1999 Kosovo Refugees. *Slovanský Prehled*, 105 (1), pp. 49–63.

Domaradzka, A. and Hamel, P. (2024) *Handbook on Urban Social Movements*. Cheltenham and Camberley: Edward Elgar Publishing Ltd.

Dupuis-Tordjenab, B. (2024) Bosnian Memories, *Blind*. Available at: www.blind-magazine.com/news/bosnian-memories/ (Accessed: 3 March 2024)

Džidić, D. (2024) In Race for Justice, Ukraine Repeats Bosnia's Mistakes, *Balkan Insight*. Available at: https://balkaninsight.com/2024/02/22/in-race-for-justice-ukraine-repeats-bosnias-mistakes/ (Accessed: 24 February 2024)

Farrell-Banks, D. (2022) 'Encounters through Kahlenberg: Urban Traces of Transnational Right-Wing Action', in S. Eckersley and C. Voß (eds.) *Diversity of Belonging in Europe. Public Spaces, Contested Places, Cultural Encounters*. London and New York: Routledge, pp. 197–214.

Frise, M. (2024) Remembering Trauma in Epistemology. *Philosophy and the Mind Sciences*. https://doi.org/10.33735/phimisci.2024.10220

Gruev, M. and Kalyonski, A. (2008) *Vazroditelniat protses: Komunisticheskiat rezhim i myusyulmanskite obshtnosti* [The Revival Process: The Communist Regime and the Muslim Communities]. Sofia: CIELA.

Grünenberg, K. (2005) Constructing "Sameness" and "Otherness": Bosnian Diasporic Experiences in a Danish Context. *Balkanologie – Reveu d'études pluridisciplinaires*, IX (1–2), pp. 173–193. https://doi.org/10.4000/balkanologie.587

Grzymski, J. (2019) Seeing Like a EUropean Border: Limits of the EUropean Borders and Space. *Global Discourse*, 9 (1), pp. 135–151. https://doi.org/10.1332/204378919X15470487645493

Haas, M. P. (1992) Introduction: Epistemic Communities and International Policy Coordination. *International Organization*, 46 (1), pp. 1–35. https://doi.org/10.1017/S0020818300001442

Harris, S. and Nawaz, M. (2015) *Islam and the Future of Tolerance. A Dialogue.* Cambridge, MA: Harvard University Press.
Haye, E. (2022) Der Bosnienkrieg und die Nachkriegszeit in der deutschen post-migrantischen Erinnerungskultur [The Bosnian War and the Post-War Period in German Post-Migrant Remembrance Culture]. *Südosteuropa Mitteilungen* 62 (3), pp. 59–68.
Henderson, D. (2021) The Place of Non-Epistemic Matters in Epistemology: Norms and Regulation in Various Communities. *Synthese,* 199, pp. 3301–3323. https://doi.org/10.1007/s11229-020-02935-2
Hirsch, M. (2012) *The Generation of Postmemory. Writing and Visual Culture after the Holocaust.* New York: Columbia University Press.
Hirsch, M. (2024) Rethinking Holocaust Memory after October 7, *Public Books.* Available at: www.publicbooks.org/rethinking-holocaust-memory-after-october-7/ (Accessed: 1 August 2024)
Hromadžić, A. (2023) On Being Too Close to It. *Genealogy,* 7 (4), pp. 1–10. https://doi.org/10.3390/genealogy7040076.
Iddon, P. (2022) 'Not Since World War II': The Worrying Precedent Many Are Evoking for the Ukraine War, *Forbes.* Available at: www.forbes.com/sites/paulid don/2022/11/29/not-seen-since-world-war-ii-the-worrying-precedent-many-are-evoking-for-the-ukraine-war/?sh=3f29ca5576a3 (Accessed: 2 January 2023).
Kamusella, T. (2019) *Ethnic Cleansing during the Cold War. The Forgotten 1989 Expulsion of Turks from Communist Bulgaria.* London and New York: Routledge.
Karabegović, D. (2024) Fixing Things from Outside? Diaspora Politicians and Transnational Political Engagement. *Globalisation,* pp. 1–18. https://doi.org/10.1080/14747731.2024.2336647
Kofman, E. (2020) Unequal Internationalisation and the Emergence of a New Epistemic Community: Gender and Migration. *Comparative Migration Studies,* 8 (36). https://doi.org/10.1186/s40878-020-00194-1
Koinova, M. and Karabegović, D. (2016) Diasporas and Transitional Justice: Transnational Activism from Local to Global Levels of Engagement. *Global Networks,* 17, pp. 212–233. https://doi.org/10.1111/glob.12128
Kola, A. F., Domachowska, A., Gemziak, Ł. and Trupia, F. (2022) Mnemonic Wars and Parallel Polis: The Anti-Politics of Memory in Central and Southeast Europe: Kosovar Women and Black/Roma Lives Matter. *Memory Studies,* 15 (6), pp. 1406–1419. https://doi.org/10.1177/17506980221134936
Krstić Radislav v. Prosecutor (2019) Judgement, *ICTY.* Available at: www.icty.org/x/cases/krstic/acjug/en/ (Accessed: 10 January 2023)
Kundnani, H. (2023) *Eurowhiteness: Culture, Empire, and Race in the European Project.* London: Hurst & Co Publishers Ltd.
Lesschaeve, C. and Glaurdić, J. (2023) The Ties That Bind: War Histories and Online Social Networks in Postwar Societies. *Journal of Conflict Resolution,* 68 (7–8), pp. 1443–1467. https://doi.org/10.1177/00220027231190917
Marinov, T. (2009) Ot "Internatsionalizŭm" kŭm Natsionalizŭm. Komunisticheskiat rezhim, Makedonskiat vŭpros i politikata kŭm etnicheskite I religioznite obshtnosti" [From Internationalism to Nationalism. The Communist Regime, the Macedonian Question and the Politics of Ethnic and Religious Minorities], in *Istoria na Narodna Republika Bŭlgariia. Rezhim i Obshtestvoto* [History of People's Republic of Bulgaria. Regime and Society]. Ciela: Sofia, pp. 481–516.
Merdjanova, I. (2013) *Rediscovering the Umma. Muslims in the Balkans between Nationalism and Transnationalism.* Oxford: Oxford University Press.
Minić, M. (2000) *Ratovi na Kosova, 1998–1999, i v Čečeniji, 1994–1996* [Wars in Kosovo, 1998–1999, and in Chechnya, 1994–1996]. Sarajevo: Rabic.

Moise, A., Dennison, J. and Hanspeter, K. (2024) European Attitudes to Refugees after the Russian Invasion of Ukraine. *West European Politics*, 47 (2), pp. 356–381. https://doi.org/10.1080/01402382.2023.2229688

Müller-Suleymanova, D. (2023) Remembering the Dealing with Violent Past: Diasporic Experiences and Transnational Dimensions. *Ethnic and Racial Studies*, 47 (2), pp. 259–273. https://doi.org/10.1080/01419870.2023.2260882

Mushaben, J. M. (2008) Gender, HipHop and Pop-Islam: The Urban Identities of Muslim Youth in Germany. *Citizenship Studies*, 12 (5), pp. 507–526. https://doi.org/10.1080/13621020802337931

Paul, J. (2023) White Armband Day: From Global Social Media Campaign to Transnational Commemoration Day. *Memory Studies*, *16* (2), pp. 352–368. https://doi.org/10.1177/1750698021995991

Pita, A. and Costa, R. S. (2022) Ukrainian Exodus could be Europe's Biggest Refugee Crisis since World War II, *El País*. Available at: https://english.elpais.com/international/2022-03-03/ukrainian-exodus-could-be-europes-biggestrefugee-crisis-since-world-war-ii.html (Accessed: 10 April 2022)

Politi, E., Gale, J., Roblain, A., Bobowik, M. and Green, E. (2023) Who Is Willing to Help Ukrainian Refugees and Why? The Role of Individual Prosocial Dispositions and Superordinate European Identity. *Journal of Community & Applied Social Psychology*, 33 (4), pp. 940–953. https://doi.org/10.1002/casp.2689

Ramberg, I. (2004) Islamophobia and Its Consequences on Young People, *European Youth Centre Budapest*. Available at: www.coe.int/en/web/youth/-/islamophobia-and-its-consequences-on-young-people?inheritRedirect=true (Accessed: 12 December 2022).

Rexhepi, P. (2017) 'Unmapping Islam in Eastern Europe Periodization and Muslim Subjectivities in the Balkans', in I. Kacandes and Y. Komska (eds.) *Eastern Europe Unmapped. Beyond Borders and Peripheries*. Oxford and New York: Berghahn Books, pp. 53–77.

Rexhepi, P. (2019) Imperial Inventories, "Illegal Mosques" and Institutionalised Islam: Coloniality and the Islamic Community of Bosnia and Herzegovina. *History and Anthropology*, 30 (4), pp. 1–13.

Rexhepi, P. (2023) *White Enclosures. Racial Capitalism & Coloniality along the Balkan Route*. Durham: Duke University Press.

Roy, O. (2013) Secularism and Islam: The Theological Predicament. *The International Spectator: Italian Journal of International Affairs*, 48 (1), pp. 5–19.

Sandal, N. A. (2011) Religious Actors as Epistemic Communities in Conflict Transformation: The Cases of South Africa and Northern Ireland. *Review of International Studies*, 37 (3), pp. 929–949. https://doi.org/10.1017/S0260210510001592

Scott, T. (2005) *The Global Resurgence of Religion and the Transformation of International Relations. The Struggle for the Soul of the Twenty-First Century*. New York: Palgrave Macmillan.

Shatanawi, M., Macdonald, S. and Puzon, K. (2021) *Islam and Heritage in Europe: Pasts, Presents and Future Possibilities*. London: Routledge.

Simms, B. (2002) *Unfinest Hours. Britan and the Destruction of Bosnia*. London: Penguin.

Southwick, K. (2014) Srebrenica as Genocide? The Krstić Decision and the Language of the Unspeakable. *Yale Human Rights & Development Law Journal*, pp. 188–227. Available at: http://hdl.handle.net/20.500.13051/5846 (Accessed: 12 September 2023)

Spivak, G. C. (1999) *A Critique of Postcolonial Reason*. Cambridge and London: Harvard University Press.

Stoyan, M. (1992) *Vazroditelniat Protses*. Teza-Antiteza. Otritsanie na otritsanieto [The Revival Process. Thesis-Antithesis. Negation of the negation]. Sofia: M&M.

Trajanovski, N. (2022) *Remembering the 2001 Armed Conflict in Macedonia: Modes of Commemoration and Memorialization*. Belgrade: Humanitarian Law Center.

Trupia, F. (2022) What Would Have Been My Name? The Post-Memory of the Revival Process of the "Generation After" in Bulgaria. *Contemporary Southeastern Europe*, 9 (1), pp. 47–64. http://dx.doi.org/10.25364/02.9:2022.1.4

Zanoni, P., Barros, M. and Alcadipani, R. (2023) Celebrating 30 Years of Organization: Epistemic Pluralism, Caring for Our Community and Politics of Hope. *Organization*, 30 (6), pp. 1179–1187. https://doi.org/10.1177/13505084231202161

Zogata-Kusz, A., Öbrink Hobzová, M. and Cekiera, R. (2023) Deserving of Assistance: The Social Construction of Ukrainian Refugees. *Ethnopolitics*, pp. 1–20. https://doi.org/10.1080/17449057.2023.2286779

# 4 Believing without Belonging?

The disintegration of Yugoslavia ended with the displacement and mass migration of about 4 million people. From 600,000 to 800,000 refugees found shelter in different European countries, whereas from 10,000 to 15,000 sought asylum overseas (UNHCR 2001–2023). Bosnia and Herzegovina and Kosovo became the hotspots of forced migration after Croat and Serb nationalist forces committed genocidal acts against the local Muslim population. By 1996, 400,000 out of some 1.2 million Bosnian refugees found durable solutions in host countries, mostly in Germany (International Crisis Group 1997), while another 350,000 Albanians fled Kosovo in the 1990s (UNHCR 1999). In Bulgaria, the collapse of the Communist regime was anticipated by a state-orchestrated campaign of name-changing against the Muslim and Turkish population,[1] which ended in a de facto ethnic cleansing (Kamusella 2019). Those who refused to comply faced exile, imprisonment in labour camps and even death, while others were forced to emigrate to the West (Baev 2015:164)

Associated with newcomers from the former Soviet Union and the long-established Turkish diaspora (Mushaben 2008:511), Muslims from war-torn Yugoslavia were seen through the imaginary lens of "the Orient" (Bakić-Hayden 1995:918). As discussed in Chapter 2, this misrepresentation led most scholars to focus on the "migration turn" in post-socialist Europe (Melegh 2023) and gloss over the much older global-local space of interactions

1 As I have discussed elsewhere (2022:48), this campaign is euphemistically called the "Revival Process". It was orchestrated by the Communist Bulgarian authorities between 1944 and 1989 when ethnic Turks and Muslims were forced to renounce their religious and ethnic identity by changing their Arabic-sounding names and accepting new Bulgarian/Christian ones. They were also forced to give up on traditional attire and cultural practices, such as speaking Turkish language, performing circumcision in the private space, wearing the female veil and so forth. The "Revival Process" was the most significant state-run attempt to impose a Slavonic "ethnic code" upon Turks and Muslims of other ethnicities (e.g. Pomaks, Tatars, Roma and Alevis). In fact, this assimilation campaign was not new in the country. Between 1964 and 1972, ethnic Pomaks were similarly targeted by Party authorities and militias for "healing" from "the wounds of Turkification". Between 1981 and 1984, about 900 Muslims were targeted for violence and about 50,000 names were changed.

DOI: 10.4324/9781003589624-5

between Balkan Muslims and the *ummah* (Merdjanova 2013). The study of diaspora has been based on the attachment to the former home and, typically, on the fantasy of return (Hirsch and Miller 2011). In this regard, Muslims from the Balkans were considered specific political entities to be repatriated and reintegrated in order to reverse genocide and ethnic cleansing endured during the wartime (Black 2001). After socialism, Southeast Europe became yet again a site at which the tensions of postcolonial and postsocialist histories and legacies remained continuously contested by various movements but also emboldened by increased recognition and support by both Europe and the EU in the project of developing a "European Islam" (Rexhepi 2019:10). Although the "spirit of Europe" was both positively endorsed and historicised in a long trajectory of intra-European migration, the debate over Turkish membership of the European Union had raised questions over whether a country with a Muslim majority could become part of a "European identity". Hence, the EU enlargement process toward the Western Balkans has turned this question *inward* and rhetorically expanded boundaries to include "internal outsiders". Throughout, Muslims in/from the region are often a subject of contention. Serbian officials in the Republika Srpska, one of the two entities of post-war Bosnia and Herzegovina (herein, Bosnia), and Serbia proper, have never really ceased to deny publicly the occurrence of the genocide of Bosnian Muslims in the manner that has been established by the International Criminal Tribunal for the former Yugoslavia (ICTY) and the International Court of Justice (ICJ).

Among the diaspora, interest and awareness about the operationalisation of national identity of the second generations has been understudied and remained at an early stage (Vathi 2015:3). Most studies have focused on the process of migration and integration rather than on the emergence of native minorities (El-Tayeb 2011: xxi) and how the latter become part of the anti-Muslim narratives in relation to hybrid and authoritarian contexts where there is a potential of clashing between domestic politics in countries of birth and residence (Karabegović 2024). Scholarly, the methodological difficulties of tracing generational changes within intimate spaces could not unravel the modes young Muslims with Balkan roots care and nurture a sense of belonging to their parental birthplace (Bougarel 2008:155; Bougarel and Mihaylova 2005:12; Lecoyer 2020:151).

Thus, this chapter is a small step in this scholarly direction by investigating how young Muslims with Balkan roots nurture their national identity and citizenship vis-à-vis their family migration heritage and Muslimness. It draws on a qualitative collection of information and knowledge respectively constructed and collected from young Muslims born and raised in Antwerp, Belgium, whose parents fled Bosnia during the 1990s, and from same-age coreligionists born and raised in former guest-worker Albanian families who arrived in Dortmund in the early 1980s. Respectively, the Bosnian Muslim community in Antwerp is originally from Republika Srpska, specifically from Banja Luka and villages nearby Sanski Most and Ključ, while those with Albanian heritage belong to the ethno-religious minority in North Macedonia, mostly Kičevo (in Albanian, Kërçovë). The following comparison is enriched at times with personal insights from another smaller group of young Muslims interviewed in Italy and Poland. Much fewer in number and living in different dynamics that in German and Belgian cities, this third group of young Muslims of Balkan origin is taken into consideration to capture similarities and affinities among the diaspora living across Europe.

Looking at these small communties of young Muslims with Balkan roots, it is argued that this post-migrant generation remains exposed, if at all, to a condition of *atopicality* (Marramao 2012:70). However, it should also be pointed out that this chapter is not about the politics of belonging, which is concerned with the boundaries of the political community of belonging and, in turn, with the boundaries that separate "us" from "them" (Yuval-Davis 2006). Nor does it focus on contestations of the participatory dimension of citizenship and the status or entitlements that such membership entails. In contrast, it sheds light on how these young generation of Muslims position themselves inside or outside the imaginary boundary line of the nation and/or other communities of belonging (Yuval-Davis 2011). It thus looks at how they hold, nurture or even deny their Muslimness vis-à-vis Europe's Islamophobia that heightens a sense of belonging to their birthplace and/or the parental country of origin.

## In Search of (Lost) Belonging

Out of the n=72 respondents among the generation after, this chapter looks at a sample of n=24 (15 males and 9 females). This group is considered along with perspectives that emerged out of the participation-observation in Antwerp and Dortmund. At the time of the interviews, respondents were between 19 and 35 years old; some held at least, or were pursuing, a bachelor's degree in a wealth of disciplines, while others were already employed in various workplaces, from academia to civil society, from STEM to the third sector.

In-depth interviews followed up participant-observation in the distinct city districts of Deurne and Borgerhout in Antwerp, and Innenstadt-Nord in Dortmund. These neighbourhoods were chosen to capture in depth and breadth the ways potential respondents nurture, reiterate and care about a sense of belonging vis-à-vis their religious salience and family migration heritage, and how they hold infra-city relationships of mutuality, solidarity and support in moments of need or danger (Sofos and Tsagarousianou 2013:96). Across the four countries this study focuses on, a sense of a locally nuanced connectedness with the neighbourhood does not resemble France's *banlieue* atmosphere (so-called, in French, "*nationalism du quartier*", see Leiken 2012). In Germany and Belgium, it rather replicates a stunted and deformed sense of identity which is somewhat different from the national pride of the core society, and from the glorification of what is despised and dreaded by most national stocks (Tsagarousianou 2016:70). In Antwerp and Dortmund in particular, intra-city dynamics show political dynamics of inclusion/exclusion, shedding light on the meanings of *belonging* (Open Society Foundations 2011) and how different ethnic and religious groups constantly negotiate their presence in town. As introduced in Chapter 1, this perspective "from below" (see Methodology) was important to avoid a heavy-handed legal description of Islam (Karić et al. 2023) and thus better scrutinise whether or not the Muslims' sense of belonging to their birthplace is burdened by their parents' struggle of integration and educational/cultural background.

Following the breakup of Yugoslavia and the demise of socialism, many Muslims in/from the Balkans lost their benefit of common citizenship. Their arrival in 'the West' coincided with the challenges of legal measures that limited the access to citizenship in the new host countries (Bougarel 2008:4). Meanwhile, the traumas of war, genocidal violence and forced migration permeated across generations and remained pervasive and long-lasting over time. Since potential respondents were born outside the Balkans, therefore socialised with national cultures and languages, the personal bond with the parental countries of origin was expected of being gradually loose or mythologised as an element of family heritage (Bobako 2015:46). Here, it was hypothesised that (post-) migration practices have not necessarily been the same among young members of the diaspora. With this in mind, in-depth interviews were also held to investigate how they care about family cultures, comply with family traditions, spend quality time at their parental birthplace, and worship Islam, or nurture a particular alternative cosmopolitan attitude (Roy 2007: xi).

After establishing a sufficient level of trust and receiving invitations to visit private places and cultural centres, two open questions were not raised to capture the ways the two groups under study adapt to religiously neutral ideals of citizenship in European liberal democracy (Karić et al. 2023). As follows:

1) How do you grapple with the legacies of your family migration experiences and religious identity while living in a post-secular and multicultural society?

2) If at all, when do you experience a sense of belonging to your place of residence and your parents' country of origin in your everyday life?

During each in-depth interview, both questions had the scope to explore whether a respondent experiences a sense of unfamiliarity with their birthplace or parental country of origin, and how this potential feeling is hijacked by Europe's unwillingness to abide citizens of predominantly Muslim heritage. In particular, the following sections discuss certain dynamics of exclusion/inclusion as they were verbalised and reflected on by the respondents here under consideration. In doing so, this chapter aims to illuminate how the personal feeling of those whose home is Belgium and Germany, but who are not yet recognised as full nationals, has nothing to do with a politics of recognition or belonging. Nor is their predicament of atopicality connected with the failure of integration and painstaking inclusion after their parents' experience of migration. This atopicality is rather embedded in the legacy of the West's hegemonic ideas of secularism and diversity that dictate the social conditions of Muslims in the contemporary European societies.

## Neither West/Erners Nor East/Erners

The thorny question of "*what does it mean to be European*" has been compounded by studies of "belonging" and "not-belonging" – namely, by the recognition of "who belongs to Europe" and the exclusion of those who do not. In its most basic sense, *belonging* implies an individual's orientation towards, and interaction with, a given environment and space. Eckersley and Vos (2023) point out three significant and interconnected dimensions: first, to fit in a spatially located place, opposite to being/feeling "out of the place"; second, to be a member of a people or community; and third, to have the right to be in a location. Respectively, "fitting in" plays a pivotal role in the individual's symbolic and physical dimension of self-identification (Tsagarousianou 2016:62). "Feeling at home" can refer to an ancestral requirement for being a true national (Fleischmann and Phalet 2018:46), while "having the right to access" a particular group (Yuval-Davis 2006:198) varies in complexities and fluid and flexible dimensions (Lähdesmäki et al. 2016).

In general, Europeans conceptualise national identities in terms of ethnic belonging – meaning having either an ancestral agency or a long family history in the country as a requirement to be a true national. Belonging has been used interchangeably with the concept of identity and is often associated with themes of citizenship and migration. It follows that normative perspectives of good (socially beneficial) and bad (more reprehensible) nationals – be they from "victim" and "labour" diaspora (Cohen 1997), "trade" and "imperial" diaspora (Urry 2000), with "a particular type of consciousness" (Bryden 2004; cf. Vertovec and Cohen 1999) – have been used to look at the governance of nation-state toward non-citizen populations, the role of the latter as political actors and lobbying forces in domestic and international politics of countries (Lyons 2006). Against this backdrop, Giacomo Marramao argues that the modern democratic idea of *belonging* fully realised in the paradigm of citizenship is no longer able to deal with the challenges of contemporary society. Rather, he adds, there is a need for symbolic identification that can never find full realisation in the sphere of citizenship – not even in its broadest imaginable or conceivable form (2012:76).

In the 1990s, the international spotlight on the Yugoslav wars and the genocidal violence against local Muslims reactivated the intertwined questions of race and coloniality *from within* Europe (Bjelić 2018:752). Talal Asad recalled (2003:164) the interview held in 1995 between Tadeusz Mazowiecki, UN Special Rapporteur for the Commission on Human Rights in the Balkans, and two French journalists, who found it strange that a Polish Christian was found defending Bosnians, many of whom were Muslims. Mazowiecki soon reassured them that the war in Bosnia was not a religious one, and that Bosnian Muslims are not a danger to Europe. As Talal pointed out, Mazowiecki's assumption (accepted without comment by his French interlocutors) was that Bosnian Muslims may be *in* Europe but are not members of it. Even though they might not arrive from Asia to Europe, and even though they may have adjusted to secular political institutions, they cannot claim a Europeanness in the same way Christian inhabitants can. Poisoned by this misapprehension, this is why the war-torn region became the venue for raising yet again the aforementioned questions, albeit in a slightly different manner: "what is Europe supposed to be?" rather than "what is Europe?" Hence, "who counts as European?" rather than "who is European?" At the same time, the demise of state socialism had accelerated the reconnection between the Muslims from/in the Balkans and the Muslim world, mainly the Middle East. Although such a reconnection was not unique (Sadriu 2017:551), the idea of belonging to the *ummah* became a preoccupation for a large circle of pundits and experts who never ceased to foresee Islam as an invasive and threatening "Trojan horse" within the white, Christian, European canon of norms and values (Sofos and Tsagarousianou 2013:15). Hence, Muslims pay a huge price for belonging (Khan 2022:61) due to Europe's cultural reluctance to come to terms with the century-long presence of Islam. As discussed in Chapter 2, this dissonance does not stem exclusively from a theological and Christian impulse and motive (Ramberg 2004:5). Nor does it come exclusively from those rigid Euro-modern philosophies that silence other local and indigenous ontologies, systems of knowledge and practices that "*do not fit*" in the West (Tlostanova and Mignolo 2012). If anything, the prescription and proscription to think of Muslims from/in the Balkans as subjects defined and constituted by and in regulation, restriction and control (Karić et al. 2023) barely address Europe's long history of racialisation. The latter ascribes implicitly a marker of not-belonging to European "others" (El-Tayeb 2011). In this respect, Coskun Canan and Naika Foroutan observe how Europe's philosophy of pluralism lies in the recognition of diversity and social integration in the majority of the core society. Yet this philosophy seems limited and contested when concerning the largest minority group – namely, Muslims in Europe. What Canan and Foroutan highlight is a paradox of today's European societies. It goes in line with the motto: "We want diversity, but without Muslims" (2016:164). This paradox speaks of Europe's cognitive dissonance in promoting multiculturalism while wishing to live in a "community without strangers" (2019:43), to use Achille Mbembe's words.

Muslims in/from the Balkans are the favourite target of otherisation (Merdjanova 2013:115) and assorted with any fellow Muslim originally from Africa, the Middle East or Asia. This subtle mechanism of equalisation has not only come to contradict Europe's attempt to define a "European Islam" and curtail it from "the extremist, suspect and fundamentalist Islam" that must remain outside (Rexhepi 2017b:53). It has also come to constitute an ahistorically fixed Muslim minority in the face of European prejudice (Karić et al. 2023; Spellman Poots 2019), preventing Muslims from and beyond the Balkans to even become part of the tolerant, secular European "we-ness" (El-Tayeb

2011:xxvi, Ramberg 2004:6). Needless to say, this Eurocentric bent aggravates the continuous conflict and negotiation between non-European Muslims originally from the postcolonial world (Cesari 2003:256) and those who were already EU citizens.

From within the European Union, a "fortress" mentality has also politically problematised its border policies and provided a rather misleading idea of representing the essence of Europe (Spellman Poots 2019:187, Grzymski 2019:136). Efforts to prevent inflows at unauthorised locations have targeted the land borders of Muslim-majority Balkan countries, which have entered the securitisation discourse in the post-9/11 era (Preljević and Ljubović 2021:264). As the borders of Muslim-majority Balkan countries merge with those of the Schengen zone, this securitisation discourse holds together the markers of any extremist, suspect and fundamentalist Muslim with any coreligionist from the Middle East and beyond. It therefore clearly defines too culturalist boundaries between an Islam that can be integrated into the EU and an "extremist Islam" that must remain outside Europe (Sofos and Tsagarousianou 2013:16; Rexhepi 2017b:53). These borders deepen the continuous conflict and negotiation along ethnic and religious lines between the host country and the country of origin of European Muslims and those originally from the postcolonial world (see Cesari 2003:256 and Merdjanova 2013:104), as well as between those who reside in the not-yet-EU Balkan EU states and those who already hold an EU passport. In the case of the latter, Piro Rexhepi argues that the EU enlargement project has so far wasted energy on the rhetoric that all people *in* [and *from*] the Balkans – including refugees, Roma and Muslims – are human too (2017b:46). Although this group is anchored in the "western hemisphere" because it is different from those coming from further east and the Global south, the intra-Europe experiences and practices of migration equalise it with those incoming. Paraphrasing Aleksandar Hemon's words, Muslims from/in the Balkans are just close enough to being Europe to keep perpetually failing at being Europe (see Bronwyn 2020). Alternatively, as Avtar Brah would say (1996:2), they would occasionally struggle to see themselves as *both* Muslims *and* Europeans.

Among post-migrant generations of Muslims born outside the Balkans, many experience a permanent condition of *migrating* in their birthplaces. Their "homeland", "host country" and even cosmopolitan references to belonging remain a project-in-the-making (Merdjanova 2013:103). This condition of atopicality holds them hostage to continuous and unpredictable displacement, exposing them to the recurrent questions regarding their loyalty to Europe and whether or not they can be considered a threat to liberal democracy. Following Madina Tlostanova (2017), they are no longer Orientals nor yet Europeans; they would never be accepted as fully Europeans because of the fact that Westerners would be unlikely to accept them as equals (Mark et al. 2019:282). To put it simply, they are often still considered immigrants – in opposition to citizens – in the country in which they were born and currently reside (Dahinden 2016). They remain trapped in a status of colonised, discriminated and racialised non-European subjects (Tlostanova and Mignolo 2012), all ascribed to a sort of "civilisational illegitimacy" (Bougarel 2008:160) which raises the question of vague and largely opinionated integration and acceptance (Merdjanova 2013:104).

This backdrop prevents Muslims from/in the Balkans from *belonging* to the ummah and being "connected" with a more cosmopoliation vision of their past (Sadriu 2017:541). In effect, when the former identify with the pleas of the latter by standing in solidarity with each other (Rexhepi 2017b:55), public fear and Islamophobia intensify in most European countries (Rexhepi 2015). Therefore, they cannot exercise genuine agency, but they tellingly internalise Islamophobia as they are embedded in a hegemonic European framework of anti-Islam arguments where whiteness and Christianity are considered the norm (Ferizaj 2023). Under these circumstances, they (un)consciously self-reiterate the Eurocentric distinctions between the whiter, local and European Islam from that of Black and brown Arab Muslims, reinforcing binary and exclusionary white/Queer/Islam divisions that prevent the emergence of intersectional solidarities and subjectivities (Rexhepi 2023:32).

## "Where are you really from?"

Throughout the fieldwork, a general view holds that integration and acculturation has been more successful for the respondents than for the older community members. Among them, not all practices and feelings of belonging are important to people in the same way and to the same extent due to the recollection of narratives, memories and stories about who they are and who they are not.

In the case of young Muslims with Albanian roots, the maintenance of transnational ties with family culture and Islam is not uniform. They particularly depend on parental goodwill and are often characterised by a wealth of transnational ways of being and belonging (Vathi 2015:34). As families of most respondents are not originally from Albania proper, but from the multicultural town of Kërçovë in North Macedonia, the trans-local reproduction of Albanian customs and traditions replicates minority-majority dynamics across time and space. The strong connection with Albanian culture, language and historical legacies is important to ease the challenges of being Muslims not only in Germany but also in the places where their parents come from. Nonetheless, the personal attachment to Albanian culture also differs from the construction and reproduction of the parental identity narratives (Yuval-Davis 2006:203). For instance, one mother is very explicit in this respect, admitting to "speak[ing] mostly German to [her] son [as she] does not want him to feel part of, or obliged to comply with, a minority in Germany". Belonging also largely depends on the socio-economic background that caused migration (and displacement) due to which experiences of integration (or lack thereof) in the host society have (not) occurred successfully.

The younger respondents do not avoid categorisation or draw uncritical conclusions about their sense of unfamiliarity to the parental place of origin. If anything, they mostly confess to feeling somehow uprooted from North Macedonia and from their parents' experiences of migration. Their parents' trauma and burden of integration impinge on their feeling of being fully integrated in, and feeling attached to, Germany. In simpler words, respondents do not reject Albanian culture and traditions intertwined or linked with Islam; hence, they are more likely than previous generations to nurture a "strategic cosmopolitanism" to avoid identity dilemmas in their everyday life. During the fieldwork, they were found to be navigating between two (or more) cultures – German, Albanian and pop-Islam (Gerlach 2006) – while juggling religious and secular ways of thinking, often crippled by self-doubt triggered by the "*halal*-or-*haram*" question (see Chapter 5). Living in Germany and visiting North Macedonia activate a sense of attachment and remoteness at the same time, as few respondents point out.

> "We have a big family [in Kërçovë] and I feel that half of the village is related to me . . . but I would not say that I am connected with the village, nor I am with the country at all".
>
> "When I go visiting my family in [North] Macedonia, I see how difficult it is to go along with same-age peers; perhaps they do not set specific goals in life as we do here in Germany. This double identity was difficult to deal with when I was younger . . . now it is not a problem anymore. But it hits back when I notice that my German friends have better opportunities than I have".
>
> "I know I was born here, that I am a German citizen and I won't live in [North] Macedonia. Yet Albanian culture was so present in my private life and I spent so much time visiting my parents' hometown [that] I can't fully identify as a German".

The burden of integration is largely salient and transmitted through a set of performative practices that do not prevent respondents from admitting that they enact different ways of belonging than the older generations. A more symbolic sense of belonging seemingly shows a variety of tendencies, orientations and opinions amidst the highly complex "global-to-local" interconnections and peculiar gender dynamics at the community level. As previous studies show (Sofos and Tsagarousianou 2013; Tsagarousianou 2016; Leiken 2012; Ripa 2023), the "local" dimension is paramount for young Muslims in the definition of "home" (in German, *heimat*) and their mobilisation outside their private space, or the neighbourhood. Tellingly, respondents praise their attachment to differently connected localities, which, in many in-depth interviews, were described as despised and dreaded by same-age peers. Respondents do not only romanticise the locality where their parents and community are originally from, but they also discuss the "simpler, rural everyday life", where "at least tomatoes are tasty and you can grow them yourself" while "the whole atmosphere around is definitely warmer and more welcoming". At the same time, other cultural legacies are openly criticised. When Albanian culture is passed down across generations, female respondents openly criticise "Albanianism" as traditionally remaining a man's world and only a matter of fathers and sons (Lowenthal 1998:42). Among others, a female respondent bursts into tears while verbalising her malaise for "being forbidden [by the father] to veil [herself] in order to better adapt to German society". She critically adds that this decision stems simply from the "common, patriarchal and double standards of the Albanian families that have nothing to do with Islam or integration". Since she herself was born and raised in Dortmund, works in town and has her life established in Germany, this type of imposition intensifies her sense of not-belonging to the rest of the veiled Muslim women in and beyond Germany, as well as to the traditional rules of Islam shared by Muslim women worldwide. In retrospect, however, her critical stance toward the overwhelmingly (and commonly) gendered dynamics show how Albanian Muslim masculinities are subordinate to European Christian or secular masculinities. In seeing her daughter veiled, the father's fear stems from having internalised Islamic practices as a foreigner to Germany (Ferizaj 2019:74). In it, "Personen mit Migrationshintergrund" (in English, "people with a migration background") are generally treated as non-white Germans (Ferizaj 2023), while Islam reiterates the burden of belonging to a country, namely North Macedonia, which is barely associated with the culturally developed Christian (white) Europe. Regardless of the level of religious salience, Islam is much less equalised with, or acknowledged as, Judaism and/or Christianity – a misconception that fuels Islamophobia and hits the nerves of the already-minoritised Albanian diaspora in their place of residence. A respondent recalls his real-life experiences as follows:

> "Once I confessed to a [German] friend to be Muslim. He was taken by surprise: 'You were born here, but your family is originally from Macedonia, Albanian and Muslim. Wait, where are you really from?' . . . I always specify my identity background. . . . Yet people assume I am not German [and] they ask: 'so, where are you really from?' . . . I have strange feelings about this question".

This question couples with verbal assaults and racist expressions in everyday life, all creating an echo chamber where young Muslims perceive the abundance of Islamophobic slurs and comments in the political discourse and social media platforms, respectively. Respondents paradoxically self-reiterate the downward spirals of alienation and dominant explanations that have contributed to the multiple converging crises and pain that Balkan Muslims have endured over the last three decades (Rexhepi 2017a). As discussed in Chapter 2, when respondents associate themselves with "European Muslimness", they yearn to take distance from "other Islams" preached by non-European Muslims in Dortmund and Germany in general. Although it is no longer possible to distinguish between 'imported' and 'local' versions of Islam from within some peripheral localities (Bardos 2014:78), most male respondents detach the self-labelled Balkan, European, secular and moderate Islam from the oriental, radical and backward forms of Islam of Africa, the Middle East and Asia. Yet again, this definition likely shows how Albanians yearn to present themselves as (white) Europeans while being burdened to belong to a Muslim-majority population from the periphery of Europe (Ferizaj 2023). They also echo the discourse of Albanian elites (be they in North Macedonia, Kosovo or Albania), who frame themselves as 'good European Muslims' as opposed to 'bad Arab Muslims' (Sadriu 2017).

Conversely, some female respondents enact postulates of solidarity with other female Muslims originally from Palestine, Kurdistan and Morocco, emphasising a special bond on a local level. Islam here creates a sense of belonging to a transnational community in which interactions are shaped by common experiences of migration (El-Tayeb 2011: xxi). They understand that Islam remains in a binary, unified and separated position from "Europe" (Bobako 2015:44), but encounters with other Muslim women soften their feeling of being unwanted, unwelcomed and sometimes hated. As much as unfair and unpleasant circumstances matter on the individual level, these women realise that the all-encompassing discourse about Islam and Muslims stigmatises them in their place of birth and residence. In this manner, Muslimness is imprinted on the bodies of female Muslims in Germany (Özyürek 2015). As a male and female respondent openly admit and complain, respectively:

> "We have a mosque in the neighbourhood; the imam calls for the prayer only once and only on Friday. That call really bothers German locals. My neighbour who really likes me and my wife . . . is racist – I must admit. . . . Another neighbour, same age of mine, ran away and went to live outside the city as he could not make it with many Muslims around him".
>
> "Why all the time do I need to explain that I do not drink [alcohol], eat pork, bet and speak German so well? . . . After working for six years in the same place, it is a bit annoying because they knowingly question me".

Innenstadt-Nord was often taken into consideration as a spatial reference to handle a sense of belonging between Germany and North Macedonia. Overall, respondents lament what the Leipzig Autoritarismus-Studie discovered in 2020: almost half of the German population (46.8%) feel like a stranger in Germany due to the many Muslims, while more than a quarter of the respondents (24.7%) believe that Muslims should be banned from immigrants (quoted in Zubair 2023:271). What a male respondent points out is the consequence of secular laws attempting to reinforce the idea that there is no space for visible signs of Islam (Najib and Teeple Hopkins 2020:452) in areas where Muslims and "new dwellers" live in a great majority, even if they represent a small proportion in Dortmund. Since the 1980s, Albanian families have clustered in this Innenstadt-Nord, along with other communities from the Balkans, Eastern Europe and the Global South. Outside this neighbourhood, respondents have a pragmatic approach to different inner-city environments. Some easily negotiate cultural diversity from within Innenstadt-Nord, while others refer to this area as a much safer and more liveable milieu for young Muslims compared to Dorstfeld, defined by one respondent as a "*Nazi-Kiez*" – literally, a "Nazi area". In Innenstadt-Nord, quotidian encounters with other same-age peers sharing a similar family migration heritage boost a transnational circuit of friendships and provide a 'safety net' against potential exclusion and lack of social capital (Vathi 2015:10). Although "street cultures", often in contradiction with Islam, surround the community under study, the postmodern and post-secular culture of German society is pragmatically welcomed thanks to the transnational Muslim friendships that de-essentialise processes of belonging to kinship and ethnic family background. Only one male respondent refers to the neighbourhood as a "ghetto", while the rest realise that intra-city dynamics and the political atmosphere may impinge on their 'being Muslims'. In their place of residence, which is often identified in the neighbourhood, Islam becomes a secondary yet connected issue with street violence and radical Muslims that might constitute a potential risk. There is little doubt that the international context has a very powerful impact on local debates and national identity (Sadriu 2017:542).

> "A 14-year-old [sic] Black kid holding a knife was shot by the police. . . . True, he had a knife, but he died on the spot for it! I was shocked, especially because it happened here, just around the corner, with a machine gun in this neighbourhood, where all people [from migrant and post-migration communities] live together with many German students".
>
> "In Innenstadt-Nord, we do have extremists: they greet you, invite you to the mosque, [but if] you are educated you cannot buy what they say, [and] this is exactly the problem: in our societies, where everyone thinks of religion as not imporant, people do not have good knowledge regarding potential misunderstanding of Islam".

The former interview insight recalls the tragic death of Mohamed Lamine Dramé, an unaccompanied 16-year-old minor originally from Senegal, who suffered from mental health issues and lived in a Catholic youth welfare institution. He was shot dead with a submachine gun in front of a youth welfare facility while he was wielding a knife. The shooting heightened the debate all over Germany, sparking protests against police brutality, racial profiling and racism after five policemen were suspended for their participation in right-wing chats and a black man was hit by the police in Berlin (Zubair 2023:270). A report by Junge Welt noted that the killing of Mohamed was not an isolated incident, but it was one of the four deaths in one week in August, three in

September and two in October 2022, many with migrant backgrounds.[2] In the case of the latter interview, instead, the respondent warns about Salafist missionizing activities and gaining new members in Dortmund and the North Rhine-Westphalia in general, a region which is considered the Salafist hotbed in Germany (Felden and von Hein 2018). While going through the city centre for a potential interview, many German converts and Salafist preachers were found handing out publications of the Qur'an and booklets on Islam. When asked to comment on what every German considers extremist interpreters of Islam, all respondents were found to be quick to condemn those who represent only a small position within the *ummah* and dangerously veer towards reductionist, fragmented interpretation of religious meaning separated from traditional roots (Robinson-Bertoni 2017:26; see also Chapter 5).

## Do Belgium and Bosnia Mirror Each Other?

Some recent data on the Bosnian diaspora estimates that 8,000 former war refugees settled in Belgium since the early 1990s. About 1,800 arrived in Antwerp (Halilović 2008:18) – making the Dutch city the "centre of the Bosnian diaspora in Belgium", as the saying goes among Bosnians themselves residing in town. While conducting in-depth interviews, most respondents verbalise a great attachment to the city. One jokes about being "proudly bigheaded" – referring to a Flemish metaphor that depicts the feeling of superiority and greatness of Antwerpians (Clapson 2023). Another respondent claims to "have lived her entire life in Antwerp and cannot imagine her future far from it". Yet another speaks of the importance of the multicultural district of Durne, where his family and many Bosnian Muslims found refuge after fleeing the war in Bosnia. He explains,

> My father fled a concentration camp in Bosnia, while my mother arrived as a refugee. Once in Antwerp, they met in a cafeteria – a "Yugo club" – which soon became a meeting point for many Bosnian Muslims back then.

This strong sense of *belonging* to the city of Antwerp takes on additional poignancy, though. When discussing the everyday dilemma of belonging related to anti-migration discourse, many restate the right of their parents to enter Belgium as members of a political community escaping war, and, once inside,

2 "Peoples Dispatch", an international media project with the mission of bringing voices from people's movements and organisations across the globe, reported that more than 2500 people followed the call of the alliance "Justice 4 Mouhamed" to Dortmund on November 19 and protested in memory of all victims of police violence. Mouhamed's death was understood as resulting from the repressive, racist and discriminatory course of action of the German police. Available at: https://peoplesdispatch.org/2022/11/28/progressives-in-germany-demand-justice-for-16-year-old-who-was-killed-by-police/

exert the right to become citizens of a pluralist society (Yuval-Davis 1991:58). In so doing, respondents recall their 'semi-diasporic situation', thereby revealing to belong to "a diaspora's diaspora" (Nelson 2011:25) whose members are often treated as having just arrived, regardless of how long they have been in the country (El-Tayeb 2017). Nurturing long-distance relations with Bosnia is particularly important (Bougarel 2008:151) as they are fully aware of belonging to the generation born outside Bosnia because of the genocidal violence against Yugoslavian Muslims. In fact, most perceive their birthplace and Muslimness not so much as a by-product of the violence endured by their communities, but as the very purpose of persecuting Muslims in Yugoslavia. Due to linguistic and institutional situations, respondents eventually feel 'minoritised' or 'not at home', as do many other Dutch speakers and citizens in the Belgian Flanders (Stroschein 2003:4). To a certain extent, this discomfort is expressed by other respondents in Germany, unlike in Italy and Poland.

In theory, such a sense of unfamiliarity inevitably makes the establishment of social ties with people from the core community more difficult ( Lesschaeve and Glaurdić 2023:8), especially in terms of the older generation's possibility (or illusion) of returning back home. The parents' national origin is a central, or even unique, marker of their identity (Riniolo and Toivanen 2023:304). Yet this attachment to Bosnia occasionally jeopardises that to Antwerp, especially when respondents experience distress in grappling with the legacies of a postmodern and post-secular society. Although many worship and care about Islam by openly manifesting their religious salience in and beyond the Bosnian Muslim community, identity contestation happens when they compare themselves with the post-migrant conditions of other Muslims in Belgium.

> "I am as much Belgian as much I am Bosnian . . . but in Bosnia, I am an outsider, and in Belgium, when I say my last name, I know that someone might think like 'he is not one of us'.
>
> "In Belgium I am Bosnian, in Bosnia I am Belgian. Yet I love Bosnia . . . and I also like Belgium for the opportunities given to my parents. . . . I can go back to Sarajevo with my education, but economic insecurity makes it difficult for me . . . also, the lifestyle there is far from Belgium's".
>
> "I always looked forward to going to Bosnia for summertime. . . . Now I go there for family business, and I have the feeling that that sense of attachment is slowly fading away. When I was a child, Bosnia looked like the perfect world to be [in] . . . now, as time passes by, it seems that there is no future there".

These interview insights show how the discourse on sameness and otherness changes, at least on the surface (Grünenberg 2005). As Fleischmann and Phalet notice, these young Muslims actively seek validation of their dual identity as Muslim and European nationals and act accordingly in order to extend the inclusiveness of European national identities to their religious minority group (2018:57). Yet their sense of belonging is articulated and formally structured, or at times politicised, when it is threatened in some way (Yuval-Davis 2011:4). Although they do not lack socialisation in their places of residence, respondents emphasise with bitterness the spatio-temporal contexts and dynamics of their parental experiences and critically reflect on the historical and political disputes in their place of birth and residence. In other words, respondents easily associate themselves with their birthplaces outside the Balkans, yet share a certain degree of distress about political development in their parents' places of origin. When they begin to recollect the events that led to their families fleeing Bosnia and settling in Belgium, they wonder whether Islamophobia can jeopardise their positions as Muslims living in Antwerp in the same way anti-Muslim rhetoric did to their parents before throughout the wars in Yugoslavia. Tellingly, this liminality was even expressed by some in Italy and Poland. These three interview insights are instructive:

> "When I say I am Italian and Bosnian, people misunderstand or perhaps they do not really grasp what I mean. I was born in Italy, I speak Italian and I think alike, however I have my story and I can't forget my past. This doable identity is often misunderstood by Italians".
>
> "I fully respect the law of Montenegro, and [this is why I] have accepted neither German nor Italian citizenship – because Montenegro has issues with Serbia, especially when it comes to speaking of the 2006 referendum. My roots are in Montenegro, though [and] this duality [of being], both Italian and Montenegrin, must be included within a European identity [because] I would like to transmit it to my children".
>
> "My nationality is Bosniak, even though my family belongs to Sandžak; it was not difficult to adapt [in Poland] because I was only one year old when my mom brought me here. I have no memories, but I am definitely attacked to Sandžak".

Another spontaneous equalisation turned out to liken the migration experience of their parents to that of non-European newcomers. In this respect, primarily male respondents self-reiterate political speculation about the domestic problems caused by the inflow of refugees and migrants into Belgium. Since many nationals are "really in need" in Belgium, in their opinion immigration raises problems in different fields of life (Preljević and Ljubović 2021) as newcomers are more likely to exploit social benefits through tax exemptions and education services, among others, consequently affecting the already-established former migration communities. As Piro Rexhepi notes (2017a:55), Balkan Muslims reflect on the abuse of European hospitality, considering themselves the good, white, European Muslims when encountering racism among colleagues, friends and same-age peers who do not know about their religious faith. While conducting in-depth interviews, two male respondents (perhaps unconsciously) self-reiterate certain anti-migration discursive strategies in explaining how they handle the unfair pressure and endure the pain of their parents' dislocation from Bosnia. A female respondent reflects instead on how Bosnian Muslim war refugees were initially welcomed and rescued, but recently populism and nativism have dangerously shifted gears throughout the Flanders and targeted them simply because they are Muslims.

> "In Belgium, we [Muslim] have much [fewer] troubles than [Muslim] Moroccans. . . . We can live easier in a [more] liberal society than people in Pakistan, [but] for Belgians it is difficult to understand Bosnia, its political system, the history and what is happening right now. I can answer their questions, but it is very difficult to explain why I am here, not in Bosnia."
>
> "My mom is from a Bosnian region where Muslims were the majority before the war; [t]here, three concentration camps were set up. . . . I am not saying that Belgium is like Bosnia [but when it comes to Islamophobia,] this is a sentiment very felt in my family. What is unthinkable to many, it is instead understood as possible by us".

Another respondent echoes a right-wing view which usually goes viral in the Belgian Flanders. He explains that "people easily get social benefits and exploit [Belgium's] 'socialistic' society . . . sometimes [expressing] anti-Belgian sentiment [and] getting advantages from Belgium to oppose the idiots in power". This argument points to the allegedly too-generous social protection and welfare policies that create a vicious circle of "welfare addiction" and penetrate so deeply to lower participation in the labour market (Van Leuven et al. 2023:62). However, all these insights warn about a tense political atmosphere across Belgium, which is not only internalised by young Muslims, but it also reactivates the plight of the traumatic war experiences that can only further inflame rampant polarisation over spatial divisions and people's distress. A female contends that "in spite of everything, Bosnia without Serbs and Croats cannot exist, although both communities are a bit different than us Bosniaks". Across time and space, a personal sense of belonging and safety (might) continue to "bleed" (Hirsch 2012:34), especially when reminded of episodes of assimilation, the mass and organised expulsion and violence, the continued destruction and erasure of Islamic sites and all that their parents have left behind (Rexhepi 2017a:54). Among others, the mass expulsion of ethnic Turks and Muslims from Communist Bulgaria in May 1989, the 1995 Srebrenica Genocide and the genocidal violence against Albanians before the 1999 Kosovo War are seminal events for the *generation after.* As discussed in Chapter 3, this process of mnemonic recollection of events and adoption to today's political atmosphere bring young Balkan Muslims to align their experiences with those of other non-European Muslims, thereby integrating them into their personal stock of knowledge, memory and consciousness (Sofos and Tsagarousianou 2013:118). This web of post-memories roams among the young generations of respondents who admit to navigating in uncertainty as they are seen, and continue to see themselves, as the "eternal newcomers" in their birthplace, divided by a longitudinal fracture in terms of a double injunction of a conflictive co-existence and/or cohabitation with Bosnia. In the realm of everyday life, they often detect the phenomenon of "nano-racism", to use Achille Mbembe's words (2019:57); that is, a series of everyday gestures that express the spiteful banter, some allusion or insinuation, a slip of the tongue, a joke, some consciously spiteful remarks that deliberately stigmatise and inflict violence to those who are not considered "one of us". To cope with this, many keep a sort of "security distance" from some communities of the *ummah* in Antwerp, mainly composed of refugees and unloved newcomers who are perceived as different and dangerous to be accepted as European Muslims.

> "[L]ooking 'white' helped me to avoid racism. Even so, there have been some pre-judgments from my name . . . I feel Islamophobia: I see people here who are genuinely racist, and when I am with them, they do not understand that I am Muslim, making racist comments".

In retrospect, none reflected on the fact that their parents' birthplace in Northwest Bosnia has again become a site for refugees and an EU-sponsored space for establishing refugee camps before entering the European Union (Rexhepi 2023:22). In their opinion, their self-described "light skin", European outfits and fluency in Dutch language constitute the concrete difference between them and other coreligionists who have just arrived. Yet again, "whiteness" is the main reason for which they easily avoid unpleasant encounters and subtle forms of discrimination. However, their investment in whiteness comes close to Albanians' (Ferizaj 2023), as mentioned earlier. To affirm their "European" identity, respondents seek unambiguous acknowledgement as being white in its socio-political meaning in the attempt to normalise the history of 'Bosnian Islam' in the European canon. In turn, these claims to whiteness reveal how the effects of racialisation and the ideology of colour-blindness operate through an active process of suppression of Muslim solidarity across the *ummah*, rather than a simple passive attitude of Islam in general (El-Tayeb 2011: xxiv).

In the multicultural neighbourhoods under observation, religious and cultural affinities particularly resonate cultural closeness with the Turkish diaspora. Türkiye is not seen as a "second homeland" as it is for the second and third generation of Turkish families. However, respondents express a sense of attachment to Türkiye and same-age peers from Turkish Muslim families rather than other Muslims from Morocco or the Middle East. At the intercultural *iftar* event at the AntwerpExpo in April 2023, a respondent says that

> "not every Bosnian feels comfortable to come here, as most people prefer going to our mosque and attending community events there. . . .

> Islam and the *ummah*, which both transcend all political borders, are the primary objects of loyalty, and not any particular nation-state".
>
> (Byrd 2017:249)

Yet the burden of the traumatic experiences of loss and discrimination still haunt the community, leading most Bosnian Muslims to prefer a familial environment to comply with practices of Islam. In this regard, there is little doubt that war legacies circulate across generations, thereby driving certain in-group dynamics and still having a grip on people's social networks ( Lesschaeve and Glaurdić 2023).

## References

Asad, T. (2003) *Formations of the Secular. Christianity, Islam, Modernity.* Stanford: Stanford University Press.

Baev, J. (2015) 'De-Stalinisation and Political Rehabilitations in Bulgaria', in K. McDermott and M. Stibbe (eds.) *De-Stalinising Eastern Europe. The Rehabilitation of Stalin's Victims after 1953.* London: Palgrave Macmillan.

Bakić-Hayden, M. (1995) Nesting Orientalisms: The Case of Former Yugoslavia. *Slavic Review*, 54 (4), pp. 917–931. https://doi.org/10.2307/2501399

Bardos, G. (2014) Jihad in the Balkans: The Next Generation. *World Affairs*, 177 (3), pp. 73–79.

Bjelić, D. (2018) Introduction. Balkan Transnationalism at the Time of Neoliberal Catastrophe. *Interventions – International Journal of Postcolonial Studies*, 20 (6), pp. 751–758. https://doi.org/10.1080/1369801X.2018.1493392

Black, R. (2001) Return and Reconstruction in Bosnia-Herzegovina: Missing Link, or Mistaken Priority? *SAIS Review*, 21 (2), pp. 177–199. https://doi.org/10.1353/sais.2001.0031

Bobako, M. (2015) Inventing Muslims in Europe. Religion, Culture and Identity in the Time of Neoliberalism. *Przegląd Religioznawczy – The Religious Studies Review*, 4 (258), pp. 43–55.

Bougarel, X. (2008) 'Balkan Muslim Diasporas and the Idea of a European Islam', in T. Dulić, R. Kostić, R., I. Maček, and J. Trtak (eds.) *Balkan Currents. Essays in Honour of Kjell Magnusson.* Uppsala: Uppsala University Press, pp. 147–165.

Bougarel, X. and Mihaylova, D. (2005) Diasporas musulmanes balkaniques dans l'Union européenne [Balkan Muslim Diaspora in the European Union]. *Balkanologie – Revue d'études pluridisciplinaires*, IX (1–2), pp. 59–211. https://doi.org/10.4000/balkanologie.577.

Brah, A. (1996) *Cartographies of Diaspora. Contesting Identities.* London: Routledge.

Bronwyn, J. (2020) The Balkans is just Close Enough to Being Europe to Perpetually Fail at Being Europe, *Kosovo 2.0.* Available at: https://kosovotwopointzero.com/en/aleksandar-hemon-the-balkans-is-just-close-enough-to-being-europe-to-perpetually-fail-at-being-europe/ (Accessed: 10 April 2023)

Bryden, D. (2004) Postcolonialism Now: Autonomy, Cosmopolitanism, and Diaspora. *University of Toronto Quarterly*, 73 (3), pp. 691–706. http://dx.doi.org/10.3138/utq.73.2.691

Byrd, J. D. (2017) *Islam in a Post-Secular Society. Religion, Secularity and the Antagonism of Recalcitrant Faith.* Leiden and Boston: Brill.

Canan, C. and Foroutan, N. (2016) The Paradox of Equal Belonging of Muslims. *Islamophobia Studies Journal*, 3 (2), pp. 160–176. http://dx.doi.org/10.18452/22484

Cesari, J. (2003) 'Muslim Minorities in Europe: The Silent Revolution', in J. Esposito and F. Burgat (eds.) *Modernizing Islam: Religion in the Public Sphere in the Middle East and Europe.* New Brunswick: Rutgers University Press, pp. 251–271.

Clapson, C. (2023) People from Antwerp are all bigheads, All West Flemings Are Hard-Working!, *Flanders News.* Available at: www.vrt.be/vrtnws/en/2023/03/29/where-do-flemings-regional-reputations-come-from/ (Accessed: 18 April 2023)

Cohen, R. (1997) *Global Diaspora: An Introduction.* London: Routledge.

Dahinden, J. (2016) A Plea for the "De-Migranticization" of Research on Migration and Integration. *Ethnic and Racial Studies*, 39 (13), pp. 2207–2225. https://doi.org/10.1080/01419870.2015.1124129

Eckersley, S. and Vos, C. (2023) *Diversity of Belonging in Europe. Public Spaces, Contested Places, Cultural Encounters.* London and New York: Routledge.

El-Tayeb, F. (2011) *European Others: Queering Ethnicity in Postnational Europe.* Minneapolis: University of Minnesota Press.

El-Tayeb, F. (2017) European Others, *Eurozine.* Available at: www.eurozine.com/european-others/ (Accessed: 9 October 2022)

Felden, E. and von Hein, M. (2018) North Rhine-Westphalia: Germany's Salafist Hotbed, *Deutsche Welle.* Available at: www.dw.com/en/invisible-and-dangerous-the-salafist-scene-in-north-rhine-westphalia/a-45949192 (Accessed: 10 June 2023).

Ferizaj, A. (2019) Othering Albanian Muslim Masculinities: A Case Study of Albanian Football Players. *OCCHIALÌ – Rivista sul Mediterraneo Islamico*, 5, pp. 71–93.

Ferizaj, A. (2023) The Desperate Desire to Be Europeans, *Kosovo 2.0.* Available at: https://kosovotwopointzero.com/en/the-desperate-desire-to-be-european/ (Accessed: 3 December 2023)

Fleischmann, F. and Phalet, K. (2018) Religion and National Identification in Europe: Comparing Muslim Youth in Belgium, England, Germany, the Netherlands, and Sweden. *Journal of Cross-Cultural Psychology*, 49 (1), pp. 44–61 https://doi.org/10.1177/0022022117741988

Gerlach, J. (2006) *Zwischen Pop und Dschihad. Muslimische Jugendliche in Deutschland* [Between Pop and Jihad. Muslim Young People in Frankfurt, Germany]. Berlin: Ch. Links Verlag.

Grünenberg, K. (2005) Constructing "Sameness" and "Otherness": Bosnian Diasporic Experiences in a Danish Context. *Balkanologie – Revue d'études pluridisciplinaires*, IX (1–2), pp. 173–193. https://doi.org/10.4000/balkanologie.587

Grzymski, J. (2019) Seeing Like a EUropean Border: Limits of the European Borders and Space. *Global Discourse*, 9 (1) pp. 135–151. https://doi.org/10.1332/204378919X15470487645493

Halilović, S. (2008) *Pregled Stanja bosanskohercegovačkog iseljeništva* [Overview of the State of Bosnian Emigration] Sarajevo: Ministarstvo za ljudska prava i izbjeglice Bosne i Hercegovine. Available at: www.mhrr.gov.ba/iseljenistvo/publikacije/default.aspx?id=940&langTag=bs-BA (Accessed: 4 March 2023)

Hirsch, M. (2012) *The Generation of Post-Memory. Writing and Visual Culture after the Holocaust.* New York: Columbia University Press.

Hirsch, M. and Miller, N. (2011) *Rites of Return. Diaspora Poetics and the Politics of Memory.* New York: Columbia University Press.

International Crisis Group (ICG) (1997) *Refugees and Internally Displaced Persons in B-H*, 30 April. Available at: www.refworld.org/docid/3ae6a6d20.html (Accessed: 17 August 2023)

Kamusella, T. (2019) *Ethnic Cleansing during the Cold War: The Forgotten 1989 Expulsion of Turks from Communist Bulgaria.* London and New York: Routledge.

Karabegović, D. (2024) Fixing Things from Outside? Diaspora Politicians and Transnational Political Engagement, in *Globalisation*, pp. 1–18. https://doi.org/10.1080/14747731.2024.2336647

Karić, D., Buljina, H. and Rexhepi, P. (2023) Feel-good Orientalism and the Question of Dignity, *Maydan. Islamic Thought.* Available at: https://themaydan.com/2023/02/feel-good-orientalism-and-the-question-of-dignity/ (Accessed: 2 January 2024).

Khan, T. (2022) *Muslim, Actually. How Islam is Misunderstood and Why It Matters.* London: Atlantic Books.

Lähdesmäki, T., Saresma, T., Hiltunen, K., Jäntti, S., Sääskilahti, N., Vallius, A. and Ahvenjärvi, K. (2016) Fluidity and Flexibility of "Belonging": Uses of the Concept in Contemporary Research. *Acta Sociologica*, 59 (3), pp. 233–247. https://doi.org/10.1177/0001699316633099

Lecoyer, K. (2020) Internormative Family Conflict Mediation within Belgian Muslim Families. *Revue Interdisciplinaire d'Études Juridiques*, 84 (1), pp. 149–177. https://doi.org/10.3917/riej.084.0149

Leiken, R. (2012) *Europe's Angry Muslims: The Revolt of the Second Generation.* Oxford: Oxford University Press.

Lesschaeve, C. and Glaurdić, J. (2023) The Ties that Bind: War Histories and Online Social Networks in Postwar Societies. *Journal of Conflict Resolution*, 68 (7–8), pp. 1443–1467. https://doi.org/10.1177/00220027231190917

Lowenthal, D. (1998) *The Heritage Crusade and the Spoils of History.* Cambridge: Cambridge University Press.

Lyons, T. (2006) 'Diaspora and Homeland Conflict', in M. Kahler and B. Walter (eds.) *Globalisation, Territoriality and Conflict in Era of Globalization.* Cambridge University Press, pp. 111–130.

Mark, J., Iacob, B., Rupprecht, T. and Spaskovska, L. (2019) *1989. A Global History of Eastern Europe.* Cambridge: Cambridge University Press.

Marramao, G. (2012) *The Passage West. Philosophy after the Nation State.* London: Verso.

Mbembe, A. (2019) *Necropolitics.* Durham: Duke University Press.

Melegh, A. (2023) *The Migration Turn and Eastern Europe. A Global Historical Sociological Analysis.* Cham: Springer.

Merdjanova, I. (2013) *Rediscovering the Umma. Muslims in the Balkans between Nationalism and Transnationalism.* Oxford: Oxford University Press.

Mushaben, J. M. (2008) Gender, HipHop and Pop-Islam: The Urban Identities of Muslim youth in Germany. *Citizenship Studies*, 12 (5), pp. 507–526. https://doi.org/10.1080/13621020802337931

Najib, K. and Teeple Hopkins, C. (2020) Geographies of Islamophobia. *Social & Cultural Geography*, 21 (4), pp. 449–457. https://doi.org/10.1080/14649365.2019.1705993

Nelson, A. (2011) 'The Factness of Diaspora: The Social Sources of Genetic Genealogy', in M. Hirsch and N. Miller (eds.) *Rites of Return. Diaspora Poetics and the Politics of Memory.* Columbia University Press, pp. 23–39.

Open Society Foundations (2011) *Muslims in Antwerp.* Available at: www.opensocietyfoundations.org/publications/muslims-antwerp (Accessed: 28 February 2021)

Özyürek, E. (2015) *Being German, Becoming Muslim: Race, Religion, and Conversion in the New Europe.* Princeton: Princeton University Press.

Preljević, H. and Ljubović, M. (2021) Re-thinking about Muslim Migration into the European Union. *Journal of Muslim Minority Affairs*, 41 (2), pp. 263–280. https://doi.org/10.1080/13602004.2021.1943883

Ramberg, I. (2004) Islamophobia and Its Consequences on Young People, *European Youth Centre Budapest.* Available at: www.coe.int/en/web/youth/-/islamophobia-and-its-consequences-on-young-people?inheritRedirect=true (Accessed: 12 December 2022).

Rexhepi, P. (2015) Mainstreaming Islamophobia: The Politics of European Enlargement and the Balkan Crime-Terror Nexus. *East European Quarterly*, 43 (2–3), pp. 189–214. Available at SSRN: https://ssrn.com/abstract=2706058

Rexhepi, P. (2017a) 'Unmapping Islam in Eastern Europe Periodization and Muslim Subjectivities in the Balkans', in I. Kacandes and Y. Komska (eds.) *Eastern Europe Unmapped. Beyond Borders and Peripheries.* Oxford: Berghahn Books, pp. 53–77.

Rexhepi, P. (2017b) Borders. *Critical Muslim*, 21, pp. 45–56.

Rexhepi, P. (2019) Imperial Inventories, "Illegal Mosques" and Institutionalised Islam: Coloniality and the Islamic Community of Bosnia and Herzegovina. *History and Anthropology*, 30 (4), pp. 1–13.

Rexhepi, P. (2023) *White Enclosures. Racial Capitalism & Coloniality along the Balkan Route*. Durham: Duke University Press.

Riniolo, V. and Toivanen, M. (2023) Future Paths in the Study of Migrant Descendants' Citizenship: Engaging with Critical Literature. *Migration Letters*, 20 (2), pp. 301–311. https://doi.org/10.33182/ml.v20i2.2890

Ripa, R. (2023) Europe Is Increasingly More Diverse – When Will City Leadership Follow Suit? *LSE Blog*. Available at: https://blogs.lse.ac.uk/europpblog/2023/01/12/europe-is-increasingly-more-diverse-when-will-city-leadership-follow-suit/ (Accessed: 15 January 2023)

Robinson-Bertoni, S. (2017) Re-Territorializing Religiosity in Wholesome Muslim Praxis. *Religions*, 8 (7), pp. 1–31. https://doi.org/10.3390/rel8070132

Roy, O. (2007) *Secularism Confronts Islam*. New York: Columbia University Press.

Sadriu, B. (2017) Grasping the Syrian War, a View from Albanians in the Balkans. *The Journal of Nationalism and Ethnicity*, 45 (4), pp. 540–559. https://doi.org/10.1080/00905992.2017.1292498

Sofos, S. A. and Tsagarousianou, R. (2013) *Islam in Europe. Public Spaces and Civic Networks*. New York: Palgrave Macmillian.

Spellman Poots, K. (2019) 'Muslim Diasporas in Transition: Islam, Gender and New Regimes of Governance', in D. Kandiyoti, N. Al-Ali, and K. Spellman Poots (eds.) *Gender Goverance in Islam*. Edinburgh: Edinburgh University Press, pp. 186–215.

Stroschein, S. (2003) What Belgium Can Teach Bosnia: The Uses of Autonomy in 'Divided House' States. *Journal of Ethnopolitics and Minority Issues in Europe*, (3), pp. 1–31.

Tlostanova, M. (2017) *Postsocialism and Postcolonialism in Fiction and Art. Resistance and Re-existence*. London: Palgrave Macmillan.

Tlostanova, M. and Mignolo, W. (2012) *Learning to Unlearn: Decolonial Reflections from Eurasia and the Americas*. Columbus: Ohio State University Press.

Tsagarousianou, R. (2016) European Muslim Diasporic Geographies. Media Use and the Production of Translocality. *Middle East Journal of Culture and Communication*, 9 (1), pp. 62–86. https://doi.org/10.1163/18739865-00901007

UNHCR (1999) *UNHCR Urges the World to Receive Kosovo Refugees as Exodus Grows*. Available at: www.unhcr.org/ie/news/news-releases/unhcr-urges-world-receive-kosovo-refugees-exodus-grows (Accessed: 11 October 2023)

UNHCR – The UN Refugee Agency (2001–2023) *Regional Representation South Eastern Europe*. Available at: www.unhcr.org/see/where-we-work (Accessed: 11 October 2023)

Urry, J. (2000) *Sociology beyond Societies. Mobilities for the Twenty-First Century*. London and New York: Routledge.

Van Leuven, A., Mertens, S., D'Haenens, L. and Mekki-Benada, A. (2023) 'The Political and Intellectual Discourse on Islam and Muslims in Flanders', in L. d'Haenens and A. Mekki-Berrada (eds.) *Islamophobia as a Form of Radicalisation. Perspectives on Media, Academia and Socio-political Scapes from Europe and Canada*. Leuven: Leuven University Press, pp. 59–74.

Vathi, Z. (2015) *Migrating and Settling in a Mobile World Albanian Migrants and Their Children in Europe*. Springer Open. Available at: https://link.springer.com/book/10.1007/978-3-319-13024-8 (Accessed: 18 July 2023).
Vertovec, S. and Cohen, R. (1999) Conceiving and Researching Transnationalism. *Ethnic and Racial Studies*, 22 (2), pp. 447–462. https://doi.org/10.1080/014198799329558
Yuval-Davis, N. (1991) The Citizenship Debate: Women, Ethnic Processes and the State. *Feminist Review*, 39 (1), pp. 58–68. https://doi.org/10.1057/fr.1991.40
Yuval-Davis, N. (2006) Belonging and the Politics of Belonging. *Patterns of Prejudices*, 40 (3), pp. 197–2014. https://doi.org/10.1080/00313220600769331
Yuval-Davis, N. (2011) 'Power, Intersectionality and the Politics of Belonging', in W. Harcourt (ed.) *The Palgrave Handbook of Gender and Development*. London: Palgrave Macmillan, pp. 367–381. https://doi.org/10.1007/978-1-137-38273-3_25
Zubair, A. (2023) 'Islamophobia in Germany', in E. Bayraklı and F. Hafez (eds.) *European Islamophobia Report 2022*. Vienna: Leopold Weiss Institute, pp. 261–284.

# 5 Halal or Haram?

"How far are we Muslims?" This question was raised by Alija Izetbegović in his famous "Islamic Declaration" (1990:17), written amidst the decolonial efforts in the Global South but only officially published in 1990 in Sarajevo. Izetbegović was not only a controversial figure for his political activism in Yugoslavia prior to becoming the first president of independent Bosnia and Herzegovina. He was also a fascinating Muslim intellectual who described capitalism and socialism as two premises of the same Western project of modernity and colonialism. To a certain extent, Izetbegović's critical viewpoints had anticipated Talal Asad's definition of *the secular* (2003) as a Eurocentric trademark to label good and "evil" enemies at home and across non-Western spaces.

Inspired by Izetbegović's provocative query and informed by Oliver Roy's concept of religiosity (2005, 2013), this chapter explores how the groups under study conceive and engage with the realm of everyday life vis-à-vis the fine line of what is "permitted" or "licit" – *halal*, from what is "forbidden" or "sinful" – *haram*. Both the significance and meanings ascribed to such a binding dichotomy are deeply rooted in a wide spectrum of values and strictures that provide direction in quotidian life (Sofos and Tsagarousianou 2013:71). However, the aim of this chapter is not to mull over the religious salience of the *generation after*, nor does it aim to detect inner divisions between the latter and the older generations of the Balkan Muslim diaspora (Merdjanova 2013:105, Bougarel 2008:155, Bougarel and Mihaylova 2005:12). In theory, intersectional and proxy factors such as generational changes, genderism, cultural and geographical features (Grünenberg 2005:189) remain simply under-researched (Lecoyer 2020:151–153) because it is extremely difficult to detect, measure and quantify them (Hurd 2008:21). In practice, all these factors may also reinforce racialised pictures of self-exclusion, low educational attainment, forced marriages, domestic violence, victimisation and others alike (Mushaben 2008:508), eventually leading scholars to bring up the wrong questions. As follows: how observant are young Balkan Muslims? May a good citizen be also a devout Muslim, or vice versa (Byrd 2017:17)? Alternatively, should a devout Muslim emulate the Western lifestyle to feel equal to a layperson (Scott 2005:41)? Against this pitfall, open questions related to being a Muslim were only raised at the time of the in-depth interviews. At times,

DOI: 10.4324/9781003589624-6

Islam and Muslimness were taken into consideration as a yardstick to assess the crisis of liberal democracy and the rampant rise of nationalist rhetoric against Muslims.

Therefore, the first part of this chapter investigates what, according to Talal Asad (2003:201), both liberals and secularists often overlook: how, when and by whom are the conditions of "the secular" set? From this perspective, the second part further discusses how the young Muslims in focus deliberately blend into non-Muslim peers, colleagues at work or public figures who do not abide by Muslims' modes of thinking, staging and everyday actions.

## A New Religiosity and a Newer Islam?

Since it was thought that secularism would free modern societies from religious interference (Azabar and Van Aelst 2023:1), political scientists have emphasised the tenets of a society without religious identity. In theory, the watchword of secularism promotes democratic institutions to represent political identities and social virtues (Boutayeb 2023:42) due to citizens' desire to live together, pursue welfare activities and deliberate about the common good (Potulski 2020:16). In practice, however, religions have never really ceased to penetrate power structures, brand the formulation of authority (Hurd 2008:121) and constitute society and communities (Scott 2005:136).

In effect, the Catholic Church and Christianity undoubtedly maintain more privileges in the Western world and cannot be considered equal in the social hierarchy of other religions (Roy 2013:10). Although Islam has become increasingly institutionalised,[1] Europe's Judeo-Christian tradition is often used as a political argument to justify the incompatibility with Islam itself (Amara 2013:647) and reinforce the popular views that the liberal state is incompatible with Islamic orthopraxis (Jones 2021). Among the four countries this study focuses on, Belgium is notable. Belgium has made agreements with other religious faiths, but the Catholic pillar has never really ceased influencing the country, as well as the "collective consciousness" of its secularised societal environment, such as education, political parties, health and social welfare services, etc.! (Driezen 2023:31).

While the relationship between Islam and democracy is considered by Western commentators to be problematic, the existence of a convergence between

1 Since the adoption of the text (recommendation 1162) ratified by the Parliamentary Assembly on 19 September 1991 (11th Sitting), Islam in its different forms is considered to have influenced and contributed to the European civilisation and people's everyday life, and not only in countries with a Muslim population such as Turkey. In presenting the new Europe as "becoming increasingly subject to influences from Islam, not only through the regions of predominantly Islamic culture such as Albania or some southern republics of the USSR, the text warned about those hostile or oriental stereotypes that contribute to having very little awareness in Europe about the importance of Islam's past contribution or of Islam's potentially positive role in European society today" (Council of Europe 1991).

Christianity and liberal democracy is more often taken for granted (Vlas and Gherghina 2012:340). The recent politicisation of the Christian heritage and its interconnectedness with Europe's national identities (Fleischmann and Phalet 2018:46) have become part and parcel of illiberal and far-right populist discourse, deepening the West's cultural reluctance to come to terms with Islam. Since there is as much Islam in the West as there is the West in Islam (Marramao 2012:55), establishing a secular society does not depend exclusively on theological and religious impulses and motives, nor does it solely pertain to the matter of religion. While Margaret Jacob spoke of a "new religiosity" in terms of the historical sentiments, beliefs and ceremonial activities that contributed to the emergence of liberal society (mentioned by Asad 2003:188), Oliver Roy differentiates religiosity from religion (2004). In theory, religiosity is a formidable subject for religious studies and particularly useful for investigating a wealth of religious tenets that are potentially attentive to traditional interpretations, communitarian roots, landscape and weather patterns, and so forth. Religiosity is also the self-formulation and self-expression of personal faith, which is different from the idea of religion – meaning a coherent body of belief and dogmas that are collectively managed by a body of legitimate holders of knowledge. In contrast, patterns of religiosity have emerged out of the porousness of the same categories of religious identity in "the West" (Robinson-Bertoni 2017:14) in the wake of the crisis of social authority (Roy 2004:8) and the alleged absence of hierarchy and supposed dependence on horizontal solidarity (Asad 2003:5).

This study refers to religiosity as a complex set of adaptive strategies for second and third generations of young Muslims with a migration heritage (Roy 2004:4). In other words, it is a "generation thing", which does not necessarily stem from a phenomenon of "de-clericalisation", as Alija Izetbegović would argue (1990:22). Rather, religiosity is a form of identity performed to align with, and orient to, the Western orbit. Put simply, it is more about "spirituality", or even "spiritualism", than religion; hence, religiosity lies in the combination of the return of traditional lifestyles with the social predication of the youth residing in unprivileged and problematic neighbourhoods on the edge of post-migrant urban spaces. Many young Muslims are engaged in do-it-yourself practices to foster that kind of "liberal Islam" that Western politicians claim they would welcome. Julia Gerlach identifies a "popular Islam", or "pop-Islam" (2006), within well-educated or economically better-off family contexts, whose tendency to adapt to fashion, rap music and media focuses more on social commitment to the pillars of Islam rather than its traditional tenets. At the same time, this "pop-Islam movement" may fail to alleviate post-migrant generations of Muslims from the pressure of postmodern dilemmas. On the other hand, however, it may reintroduce a more conservative lifestyle and ideas typical of the Muslim Brotherhood but not accepted by Salafi Muslims (Mushaben 2008:508).

With this in mind, a large number of scholars contend that there is not a European Islam and it is no longer plausible to talk about a singular Islam.

A plurality of Islams, replete with sects, denominations and variant readings, have instead emerged out of a series of not always coherent and foreign attitudes appealing to a variety of publics (Harris and Nawaz 2015:12; Allievi 2017:75). Among others, Oliver Roy's concept of religiosity suggests redefining and reconstituting a cult of new Islamic regulation rather than understanding it through the prescriptive lens of restriction and control. Moreover, the new forms and expressions that have emerged among Muslims in the post-Cold War period have also become immune to attacks on secularism. Muslims have found the capacity to deter the corrosive nature of secularism (Byrd 2017:9) by *formatting* the theological set of codes, norms and values of Islam. Roy here employs the Italian word "*aggiornamento*" – literally *update* (Roy 2013:16) – describing a process that Ahmed Akbar (2007) tries to classify into actions of "accepting" (reaching out to the faith), "preserving" (traditional attachment) and "synthesising" (finding a common space with other non-Muslims and secular systems) Islam in everyday life. In studying Muslim practices in Belgium, Corinne Torrekens (2021:7) introduces the definition of "bricolage" to describe the religious identity of those Muslims who always eat *halal* but do not necessarily observe Ramadan, who pray regularly but might at times consume alcohol, who worship Islam but do not go to the mosque for various reasons. This identity stems from the selective interpretation and negotiation (sometimes unease) of norms and traditions in an attempt to live as Muslims in an urban space where Islam faces internal and external criticism and pressure. Another study by Easat-Daas (2020) shows that Belgian Muslims are inclined either to abandon Islam in favour of a secular humanistic ethos or to import Islam from the Middle East along with its attendant anachronistic excesses. Dustin Byrd (2017:3) presumes that young Muslims may also opt either for abandoning Islam, engaging in "religious dissimulation" (taqīyah), or retreating into fundamentalism. Either way, this "bricolage of Muslim identity" is about adaptability and suppleness (Mukherjee 2014:23), aiming to hone and train the psyche and the body to imbibe, ingest and incarnate Islam while engaging in a never-ending struggle to purge perceived impurities of late capitalism and the secular world. Even when disconnecting from the loss of cultural identity or detaching from any given culture (Roy 2013), Muslims struggle to feel European or anything in particular. In theory, this identity vacuum is the best possible situation in which to become a real Muslim and live Islam like a pure religion through a set of norms and values without any social or cultural content. However, there are many other proxy *ethnic*, *cultural*, *political* and *religious* factors (Sander 2014:129–132) that hinge young Muslims on their family heritage, experiences of migration and long-lasting traumas that circulate at the community level. The *national* regularly (if not primarily) invokes a "form of Islam", such as "British Islam" (Jones 2021), "Belgian" or "French Islam" (Easat-Daas 2020), as well as Danish, German and Italian Muslims (Leiken 2012:103), which links religion and post-national identities at the personal and community levels (Bougarel and Mihaylova 2005). Among Muslims in/from the Balkans, a serious thought has been given to the ethnicization of "Bosnian Islam", which played a crucial role in combining a Western lifestyle with the binding pillars of Islam after the Yugoslavian wars.[2] Just as "Bosnian Islam" goes in tandem with a "Bosnian way of being Muslim", so "Albanian Islam" is also the result of the adaptation of the strong sense of Albanian identity to Islam (Bakić-Hayden 1995:926).

Nevertheless, this string of reduction brings most Western academics and scholars (here understood as white, Christian, European) dangerously close to the stereotype of Balkan Muslims being barely Muslim anymore (Karić et al. 2023). It also gives credit to the tautology of a secular society which has to be modern in order to be secular, and to be secular it has to relegate religion to a non-political space. Both spatially and historically, this ethnicisation depoliticises rather than de-clericalises Muslims *in* and *from* the Balkans. In retrospect, it shows the always-present symptom of anxieties about non-Europeans (Asad 2003:161) whose integration has concerned Europe (here understood as Western, white, colonial) since the collapse of the Ottoman Empire (Bakić-Hayden 1995:925). In fact, these ubiquitous associations of Islam with the different national identities in the Balkans, and in turn with Europe as a whole, overshadow past cruelties and a series of policies of coercion and control that Balkan Muslims themselves have endured from the time of the Habsburg occupation and the five decades of Yugoslav-sponsored atheism until the recent integration to Euro-Atlantic institutions (Rexhepi 2023:68; Asad 2003:162; Kostadinova 2023). Rather than confronting this longue durée of violence and otherisation, the ubiquitous associations of Muslims in/from the Balkans to the national identity of the region convey a gross mischaracterisation. As discussed in Chapter 2, the groups under study admit that their Islam has been locally inflected and become malleable over time. They argued that the historical willingness of Balkan Muslims to seek integration into whatever European nation's corpus, and at times even volunteering for it (Bakić-Hayden 1995:927), also accelerated their identification with "Europeanness". Yet a paradox hits their everyday reality: as European Muslims, they uncouple with the non-European (and perceived non-secular) *ummah* where black, brown and Arab Muslims worship Islam; in turn, as Muslims from/in the Balkans, the rampant rise of Islamophobia and far-right discourse in Europe refuse to recognise them as full Europeans because they are members of a distinct religious minority group.

## The Islam of the Young

In a conversation with a devout Muslim, Dustin Byrd (2017:20) was told that "Europeans can keep [their] Gucci, Prada, and Mercedes-Benz, and [they, Muslims], will keep faith, traditions, and family customs". A rhetorical questions was instead raised by Mustafa Cerić, a prominent figure of Muslims

2 Interview with Prof. Yasemin Karakaşoğlu, Bremen University (Germany), 25 May 2023.

in Bosnia, to Ina Merdjanova (2013:120): "Are we not perhaps suitable for Europe if we don't accept homosexuality as a way of life? Must we drink alcohol to be counted as European Muslims?"

Throughout the fieldwork, respondents were found less polemic and asserted a rubric of meaning and significance upon Islam. The latter was mainly considered a guidance for complying with moral and ethical commands, thereby "giving them boundaries" and "teaching them how to respect the other". Those respondents who "really love Islam" undergo a series of recalibrations vis-à-vis non-*halal* food and sexuality, ethical gestures and family values, among others (Mukherjee 2014:23). Some deem Islam necessary to connect authentically with the *self*. At times, Islam becomes "a sort of discipline" similar to a form of resistance and embodied pedagogy against temptations and wrongdoings. Islam does not only "guide the everyday life" according to most respondents; it also "empowers the man rather than restricting his freedom" by "teaching the ethical principles to live by", along with showing the "different ways of thinking about today's society" and "respect for others at the very least".

To borrow here another definition by Oliver Roy (2017), this "Islam of the young" did not seem to question "who does or does not have faith" and thereby classify "who is Muslim from who is not". Nor does it allow respondents to mull over the personal values of same-age Muslims in relation to the Western canon. Despite the permanent confusion over Islamic values and symbols (Roy 2004:11), in Italy a respondent expresses his attachment to the flag of Montenegro, "which has three [Christian] crosses but it undoubtedly remains [his] flag". Another self-identifies as "Westerner [as his] culture is, after all, imbued with Christian values if considering where [he] was born and raised, what [he] studied, and the environment that shapes his personhood". Often Islam was also approached with modesty and did not spark any political contestation when respondents emphasised their "attempts to practise Islam diligently" in order to comply with viable models of secularism and mundane practices, sexuality, food and medical ethics, and so forth.

Previous studies show that, among the older generation of Muslims from the Balkans, the consumption of alcohol has taken on a symbolic dimension in the host-state societies (Bougarel and Mihaylova 2005:10). For the *generation after*, instead, assessing what is *halal* and *haram* has a specific psychology (Szovati 2014). Various respondents undergo purifying practices to remove obstacles, "impure" thoughts, or avoid identity dilemmas without the need to pray five times a day, reading the Qur'an regularly or fasting during Ramadan, and so forth. Keeping up with Islam means more likely refraining from unfaithful and prohibited (haram) actions rather than self-imposing strictures and obligations. In other words, many tend to adapt pragmatically to the demands and the pressure of secularisation and secularism by *formatting* their faith rather than strictly obeying a set of normative practices. For those who self-identify as "cultural Muslims", meaning they are socialised with Islamic practices at home since childhood (Grünenberg 2005:181), Islam is more a privatised and family business (Cavenaugh 2018:314). Especially in Poland and Italy, respondents are aware of the corrosive effects of Westernisation upon their lives (Byrd 2017:11) and more likely to hold a much looser relation with Islam than their parents (Harris and Nawaz 2015:73). Although some strip Islam down until it is no more than a series of practices, food restriction (mostly pork) and Ramadan fasting are scrupulously observed. None stand against the "modern life", but rather express the desire to keep up a certain way of living without resenting or rejecting other people's modern worldviews and lifestyle (Rippin 2001:169).

> "I do identify as a Muslima, and I do practice Islam: I know Arabic and I read the Qur'an. I pray, not every day, but I have my praying time. And I fast. I just do not veil myself, but this is not an issue for me".
>
> (Antwerp, Belgium)

> "The peer pressure of moving on, modernising yourself – meaning to leave your culture behind – is salient. . . . I have noticed some changes between my parents' and our generation, like the consumption of alcohol and food . . . [but Islam] is not just about fasting – meaning, staying away from non-*halal* food and alcohol. It is about staying connected with the spiritual self, thinking about people who do not have much, and reflecting on the conditions I live on a personal level".
>
> (Antwerp, Belgium)

> "My relation with Islam fluctuates. Once I spent a few months in Bosnia, at my grandparents'; I came back to Belgium veiled and with the idea of being fully a Muslima. I wanted to clarify that I was proud of my background and I thought of my future children: they won't need to feel embarrassed for having been raised as Muslims, as I and my generation feel. Now, however, I worship Islam very little, but I still go to the mosque, fast during Ramadan and attend *iftar* with my father's community here".
>
> (Ghent, Belgium)

> "I know when to be religious: during funerals, festivities and other Muslim rituals. I know how to *wudu* and pray during Ramadan. Yet, I am Albanian and I was born in Germany, so I can't be that religious".
>
> (Bremen, Germany)

> "I pray five times a day, and I managed to get a private room at work for doing that. But I am an independent Muslima. I have my own mind; when you [belong to] a family where the father is always suggesting how you should live your life, and he often relies on Islam as a guide to your lifestyle, it is not easy at all".
>
> (Dortmund, Germany)

> "I am somehow Muslim. I keep up with obligations: going to the mosque, avoiding pork and alcohol. But I have changed: now, as a young father, unlike when I was younger, I pay more attention to Islam".
>
> (Bremen, Germany)

> "If my parents would like an Islamic funeral, I will do so. If they want to pray or fast during Ramadan, I follow up. But my everyday life is far from complying with Islam".
>
> (Piacenza, Italy)

The Islam of the young shows how polyvalent *halal* and *haram* can be, and how the fine line between the two categories can be subjected to free will and outlandish practices (Mukherjee 2014:39) vis-à-vis potential conflicts, hurt feelings and controversial ambitions with Islam itself. During some of the in-depth interviews, practices of "liberal *halal*" – or alternatively, "sort of *halal*" – were verbalised to explain how young Muslims deal with the "very high level of drinking and doping among same-age peers", the "different drugs and social media addictions", the "online gambling" and some "toxic masculinity behaviour that is unethical for Muslims yet occasionally enacted within certain post-migrant dynamics".

Granted, certain aspects of the Islamic orthopraxis are influenced by the personalised interpretation of individual decisions and strategies (Kostadinova 2023). Hence, most respondents (attempt to) get engaged in the social world in spite of the restrictions that Islam imposes. This constant negotiation is part and parcel of their Muslimness and the ethical sheer values they stand for in a society where they express their right to exert a lived form of Islam. Everyday worries coupled with identity dilemmas are also used as a means to reflect on some "conservative" and "radical Muslims". Criticism was particularly oriented toward the bad habit of grand/parents who mix up "Islam" and "culture" for their vested interests. In this regard, the special relationship of many respondents with the Qur'an was noticed. Given the new production and distribution of the latter, as well as the alternative sources of religious knowledge that facilitate the reading of this sacred text (Jones 2021:33), most respondents were found to be knowledgeable about how the Qur'an was revealed to Prophet Mohammed and how it should be read and lived accordingly. What they pointed out was the various jurisprudential, philosophical, linguistic, historical and political interpretations which, when reading the Qur'an, need to be borne in mind using common sense and understanding of Islamic ethics and values according to today's issues (Mourad 2014:21; Harris and Nawaz 2015:74; Cesari 2013:198). In other words, respondents argued that the Qur'anic text should be interpreted as the actual word of God, but always filtered through the interpretation of humans. Many remain open to self-doubt in everyday circumstances. "What the Qur'an says", or, more properly, "what does the Qur'an *really* say?" are the two questions that help the groups under study reflect on dealing with everyday identity dilemmas beyond what is considered *halal* or not. A closer engagement with the Qur'an and the hadith helped respondents to navigate the *halal/haram* dilemma. What some respondents really cared about was emulating the prophetic ideals and life of the Prophet Muhammed, thereby complying with the *sunnah*, whose corpus of opinions is what a Muslim goes by (Mourad 2014:28). When the *sunnah* has little to add to the doctrine (Jomo 1992:240), even contradicting the Qur'an, the interpretation of the sacred text is not confined to favouring an inclusive theology (Sandal 2011:944). Instead, a respondent in Antwerp refers to Imam Abu Hanifah's teaching "*Don't follow me blindly*" to explain how to find the proper answer when trapped in self-doubt.

> "We, humans, have been [given rationality] by God, and we do not find it from people's answers but from their arguments. The person can make mistakes, but the argument is different. Two Muslims can disagree over a specific matter, but this is the beauty of Islam: we can learn from each other, the Maliki Muslims from the Hanafi Muslims, the old generations from the young ones. . . . Although we may worship differently and we handle everyday issues accordingly, these differences are beautiful under the same God".

In saying so, he wanted to emphasise the distinction between the Prophet and the life of the *shahaba* – the companions of the Prophet – and how they differ from one another. "When it is impossible to extract the laws of Islam from the sources, mainly the Qur'an", he added, "then we follow the person who has this ability of [interpreting] such knowledge". The respondent drew clearly on the *taqlid*, reciting the Qur'anic Sura Al-Anbiyaa, verse 7, "So then ask the people of the reminder if you do not have any knowledge". If this sophisticated reading of the Qur'an was verbalised by a very knowledgeable respondent of the Bosnian Muslim community, the reference to the sacred text and interpretation of Islam beyond the Qur'an was nonetheless consistent among other respondents with Albanian and other Slavic roots. "Do not follow me blindly" was often taken into consideration to evaluate what is *halal* and *haram*, thereby marking a new disposition for actively incorporating Islam into their social, cultural and political realities.

Last but not least, this constant reference to the Qur'an often leads to strong accusations against the language of Salafism and political Islam. The latter was understood as a malignant instrument to spread hatred and pour scorn on Muslims and people in general, thereby serving vested interests for making inroads into politics. The former was likewise accused of uncoupling the dominant Hanafi legal school of interpretation of Islam to which Balkan Muslims comply with traditionally, as well "undoing Islam" and "selling radical and extremist ways of living as Muslims in and beyond Europe". Respondents proved wrong the premise that the more zealous a Muslim is in his religious salience, the more radical he is, and the more Islam penetrates into the life of Muslims, the higher the chances to oppose, contest and eventually refuse secularisation (Byrd 2017:285). On the contrary, most respondents do respect Islam and live accordingly, yet without endangering the idea of secularisation and interfaith dialogue. Even when Islam comes back to their lives, this return to faith was not seen as a form of self-colonisation, nor as a defiance of westernisation, fulfilling the promises that capitalist and liberalist lifestyle have broken. In Biella, Italy, a young Bosnian Muslima recalled,

> "A very close friend of mine did not care about Islam at all; we could not say much, nor did we judge him. Lastly, he started praying and reading the Qur'an. . . . He used to drink, smoke and enjoy life, but now he is completely different. Not even [I], a Muslima, read the Qur'an as much as he does now".

Outside the domain of performing *halal* and rejecting *haram*, some societal issues are approached critically. The "veil debate" and so-called "gender theories" (often dubbed as "ideology") are considered thorny questions in and beyond the Muslim community. While discussing these critical themes, most male respondents claim that the parents' rights to determine their children's education and right to life over the right to abortion are non-negotiable because they are clearly part of God's order of nature. Veiled respondents instead shared their feelings of frustration at (and often actually being) being surrounded by glass walls that bar their access to public- and private-sector jobs. It goes without saying that the veil signifies a higher level of commitment to Islam (Carrim and Paruk 2020:12) while redefining (and reclaiming at times) some aspects of their Muslim femininity. In fact, the veil can be a brand (Mukherjee 2014:44) and a symbol of Muslim feminine pride, rather than merely "a backward object" associated with oppression and subordination of Muslim women. Simply put, "the veil" is not just a traditional Muslim attire and cannot only be understood as a lens through which Muslim mothers, sisters and girlfriends can be singled out on the street. A male respondent stated that his "girlfriend, who is neither Muslim nor of Bosnian origin, must veil herself when entering the mosque, visiting the graveyard and attending *iftar* or other festivities". In this case, he identified the veil as a matter of respect and not a religious obligation in the realm of everyday life.

Interestingly, both females and males pointed out that one should comprehend the value of wearing the veil only after (re)considering the historical context of secularism along with the sociopolitical implication of colonial history at the local and international level (Carrim and Paruk 2020:12–13). As a respondent said, "If a nun can veil herself and be accepted as such, why can't Muslim women do the same and expect the same recognition and respect in society?"

### *We are* What *(and* Where*) We Eat*

To summarise the preceding section, *halal* is first and foremost a strategy (Mukherjee 2014:24) to navigate religious strictures and secular worldviews.

This is also part of a personal strategy to self-identify with "European perspectives" of "being Muslim" and avoiding potential "othering" that may bar them from having a social life with their same-age peers. Thus, there is very little doubt that the *generation after* is much more prepared than older generations to accept newer interpretations of what is *haram* and reconsider an inclusive definition of *halal*.

Among others, *halal* food was the most verbalised issue to deal with. Only a few identify the "[tenderising] salsas and the vinegar" and even "some meds" as *haram* as they contain either ethyl alcohol or porcine materials. At the same time, no political critiques toward the food industry were expressed, nor concerns over consuming meat products ethically (Robinson-Bertoni 2017). While juggling with the *halal* and haram question, the latter shows a broader socialisation issue in the realm of everyday life. For instance, most respondents were quick to complain about a ubiquitous lack of sensibility of classmates, coworkers and friends who misunderstand, or are unable to pretend to understand at all, their *halal* habits. In Germany in particular, many chose irony to express their frustration over the fact that "there are more Muslims than vegans in the country, but more veggie burgers are available than *halal* food". In Dortmund, a young Muslima explained that "after years of working together, [her] colleagues keep asking why [she does] not eat pork and drink beers". These non-actions are considered as a sort of "un-German behaviour", which cast dark shadows on the alleged unwillingness of Muslims to become fully German – at least on cultural grounds (Ferizaj 2019:78). Moreover, the youngest respondents admitted that their "non-Muslim friends get a bit disappointed by their restrictions [and] usually get bored [as] they cannot have fun together". A female Muslim with Albanian roots complained about "living boringly" and, more precisely, "having stricter rules and more no-goes than her German peers whose freedom [and what that implies] is respected but not accepted". The groups under study are nonetheless influenced by their same-age peers and "street culture", where "Europeanness" is not required and ethnic diversity is even more appreciated. Ascribed by the ambiguous logics of othering, some younger males could not refrain from criticising the counter-effects of the principles of tolerance and secularism in today's society. Among this group, many contended that respect is not reciprocated when it comes to acknowledging Muslim rituals, such as Ramadan or *Bajram*. Although the latter can be equated with Christmas and other Christian celebrations due to the similar spirit of togetherness and community they are celebrated for (Byrd 2017:20, Grünenberg 2005:188), criticism is always on the rise and sparks anger among the wider public. During the period of Ramadan in Antwerp, however, a local Catholic organisation provided space for an intercultural and interfaith *iftar* for the Muslim communities originally from Kosovo, Albania and North Macedonia. During the welcoming speech, the Macedonian ambassador to Belgium pointed out that in his country, Christians and Muslims were celebrating the "Velikden" – Easter Monday for Orthodox Christians – and Ramadan together and at the same time.

In theory, Roni Mukherjee complicates the matter of the *halal/haram* fine line (2014:23) by arguing that such a binding dichotomy cannot simply be about meat or religious salience. *Halal* is not just a way of life, but also a preferred locus of congregation and dining. In fact, Islam does not "come out of nowhere" across time and space but rather endures a re-territorialisation of space in which community life is conceived in both national and transnational contexts. In the German and Belgian cities where fieldwork was carried out, some neighbourhoods were identified as "*halal* environments" and "*halal* zones". These spaces are generally perceived as a new type of dietary urban apartheid that is interspersed with even more evidence of creeping Islamisation, such as veiled women, the proliferation of mosques and marking new forms of separations along ethnic, ideological and generational lines (Mukherjee 2014:25, Mushaben 2008:508). In effect, it cannot be denied that the large concentration of Muslim diaspora may mistakenly give rise to the idea of a non-secular space whose communitarian lifestyle may erode multiculturalism and its dreams of tolerance. After triangulating field notes and in-depth interviews, the so-called "*halal* spaces" under observation came to reveal another critical angle of investigation. If *halal* is centreless due to the social function Islam and the *ummah* have, the idea of "*halal* neighbourhoods" is conceived by a rapid spatialisation of Islamophobia rather than the diffusion of Islam and the arrival of Muslim newcomers in Europe (Nijab 2022). As further discussed in Chapter 7, spatialised Islamophobia debunks Oliver Roy's paradigm of the "de-territorialisation" of Islam (2004) by showing a re-territorialisation of Islam (Robinson-Bertoni 2017:14). Within Muslim-majority neighbourhoods, *halal* turns out to be a matter of trust (Mukherjee 2014:23) because clubs, coffee or tea houses and restaurants secure dwellers (particularly males) in a safer *halal* space than the "city centres". In a moment of need or doubt, the "*halal* neighbourhood" provides a venue of mutual respect and support for congregation and social life.

A vignette about the fieldwork is telling here. In order to kick off in-depth interviews, potential respondents were invited to choose a proper and safe place themselves. Almost always, they chose cafeterias, canteens or recreational spaces nearby the mosque and in the neighbourhoods where they reside. Chosen as the best place to meet up and speak freely, these spaces were preferred to meeting up downtown where, at times, respondents were noticed acting more carefully in choosing what to drink and eat, or simply being more attentive to people in their vicinity. Although cities like Ghent and Antwerp, as well as Bremen, Warsaw and Piacenza, are multicultural and deeply diverse, respondents perceived Islamophobia spatially by being (unconsciously) pushed into marginal and private spaces and away from dominant and privileged city centres (Nijab 2022:51). These space-related feelings of in/security were openly verbalised during the in-depth interviews:

> "I barely go downtown because [in Gröpelingen] I have what I need. Food, friends, the mosque is nearby, and everyone I know lives here, so I do not really have the need to go somewhere else".

> "When I have to celebrate something, I never do so with Germans, but with my friends from Albania, Kosovo, Pakistan and other countries. We stay in Gröpelingen because it is here where we all work, study or live with our families".

As consumers and residents of those neighbourhoods, respondents were much more relaxed in not verifying the "halal credentials" of the slaughterman. They did not have to inspect the abattoir to assure themselves that what was being ordered was actually *haram*-free. In general, respondents were inclined to consider the "city centre" as a space of mixing and unknowing, where they need to think twice and act carefully to safeguard their halal rigour. Thus, the latter is not only about food production standards and alcohol-free beverages, but also a social space of trust and purity for religious leaders and the Muslim community, the slaughterers and the local imam (Mukherjee 2014:38). In Bremen, for instance, Gröpelingen is a space where most young Muslims establish their life. A respondent with Albanian roots admitted to "barely going downtown because [in the neighbourhood he] can trust people, eat *halal*, go to different mosques and hang out without any pressure".

## From School to the Mosque

According to most respondents, respectfulness is at the centre of Islam. Since "being human" is by far the hardest action to abide by when relating to other fellow humans, Islam is by no means a resource of violence, but an ethical manifestation of divine grace that only a properly educated soul can perform by valuing diversity and care for others (Kostadinova 2018:82). In this regard, respondents often reiterate that Muslims, Christians and Jews have lived side by side without being overcome by the need to kill each other. The following interview insight is instructive:

> "Our Prophet, peace be upon Him, has never taught us [Muslims] to mistreat those who believe otherwise: when he conquered Jerusalem, he let Jews and Christians live, and only the polytheists who did not accept coexistence, could simply leave the city. . . . Explaining [respect] is very important to me . . . my little brother argued with other people at school, and I told him to calm down: often religion has nothing to do with what people say".

As introduced in the previous section, the Qur'anic principle of respectfulness is employed as the only way to avoid unpleasant experiences and incomprehension on a daily basis. What is considered an obstacle to God is also an obstacle to human relations. In Toruń, a man originally from Sarajevo shared the importance of teaching "respect for others" to his three children who had been born and raised in Poland. He argued that "even at the mosque, [nobody] can tell to the person nearby how to be a good Muslim, or judge him, or teach him how to pray". Another younger father in Bremen pointed to the fact that "the Qur'an clearly says that [a Muslim is] forbidden to impose their beliefs upon someone else. That's it! [Nobody] can say 'you must'". Respectfulness verbalised during other in-depth interviews prompts a focus on how the centre of gravity of today's societies has shifted from the cornerstone of tolerance to that of respect (Marramao 2012:183).

Unlike what one may think of Muslims being unable to adapt their religion and values to a post-secular society (Himmat 2014:86–87), the groups under study distinguish liberal arts from propaganda, fiction from disinformation, religious ethics from politics, and vice versa. On the other hand, however, such relevance given to respectfulness may at times produce a side effect due to the wealth of postmodern (identity) dilemmas entailing constant confrontation with Muslims on a daily basis (Van Leuven et al. 2023:62). While discussing the issue of tolerance with an Albanian imam born in Skopje, North Macedonia, at the Al-Albani Moskee in Ghent, he himself took up a pamphlet, "A glimpse of Islam"[3] by Rasheed Barbee. While leafing through it, he pointed to a paragraph listing the "Merits of Islam" (2020:12). Respect for the elderly and the deceased, along with the importance of kindness to women, neighbours and animals, as well as the principle of racial equality and diversity (with a specific reference to Arab/non-Arab relations), were taken up to discuss the openness of the mosque to non-Albanian Muslims and non-Albanian speakers. If Arabic was used for reading the Qur'an, Dutch was spoken occasionally outside the praying time. This linguistic aspect is important for observing how certain Muslim communities in Belgium barely use the Dutch language as some imams are trained either in a foreign state or in their countries of origin. Therefore, they have a rudimentary understanding of the languages of Belgian society – be that French or Dutch – with sermons often a cause for alarm among the central authorities and the rest of the local Muslim community (Torrekens 2021:8).

When in Bremen I partook in a few Qur'anic classes at the local Albanian and Bosnian mosque. The hodža, a middle-aged Albanian man originally from Skopje and Sarajevo-educated, spoke only in German, and one of his students sat next to me to provide simultaneous translation. After being welcomed and accepted by every attendee, I sat down to observe the teaching. Rather than coaching young students in their mother tongue, the goal of the class, the hodža pointed out, was to "help young Muslims master the German language and not only the language of their parents who might still struggle with integration". After focusing on students' memorisation of the Qur'an through the correct pronunciation of its Arabic verses, the hodža began to address the pitfalls and threats of contemporary society in and beyond Germany. He addressed the nuances of the problem of Islamophobia, highlighting the role

3 My translation from Dutch, "*Een glimp van de Islaam*".

of the *ummah* as constituted by the authority of the Prophet (Mahomed 2022:30). Hence, he also referred to radicalism and extremism, as follows:

> "How dare you say 'Allahu Akbar' while killing people? These people are not Muslims regardless of what they say! We do not only respect each other as Muslims, but we also respect others who are not. . . . because of these people, in Germany we have a very high level of Islamophobia. What is Islamophobia? It is not only the fear of Islam, but it is the fear of the other person . . . Islamophobia, Christianophobia, Jewphobia, they are all the same. But being Muslim does not mean to fear. . . . Look at Francesco, he is here with us, and he is not Muslim. He comes from Italy, a Christian country where the pope guides Catholics. Let's take the Qur'an – you see [pointing at the text], Jesus is "*al-Masīḥ*", a servant of Allah. We share Jesus with Christians, even though for us [Muslims] he is not the last, because Prophet Mohammed, Peace Be Upon Him, is the last one".

The hodža's approach definitely challenges the premise that religious figures no longer produce knowledge for practical everyday issues (Roy 2013). In an attempt to "protect" his students (and the community as a whole) from

*Figure 5.1* A short break during the Saturday class at the Albanian mosque in Bremen. Photo by the author.

undesirable encounters and sinful acts (Jones 2021:114), he moved on. Closing the Qur'an, he opened up other thorny and much-debated issues among the class: from the different attitudes of parents toward the younger generations, to the experiences of migration from the Balkans and adaptation in Germany, among others. Some intimate experiences of Muslim life were also taken into consideration, such as the ritual bath of ***wudu***, that is, the partial ablution which Muslims have to perform following sexual intercourse and menstruation. Although some tried to hide their sniggers, the hodža brought everyone's attention to the seriousness of what was being discussed.

After one of the classes, I continued to talk with Gëzim, a young student with Albanian roots whose parents settled in Bremen after escaping Kosovo in the 1990s. Since schools and educational environments in general are interesting settings to study processes of collective identity formation (Driezen 2023:62), I decided to delve deeper. Gëzim shared his pleasure and genuine interest in attending those classes, valuing the learning process through Arabic and German languages, both paramount in knowing how to better deal with identity dilemmas in his life. When I asked specifically about the rather intimate issues the hodža openly discussed, Gëzim was surprised by the question. Summarising his words, the hodža did not want to know about their intimate life. He was simply attempting to help young Muslims born in Germany in taking care of their religious identity while coming to terms with the postwar legacies and postsocialist heritage still salient within the family circle. In other words, classes are about establishing a spiritual companionship with the hodža and attaining a type of experiential knowledge that helps them embody the *adab* in both their public and private life (Kostadinova 2018:81, Sandal 2011:934). In doing so, he did not regret spending time during the weekend at the mosque rather than with friends; the mosque is in fact the physical and sacred space essential for taking care of yourself as a Muslim.

Gëzim's words counter the interpretation of mosques as hotbeds of radicalisation and the loci of dominant public theology where local imams and community representatives do not convey the right message to the Muslim community. In turn, Gëzim's words also subvert the idea of young Muslims being unable to relate to local imams during the teaching of Islam (Mandaville 2002:3). As pointed out by Yasemin Karakaşoğlu, Balkan imams and other religious representatives are the backbone of Muslim integration in the federal state of Bremen. They do not simply play the role of religious figures but also cooperate positively with state institutions. This opinion was later confirmed by two representatives of a local NGO based in Gröpelingen which was visited during the fieldwork in the neighbourhood. Their mission involved running cultural projects for young Muslims and training state representatives, such as teachers, policemen and practitioners, to foster mutual respect and tackle the phenomena of radicalisation. The latter are at times supported by diaspora organisations, such as the Turkish *Millî Görüs* (National Vision) and the *Garmisch-Partenkirchen Union der Anstalt für Religion* (DITIB) as both organisations bear responsibility for failure to participate in state-backed imam trainings while encouraging the opening up of new mosques and parallel Islamic schools that spread anti-European, anti-Western and anti-Semitic ideas.

> "At school, most teachers' blunt descriptions of Erdogan and Turkey, i.e. as a dictator and authoritarian regime respectively, disturb many pupils and students with Turkish and Muslim background."[4]

Issues of radicalisation and extremism were often discussed throughout other in-depth interviews. Most male respondents addressed "Islamic extremism as a product of the West, because, [in the Balkans and the Middle East], Muslims know what comes after extremism". This general assertion often went hand in hand with the importance that respondents themselves gave to the role of schooling and education as a whole. To a certain extent, the latter has always been part and parcel of Muslim everyday life in and from the Balkans. Džemaludin Čausević (1870–1938) campaigned in Bosnia for boosting the role of schooling and educational institutions to promote Islamic knowledge, especially with regard to some requirements for Muslim women, such as the *niqab*, which he did not consider a requirement of the faith (Khan 2017:207). On the basis of the negative experiences that some had endured in the past, and others still do in the present, discrimination was often associated with school.

In Belgium, some complained more about the state-sponsored model of *laïcité* rather than the fact that public education is partly still organised through the Christian Catholic culture (Driezen 2023:33). According to a young male respondent of Bosnian origin, there is "not much sense for female students to unveil before school hours and then veil again before going out" or "hiding their crosses in class to respect those who may not be Christian". A young Muslima recollects the "tense atmosphere that arose in class once the teacher matter-of-factly explained the absence of God", as well as when "[her] surname and that of another classmate, born in a Moroccan family in Belgium, brought the same teacher to ask about their family histories and religious heritage". In the Flemish educational system, which still puts forward a culturally and linguistically unified representation of the "Flemish" nation, the low educational attainment among Muslim youth is often associated by teachers with an incompatibility of Islamic norms and values with the dominant values of the Belgian society. However, as described by Ariadne Driezen's doctoral project (2023), students belonging to different ethnic and religious family heritage than Belgian often experience stigmatisation and discrimination. In this regard, teachers also tend to anticipate lower school attainments for students with a migration background, whose class performance is often compared to

4 Interview with a practitioner from NGO Schura in Gröpelinger Bremen (Germany), 17 May 2023.

that of native students. While the latter are used to multiculturalism at school and higher education, the former are instead more likely to continue their education into a vocational school, where students with migration family heritage are proportionally more numerous, and also less likely to pursue higher education. This is why teachers were described as the most significant other that – in the eyes of respondents – represent the inclusive or exclusive character of a school towards students' identities.

In Germany, schools offer unified religious lessons that include education on different faiths, Islam included. Similar to Italy, however, cases of discrimination and Islamophobic comments are influenced by the political climate and outcry against Islam when sensitive topics related to such religion become a subject of discussion at school (Khan 2022:55), especially in relation to the potential wearing of the veil in class or when Islam challenges the majoritarian Christian canon of teachers and students.[5] Everyday racial connotations hit a few respondents the hardest during the 1990s, such as: "although a mouse is born in a stable, it does not mean it becomes a horse", or "you should go back to [Bosnia] and get killed there", or "look at you, curly-haired bastard!"

In Poland, the positive experiences of Adin, who was found "preparing a class presentation about Muslims in Spain", were partially contradicted by his mother. In a different in-depth interview and place, she recollected her chat with the school psychologist after noticing some bullying at the primary school, and how she was carefully parenting Adin during his childhood. A similar experience was shared by another mother originally from North Macedonia, now residing in Katowice. Her

> "children, born in Poland, are surrounded at school by Christian symbols and comply with praying time and festivities triggering certain dissonance at home after they see their mother's different approach toward *those* symbols, and the different practices, rituals and signs at their grandparents' while spending summertime in North Macedonia".

While interviewing a few university students in Belgium, some confirm that the political climate intensifies antagonism and suspicion against Islam – even at the university level. In Ghent, a young female journalist with Bosnian Muslim/Flemish Christian family heritage complained specifically about the curricula that are only based on Western philosophy in Belgium. In Italy, two university students in International Relations and Languages complained respectively about some suspicious questions raised by the professor about "le

5 In April 2024, the Italian Prime Minister, Giorgia Meloni, banned Italian schools with Muslim-majority classes from closing for a day to mark the end of Ramadan. The decision of the "Istituto Comprensivo Iqbal Masiq" at Pioltello in Milan, having 40% of Muslim students, sparked outcry and the anti-migrant discourse, which depicted the event as an act of intolerance rather than civilisation in Italy.

Foibe",[6] and the unequal treatment of the 1915 Armenian Genocide and the Genocide in Srebrenica in 1995:

> "While the latter was barely mentioned as a simple chronological event, pre-empting its historical importance for Bosnia and Europe as a whole, the former was discussed in detail and often depicted as the first genocide of Ottoman Turks, [reinforcing the stereotype of] Muslims killing Christians".

Across the four countries where fieldwork was carried out, different forms of opposition toward the provisions of a *halal* menu at school canteens and negotiation regarding acceptable school attire (Sofos and Tsagarousianou 2013:11) were particularly noticed. They all reduce school to a symbolic space where promises of equity, integration and preparation for future opportunities are broken (Ceretti and Cornelli 2018:68); as well as being an open space that espouses education as a human right, it can also contribute towards inclusion and social justice (Gomolla 2021). The breadth of the data collected across the four countries shows Germany as an instructive case in terms of looking at how racial discrimination occurs at the school level. Edin's words summarise what many other respondents in Germany verbalise at large:

> "The schooling system is organised and sustained by teachers, in a way that children with a migration background will be prepared for working in job sectors that Germans do not aspire to work in anymore. [These students will only be able to pursue] professional careers that Germans do not aspire to anymore, [including] their future generation".

What Edin meant at the time of the interview was referring to the two-year period of orientation which follows the years of primary school (in German, *Grundschule*), where pupils receive the same education and face no formal ability grouping by teachers. After these two years, many accused the teachers of having preconceptions and culturally biased ideas about pupils with migration heritage. Here they also argue that their parents were misled by teachers' track recommendations about their future achievement as teachers often recommended a vocational-oriented school – namely, either *Hauptschule* or the *Realschule* – only on the basis of guest worker legacy in Germany. Even those who went on to *Gymnasium*, which provides an entrance ticket to university through the *Abitur*, i.e. the maturity certificate, they recall the experiences of their siblings and friends, mainly males, whose parents opted for an intermediate level of general secondary education (*Realschulabschluss*) or even the

6 "*The Foibe*" refers to the reprisal killings and forced deportations of Istrian and Dalmatian Italians and Slavs, primarily members of fascist and collaborationist forces, committed by Yugoslavian partisans and authorities in the then-controlled Italian territories.

basic level (*Hauptschulabschluss*) after teachers misjudged their potential and abilities at school. As Edin bitterly states, "I got two masters in Law here in Germany, speaking and studying in German. That means I was not that stupid, right?"

What respondents also complain about here is a subtler example of discrimination which is barely mentioned (Gomolla 2021:184), yet it is confirmed by a broad body of prior research and reports since at least the late 1980s (Wenz and Hoenig 2020). Even today, immigrant families have poorer chances of higher education than other children in Germany, suggesting that the link between socio-economic background and education outcomes is relatively strong, with youth dropping out early from the education system having poor lifetime job prospects. While experiences of migration can put a student at risk during different educational stages, it has also been proven that gateways for practices of disadvantage and exclusion have been found in teachers' potential discriminatory practices. In turn, large disparities between the children of (former) German guest workers and those of German (white) families have severe consequences throughout education and beyond educational attainment (see Diehl and Granato 2018; Wenz and Hoenig 2020; Gomolla 2021, among others).

## References

Akbar, A. (2007) *Journey into Islam, The Crisis of Globalisation*. Washington: Rowman & Littlefield Publishers

Allievi, S. (2017) *Conversioni: verso un nuovo modo di credere? Europa, Pluralismo, Islam* [Conversions: Towards a New Way of Believing? Europe, Pluralism, Islam]. Napoli: Guida Editori.

Amara, M. (2013) Sport, Islam, and Muslims in Europe: In between or on the Margin? *Religions*, 4 (4), pp. 644–656. https://doi.org/10.3390/rel4040644

Asad, T. (2003) *Formations of the Secular. Christianity, Islam, Modernity*. Stanford: Stanford University Press.

Azabar, S. and Van Aelst, P. (2023) Religion Works in Different Ways: An Intersectional Approach to Muslims' Noninstitutionalized Participation. *Acta Politica*, 59, pp. 416–438. https://doi.org/10.1057/s41269-023-00300-y

Bakić-Hayden, M. (1995) Nesting Orientalisms: The Case of Former Yugoslavia. *Slavic Review*, 54 (4), pp. 917–931. https://doi.org/10.2307/2501399

Barbee, R. (2020) *Een glimp van de Islam*. Durham: As-Sunnah Publications. Available at: https://ugc.production.linktr.ee/26fd9c8f-8d27-40c8-8a48-7c60f18b910a_E-Book-Glimp-van-de-Islam.pdf (Accessed: 12 April 2023).

Bougarel, X. (2008) 'Balkan Muslim Diasporas and the Idea of a European Islam', in T. Dulić, R. Kostić, I. Maček, and J. Trtak (eds.) *Balkan Currents. Essays in Honour of Kjell Magnusson*. Uppsala: Uppsala University Press, pp. 147–165.

Bougarel, X. and Mihaylova, D. (2005) Diasporas musulmanes balkaniques dans l'Union européenne [Balkan Muslim Diaspora in the European Union]. *Balkanologie – Revue d'études pluridisciplinaires*, IX (1–2), pp. 59–211. https://doi.org/10.4000/balkanologie.577

Boutayeb, R. (2023) 'In Praise of Coldness: The Open Neighbourhood and Its Enemies', in C. Royer, and L. Matei (eds.) *Open Society Unresolved. The Contemporary Relevance of a Contested Idea*. Budapest: Central European University Press, pp. 38–48.

Byrd, J. D. (2017) *Islam in a Post-Secular Society. Religion, Secularity and the Antagonism of Recalcitrant Faith.* Leiden, Boston: Brill.

Carrim, N. and Paruk, Z. (2020) Do We or Don't We? Muslim Women Wearing the Hijab in the South African Work Environment. *Journal of Religion in Africa*, 50 (1/2), pp. 11–31.

Cavenaugh, K. (2018) 'Policing the Public Sphere: Regulating Religion in Europe', in A. Biró (ed.) *Populism, Memory and Minority Rights. Central and Eastern European Issues in Global Perspectives.* Leiden: Brill, pp. 313–341.

Ceretti, A. and Cornelli, R. (2018) *Oltre la Paura. Affrontare il Tema della Sicurezza in Modo Democratico* [Beyond Fear. Facing the Issue of Securty in a Democratic World]. Milano: Feltrinelli.

Cesari, J. (2013) *Why the West Fears Islam. An Exploration of Muslims in Liberal Democracies.* New York: Palgrave Macmillan.

Council of Europe (1991) *Contribution of the Islamic Civilisation to European Culture.* Available at: https://assembly.coe.int/nw/xml/XRef/Xref-XML2HTML-en.asp?fileid=15196 (Accessed: 20 September 2022)

Diehl, C. and Granato, N. (2018) 'Germany: Intergenerational Inequalities in the Education System and the Labour Market for Native-Born Children of Immigrants from Turkey and the Former Yugoslavia', in *Catching Up? Country Studies on Intergenerational Mobility and Children of Immigrants.* Paris: OECD Publishing, pp. 71–92. https://doi.org/10.1787/9789264301030-5-en

Driezen, A. (2023) Youth Navigating the Superdiverse City of Antwerp: Constructing and Negotiating Ethnic and Religious Symbolic Boundaries, *University of Antwerp.* Available at: https://repository.uantwerpen.be/docman/irua/986f79motoM53 (Accessed: 2 March 2024)

Easat-Daas, A. (2020) *Muslim Women's Political Participation in France and Belgium.* Cham: Palgrave Macmillan.

Ferizaj, A. (2019) Othering Albanian Muslim Masculinities: A Case Study of Albanian Football Players. *Occhialì – Rivista sul Mediterraneo Islamico*, 5, pp. 71–93.

Fleischmann, F. and Phalet, K. (2018) Religion and National Identification in Europe: Comparing Muslim Youth in Belgium, England, Germany, the Netherlands, and Sweden. *Journal of Cross-Cultural Psychology*, 49 (1), pp. 44–61. https://doi.org/10.1177/0022022117741988

Gerlach, J. (2006) *Zwischen Pop und Dschihad. Muslimische Jugendliche in Deutschland* [Between pop and jihad. Muslim young people in Frankfurt, Germany]. Berlin: Ch. Links Verlag.

Gomolla, M. (2021) 'Educational Inequalities, Vulnerability for Discrimination and the Politics of School Change in Germany as a Post-migration Society', in N. Fromm, A. Jünemann, and H. Safouane (eds.) *Power in Vulnerability. Studien zur Migrations- und Integrationspolitik.* Wiesbaden: Springer VS, pp. 175–198. https://doi.org/10.1007/978-3-658-34052-0_9

Grünenberg, K. (2005) Constructing "Sameness" and "Otherness": Bosnian Diasporic Experiences in a Danish Context. *Balkanologie – Revue d'études pluridisciplinaires*, IX (1–2), pp. 173–193. https://doi.org/10.4000/balkanologie.587

Harris, S. and Nawaz, M. (2015) *Islam and the Future of Tolerance. A Dialogue.* Cambridge, MA: Harvard University Press.

Himmat, H. (2014) 'Islamophobia and Its Consequences on Young Women', in I. Ramberg (ed.) *Islamophobia and Its Consequences on Young People.* Budapest: European Youth Centre Budapest, pp. 85–92. Available at: www.coe.int/en/web/youth/-/islamophobia-and-its-consequences-on-young-people?inheritRedirect=true (Accessed: 12 December 2022).

Hurd, S. (2008) *The Politics of Secularism in International Relations.* Princeton: Princeton University Press.

Izetbegović, A. (1990) *Islamic Declaration.* Available at: https://archive.org/details/3IslamicDeclarationEng/mode/2up?view=theater (Accessed: 3 January 2023)

Jomo, K. S. (1992) *Islamic Economic Alternatives: Critical Perspectives and New Directions.* London: Macmillan Academic and Professional.

Jones, H. S. (2021) *Islam and the Liberal State. National Identity and the Future of Muslim Britain.* London: I.B. Tauris.

Karić, D., Buljina, H. and Rexhepi, P. (2023) Feel-good Orientalism and the Question of Dignity, *Maydan. Islamic Thought.* Available at: https://themaydan.com/2023/02/feel-good-orientalism-and-the-question-of-dignity/ (Accessed: 2 January 2024).

Khan, M. M. (2017) *Great Muslims of the West: Makers of Western Islam.* Leicester: Kube Publishing Ltd.

Khan, T. (2022) *Muslim, Actually. How Islam Is Misunderstood and Why It Matters.* London: Atlantic Books.

Kostadinova, Z. (2018) 'And When the Heart is Sick, the Whole Body is Sick'. Repairing the Person and the Urban Fabric through Everyday Sufi Ethics in Postwar Sarajevo. *Comparative Southeast European Studies*, 66 (1), pp. 69–93. https://doi.org/10.1515/soeu-2018-0005

Kostadinova, Z. (2023) Edep: Ethical Imagination and the Sunna of the Prophet Muhammed. *Contemporary Islam*, 18, pp. 87–109. https://doi.org/10.1007/s11562-023-00548-3

Lecoyer, K. (2020) Internormative Family Conflict Mediation within Belgian Muslim Families. *Revue Interdisciplinaire d'Études Juridiques*, 84 (1), pp. 149–177. https://doi.org/10.3917/riej.084.0149

Leiken, R. (2012) *Europe's Angry Muslims: The Revolt of The Second Generation.* Oxford: Oxford University Press.

Mahomed, N. (2022) The Elusive Ummah: Between the Political, Sectarianism, and Authority. *ReOrient*, 7 (1), pp. 27–45. https://doi.org/10.13169/reorient.7.1.0027

Mandaville, P. (2002) 'Europe's Muslim Youth: Dynamics of Alienation and Integration', in S. Hunter and H. Malik (eds.) *Islam in Europe and the United States.* Washington: Center for Strategic and International Studies.

Marramao, G. (2012) *The Passage West. Philosophy after the Nation State.* New York: Verso.

Merdjanova, I. (2013) *Rediscovering the Umma. Muslims in the Balkans between Nationalism and Transnationalism.* Oxford: Oxford University Press.

Mourad, S. (2014) Riddles of the Book. *New Left Reviews*, 68, pp. 15–52.

Mukherjee, S. R. (2014) Global Halal: Meat, Money, and Religion. *Religions*, 5 (1), pp. 22–75. https://doi.org/10.3390/rel5010022

Mushaben, J. M. (2008) Gender, HipHop and Pop-Islam: The Urban Identities of Muslim youth in Germany. *Citizenship Studies,* 12 (5), pp. 507–526. https://doi.org/10.1080/13621020802337931

Nijab, K. (2022) *Spatialised Islamophobia.* London: Routledge.

Potulski, J. (2020) The Civic Culture: Between Analytical and Normative Ideal. *Civitas – Studia z Filozofii Polityki*, 27, pp. 15–44. https://doi.org/10.35757/CIV.2020.27.02

Rexhepi, P. (2023) *White Enclosures. Racial Capitalism & Coloniality along the Balkan Route.* New York: Duke University Press.

Rippin, A. (2001) *Muslims. Their Religious Beliefs and Practices.* London: Routledge.

Robinson-Bertoni, S. (2017) Re-Territorializing Religiosity in Wholesome Muslim Praxis. *Religions,* 8 (7), pp. 1–31. https://doi.org/10.3390/rel8070132

Roy, O. (2004) *Globalized Islam: The Search for a New Ummah.* New York: Columbia University Press.

Roy, O. (2005) The Crisis of the Secular State and the New Forms of Religious Expression, *France Diplomatique*. Available at: www.diplomatie.gouv.fr/IMG/pdf/0101Roy_gb.pdf (Accessed: 19 October 2021)

Roy, O. (2013) Secularism and Islam: The Theological Predicament. *The International Spectator: Italian Journal of International Affairs*, 48 (1), pp. 5–19.

Roy, O. (2017) *Jihad and Death: The Global Appeal of Islamic State*. Oxford: Oxford University Press.

Sandal, N. A. (2011) Religious Actors as Epistemic Communities in Conflict Transformation: The Cases of South Africa and Northern Ireland. *Review of International Studies*, 37 (3), pp. 929–949. https://doi.org/10.1017/S0260210510001592

Sander, Å. (2014) 'Negative European Attitudes towards Muslims. Questions, Theories and Possible Explanations', in M. Deland, M. Minkenberg, and C. Mays (eds.) *In the Tracks of Breivik. Far Right Networks in Northen and Eastern Europe*. Vienna and Berlin: LIT Verlag, pp. 127–140.

Scott, T. (2005) *The Global Resurgence of Religion and the Transformation of International Relations. The Struggle for the Soul of the Twenty-First Century*. New York: Palgrave Macmillam.

Sofos, S. A. and Tsagarousianou, R. (2013) *Islam in Europe. Public Spaces and Civic Networks*. New York: Palgrave Macmillian.

Szovati, H. (2014) 'What Is a European Muslim Identity?', in I. Ramberg (ed.) *Islamophobia and Its Consequences on Young People*. Budapest: European Youth Centre Budapest, pp. 63–65. Available at: www.coe.int/en/web/youth/-/islamophobia-and-its-consequences-on-young-people?inheritRedirect=true (Accessed: 12 December 2022).

Torrekens, C. (2021) The Non-Impact of Religious Practices on the Process of Inclusion and Participation of Belgian Muslims. *Journal of Muslim Minority Affairs*, 41 (1), pp. 141–156. https://doi.org/10.1080/13602004.2021.1894384

Van Leuven, A., Mertens, S., D'Haenens, L. and Mekki-Benada, A. (2023) 'The Political and Intellectual Discourse on Islam and Muslims in Flanders', in L. d'Haenens and A. Mekki-Berrada (eds.) *Islamophobia as a Form of Radicalisation. Perspectives on Media, Academia and Socio-political Scapes from Europe and Canada*. Leuven: Leuven University Press, pp. 59–74.

Vlas, N. and Gherghina, S. (2012) Where Does Religion Meet Democracy? A Comparative Analysis of Attitudes in Europe. *International Political Science Review*, 33 (3), pp. 336–351. https://doi.org/10.1177/0192512111415983

Wenz, S. and Hoenig, K. (2020) Ethnic and Social Class Discrimination in Education: Experimental Evidence from Germany. *Research in Social Stratification and Mobility*, 65, pp. 1–38. https://doi.org/10.1016/j.rssm.2019.100461

# 6 Political Sensitivities and Civic Responses to Islamophobia

After 1989, the political turmoil in the Muslim world replaced the Soviet-Western standoff, and Islam became the constitutive threat for the whole Western orbit. Muslims from former socialist countries arriving in different European cities were ascribed with imagery of economically exploited and racialised non-Europeans (Tlostanova and Mignolo 2012). If the foundations of these racial stereotypes were laid up until the events of 9/11, the War on Terror gave a new dimension to the anti-Muslim vocabulary. Baseless headlines began reporting on the issues of integration (or lack thereof) as the main reason why Muslims, born and raised in the West, would likely carry out terrorist attacks. At first, pundits and security experts argued that they were attracted by religious extremism because they failed to integrate (Khan 2022:33). However, a disproportionate number of generally young Muslim terrorists and radicals with highly educated backgrounds proved that violence and radicalisation are more likely to stem from a whole host of social factors as opposed to ideological drivers (Harris and Nawaz 2015:12, Jones 2021:30). What gnawed at young generations of Muslims has been as much about identity as about generational conflicts and education (Easat-Daas 2020:26, Cesari 2013) rather than welfare payments, housing subsidies or any related issue thereof (Leiken 2012:38). On the other hand, Europe's fear of the loss of colour identity brought millions of Muslims to perceive and experience an atmosphere of hate and hostility (Ceretti and Cornelli 2018:63). As discussed in Chapter 4, their feeling of atopicality leads post-migrant generations to mobilise on claims in their "host countries" as this is (arguably) where they are politically socialised and their rights are best represented (Hess and Korf 2014).

Since contestation over the relationship between Islam and democracy weighs heavily in "the West", numerous competing models have sought to explain what motivates Muslims to participate in politics and the conditions under which they do so. It has been proven that these traditional models alone do not best contribute to explaining the nature of political motivations, nor do they help in understanding the particularly complex web of obvious issues for which Muslims engage or pursue specific forms of political participation (Easat-Daas 2020:38). Political participation can be

DOI: 10.4324/9781003589624-7

also difficult to explore due to a wealth of proxy factors (gender, age, birthplace) that do not reveal, unlike economic indicators or electoral turnout results, potential participation (Azabar and Van Aelst 2023:14) in collective actions, civic and social movements, or in different spaces of democratic participation and community organising, e.g. social networks, social capital, volunteerism, stakeholder theory, among others (Andriof et al. 2002; Della Porta and Diani 2006; Rubin and Rubin 1992, among others). Meanwhile, intense anti-Muslim discourse overshadows their large degree of exclusion from the core society and the related everyday issues that Muslims grapple with (Sofos and Tsagarousianou 2013). As discussed in Chapter 2, foregrounding the *ummah* shows a series of critical responses to the conflicting tensions that traverse the Muslim world at present. This is especially true for young mosque-goers who discover the *ummah* through postulates of solidarity and (re)create strong and visible in-/out-group dynamics in support or rejection of the specific idea or political concerns (Azabar and Van Aelst 2023).

Granted that Muslims from sizable Balkan diaspora families are first and foremost concerned with integration and democracy (Bougarel 2008), this chapter delves into the civic dimension of their political participation. Therefore, it explores their attitudes and engagement with public and political affairs in a time of crisis for liberal democracy, where liberal principles tend to be suspended when Muslims are involved (Jones 2021:147). The following sections consider those attitudes that go beyond the traditional and conventional practices of political participation, yet without excluding party politics when it was encountered during the fieldwork.

Two enquiries guide this chapter: do young Muslims with Balkan heritage participate in the political life of their place of residence? If at all, how does Muslimness guide their everyday responses to the current crisis of liberal democracy and multiculturalism? In addition, both questions were raised during in-depth interviews to intercept potential changes within the associative landscape after the disappearance of the Yugo clubs (Bougarel 2008) and shed light on any sort of public/civic engagement. While carrying out in-depth interviews, the main intent in investigating how civic responses were influenced and often driven by the public/private divide, was to look at the everyday personal responses to identity dilemmas and everyday encounters within a specific urban space (Posłuszny 2019:59). At this intersection, normative elements of rights and citizenship infringe on Muslimness (Sofos and Tsagarousianou 2013:64; see also Chapter 4 and 7).

Each interviewee was invited to reflect on any sort of public/civic engagement in the everyday life of any familiar locality in town. Although most respondents did not pin down their political participation, spontaneous answers reveal a wealth of civic responses and eventually the untapped ways in which respondents articulate and frame their civic actions against the political overtones of the current instability of liberal democracies and the alarming rise of exclusionary nationalism and Islamophobia.

It should be said here that this chapter considers only first-hand information extracted from the interview material, along with other related information obtained from second-hand sources collected during the period of fieldwork. Hence, the following sections focus on the political sensitivities and concerns of the postsocialist, post-war and post-migrant generations of those interviewed in and beyond their place of residence.

## Whose Secularism?

According to the four countries this study examines, secularisation has emerged from cultural processes that have not been legislated (Roy 2005) in light of the ambiguous and complex relationships between religion and politics (Carrim and Paruk 2020). Germany, Italy and Poland have concluded a church-state agreement that gives preference to a particular religion, namely the Roman Catholic Church, conferring special status and some privileges to the latter. Belgium instead shows the bifurcation of the state and official religions. This model includes a Dutch-Belgian version of *laïcité*, which differs from the French model in being less about removing religious symbols from public view and more oriented towards providing an equality of space for confessional and non-confessional organisations (Cavenaugh 2018:317).

As a major trait of European liberal democracies, secularisation does not in fact deny religion but rather it shapes its recomposition, thereby raising concerns over the impact of religion on social and political practices (Torrekens 2021:8). In this regard, Muslims have come to challenge secularism, since Islam does not provide an exit strategy from public affairs, nor a separate grounding for private and public life (Fleischmann and Phalet 2018:46; Rippin 2001:177). Put simply, Islam cannot be relegated or isolated at home. For Muslims, their religion is the conjunction of faith and knowledge, morals and politics, ideals and interests. By recognising the existence of these two worlds, the natural and the interior, Islam teaches that it is man who bridges the chasm between them. Without this oneness, religion tends towards backwardness and knowledge towards atheism (Izetbegović 1990:8). The debate is particularly rife regarding whether European unity, and therefore its external and internal boundaries, should be defined by its modern secular values, i.e. liberalism, universal human rights, political democracy, a tolerant and inclusive multiculturalism. Oliver Roy (2005) argues that current political secularism is the result of a compromise between institutional actors, the church and the state. This compromise, however, Kathleen Cavanaugh points out (2018:315), is no longer the absence of government involvement in religious affairs; rather, it is an ideology or belief that polices what is compatible with the traditions and values of European states and what is not. This analysis therefore reveals the background of a seemingly Islamophobic laïcité, which either accuses Muslims of lurking in the background to defy secularism, or regulates the extent to which they should "bracket" their power when entering into politics (Jones 2021:13). The frequent associations of so-called "political

Islam", or alternatively "politicised Islam", is today coupled with the parallel failure of the neoliberal prescription of free markets and open economies that produce more inequality than development. Moreover, the ubiquitous associations of Muslims with images of headscarves, mosques and minarets are still widespread due to the perceived failure of the West's secular, state-run and democratic model of multiculturalism (Scott 2005:41, Cesari 2013:xiii). On political grounds, Muslims' alleged desire to gain unfair influence against the social cohesion of "the West" (Hurd 2008:127) has increased people's fear over their potential political mobilisation. If assimilation policies for Muslim refugees and newcomers signified, in concrete terms, their exclusion outside the political field and public sphere (Khiari 2016:96), the steady rise of Islamophobia is neither exclusive to, nor isolated within, the marginal far-right movements, but is rather part of a broader mainstream public discourse (Rexhepi 2015:191). The so-called 2015 migration crisis in Southeast Europe came to associate Europe-born Muslims with "illegal migrants" and legitimise an Orbánesque far-right agenda within democratic institutions. Muslims were once more depicted as the biggest threat to Europe's Christian culture (Merdjanova 2013:112), empowering an assemblage of Islamophobia that also affected the families of Balkan Muslims who had escaped or fled their countries after the demise of state socialism. Although members of the *generation after* are not sojourners, newcomers or guests in their place of residence, they often remain unrecognised as Europeans despite holding European citizenship through residency, birth and/or nationality. They are instead likened to the most recent groups of newcomers arriving from non-European countries (Rexhepi 2023; Ferizaj 2019), and therefore are paradoxically associated with the strain on public services in the healthcare and education sector, job markets and lack of housing, rather than their legal and socio-political assets of contributing to justice, local economies, bolstering a younger workforce and mobilisation in public affairs, among others (Basheska and Kochenov 2024). While sharing similar goals, problems, fears and aspirations, young Muslims navigate between the effects of illiberal politics and anti-Muslim rhetoric encountered on a pan-European level.

At present, Islamophobia is part of what Kathleen Cavanaugh refers to as a hegemonic knowledge regime of secularism – namely, an illiberal secularism expressed through illiberal restrictions on religion in the public sphere. Thus, the philosophy of pluralism grafts to traditional (and dominant) European norms and values where the dominant reading of religion as a private belief justifies active intervention, ensuring that people's faith conforms to this homogenous conception of religion (2018:341). In fact, the premise is that the more zealous a Muslim is in his religious salience, the more radical he may become in his political activities. Basically, the more a Muslim prays, the more prone he is to perpetrating terrorist acts (Roy 2013:9). Against this pitfall, Fatima El-Tayeb refers to the experiences of "Queer Muslims" for describing the multiple positionalities in line with unstable, strategic and always-shifting performative identities (2011:xxxvi). Gerlach coined the term "popular Islam", better known as "pop Islam" (2006), to describe the tendency of young, post-migrant Muslims to merge their system of religious beliefs into fashion, music and the media along with their national identity. Khankan speaks of "Critical Muslims" to highlight a different engagement between coreligionists from the West and the Middle East on theological, cultural and political grounds (2018:60). Sofos and Tsagarousianou generally argue (2013:82) that the political participation of European Muslims may correspond to a high level of religious salience. In other words, when Islam shapes the fabric of daily life – even in the most mundane circumstances – Muslims' claims and demands penetrate more into the field of advocacy, citizenship, inclusion and anti-racist platforms. Both scholars also contend that young European Muslims make sense of their Muslimness through experiences of understanding and solidarities, rather than associating their religious identity with a religious sense of the term (2013:63). For instance, Muslims often use homophobic tropes when discussing themes of LGBTQI+ rights (Law et al. 2019). However, many have supported LGBTQI+ rights and criticised old-fashioned religious organisations (Khankan 2018:61), while even founding mosques for only women with female imams (so-called "Femimam"), standing up for progressive forms of Islam and embracing feminist philosophies. In the same way, others have particularly debunked the myth of homophobia and homosexuality by pointing out how the latter was even decriminalised by Ottoman Turks a century before America and Britain, and by assessing the former as a Western import of puritanical Europeans to undermine Islam's permissive civilisation during the colonisation age (The Economist 2021).

Nonetheless, ordinary Muslim voices remain either largely unheard (Finkelstein 2023:10) or subaltern to much louder Islamophobic mainstream and radical Muslims (Sofos and Tsagarousianou 2013:14). In light of a muscular liberalism aimed at protecting the Western values of tolerance, acceptance and non-conformity by whatever means (Triadafilopoulos 2011), Muslimness is mistakenly essentialised and implicitly depicted through a monolithic image of otherness (El-Tayeb 2012). As discussed in Chapter 2, Muslims from/in the Balkans have been subjected to coercive integration measures and restrictive migration and citizenship laws. In the purported "liberal" European Union, the need to declare the failure of multiculturalism (Trupia 2024) brought Western institutions to frequently suspend allegedly liberal norms of governance when Muslims are involved. This newly emerged forms of muscular liberalism take the gloves off secularism (Asad 2003), which lies in a civilisation project that has, from its very origins, involved the denigration of racialised and colonised subjects (Jones 2021:147).

A few decades after the dissolution of Yugoslavia, a vast array of studies have focused on the role of the Balkan Muslim diaspora, whose members have drastically shaped new relationships with state institutions, coreligionists and non-Muslim groups, actively participating and initiating activities for solving problems on individual and community grounds. Despite the process being long, painstaking and carrying the weight of the colonial and racial hierarchy within Europe, the Balkan Muslim diaspora has quickly developed institutions of sociability and solidarity (Sofos and Tsagarousianou 2013:49) by holding a non-radically connected position with political Islam (Mark et al. 2019:169). Studies have focused on socioeconomic and professional aspects of integration in an attempt to construct knowledge of the demographics of the diaspora (Halilovich et al. 2018), despite the lack of "hard data" regarding the different communities (Sahadžić, University of Antwerp 2021). Among others, Koinova and Karabegović analyse the subfield of transitional justice with regard to the Bosnian diaspora (2016), whose political participation and mobilisation in the wake of traumatic experiences of concentration camps in northwest Bosnia, the siege of Sarajevo (1992–1996) and the 1995 Srebrenica Genocide have gone beyond the causal mechanisms of coordination and commemoration initiatives (Karabegović 2014, 2019).

## Political Sensitivities and Disillusion

At the monthly meeting of "Solidarisch in Gröpelingen", a neighbourhood collective defending workers' rights and providing consultancy to residents with migration heritage, a very young Roma couple and their two children showed up. After taking their chairs and sitting down next to the other activists, Ahmed introduced himself and his family. By speaking in Bulgarian, he greeted everyone:

> "As-salamu alaykum, I am [Ahmed] and I am here today because after participating in the protests at the Job Centre, I managed to find a good apartment for my wife and my children. Now, I need to stand for my rights as a worker in Bremen."

While Bulgaria's Roma activists argue that recent public policies undertaken within Roma quarters are specifically meant to lower political participation (Fileva 2023) and disempower any leadership within the community (Mishev 2023), Germany shows a different set of circumstances. For example, in Duisburg, on October 23rd, 2022, more than three thousand "guest workers" of ethnically segregated Roma groups from Bulgaria and Romania, took to the streets nearby the gates of ThyssenKrupp Steel, Bruckhausen. They called for justice after the death of Refat Süleyman, a 26-year-old migrant worker from Stolipinovo, another unprivileged neighbourhood in Plovdiv, southern Bulgaria. Süleyman's body was found a few days after his natural death and kilometres away from his assigned workstation, in a designated safety zone servicing toxic waste.[1] In Bremen, the struggle of some Roma residents also concerned their labour rights.

1 Since October 2023, Stoliponovo in Europa has offered social counselling in Bulgarian, Turkish, Romanian and Romani language for people in Duisburg-Marxloh and the surrounding

*Figure 6.1* Monthly meeting of "Solidarisch in Gröpelingen" in Gröpelingen, Bremen. Photo by the author.

After taking a copy of "Voices from the neighbourhood", a bulletin written entirely in Bulgarian for the residents of Gröpelingen, I spoke with Ahmed and his wife, Mariya. While being the gatekeeper of the activists to the rest of the Roma community residing in the area, Ahmed's engagement with the collective was motivated by his fear of losing his job. His complaints about his boss, a Turkish Muslim man "who does not really respect [his] rights and simply asks [him] to 'push, push and push' without proper remuneration", were relevant yet different from Mariya's. She was more concerned about her children's education: "They must go to school and learn German very well", she added, and " 'Solidarisch' could advise [her] to enrol the children in a kindergarten in Gröpelingen".

As a Bulgarian- and Turkish-speaking couple originally from Shumen, Northeast Bulgaria, Ahmed and Mariya did not face any particular challenge living in Gröpelingen. After all, Ahmed himself described that area as a "*mahalla*" where "most residents are originally from villages around Shumen".

area. The association was found by a group of migrants, activists, journalists and scientists committed to combating the unequal treatment of minorities and unfair working and freedom of movement conditions within the European Union for years.

Yet he voiced the issue of minoritisation and socio-economic exploitation that had hit hardest those Roma who are often racially profiled on the street by the police through ID'ing.

Ahmed's words resonated with those of two young sisters of Kosovo Albanian origin, who confirmed that, in Bremen and across Germany, the plight of Roma does not elicit as much compassion as that expressed for other minority groups. The director of the neighbourhood library also bitterly admitted that Roma residents are constantly scapegoated by Germans and even Muslim residents in Gröpelingen.

The issue of Muslim Roma and their relations to Islam would warrant a separate study and future fieldwork. However, my qualitative data indicate that Ahmed's and Fatima's civic responses to labour exploitation and lack of access to education rights and housing are not exceptions. A few other respondents of Bosnian origin verbalised their concrete commitment to party politics. They stand for social-democratic values and express their political positioning on the left side of the political spectrum. In Italy, one self-identified as a "Titoist" and regrets the "loss of Yugoslavian identity among the Bosnian diaspora". He also adds, "if Yugoslavia were still alive, [he] would definitely identify as a Yugoslavian". Since the time of state socialism, anxieties and everyday worries around Islamic activism had much in common with leftist activism and were coloured by an anti-imperialist ethos. During the 1990s, the arrival and activities of the mujahideen in Bosnia and Herzegovina contrasted sharply and led to friction with the Muslim-Bosniak military leadership. After decades, however, that experience constituted a source for the engagement of a number of radicalised Bosnian Muslims in the Syrian battlefield in 2015 (Metodieva 2020; Sadriu 2017). After the fieldwork, the 2023 Israeli-Palestinian conflict in Gaza reactivated a sense of solidarity that was already being verbalised by respondents (see Chapter 2). Pundits warned about the solutions to the conflict given by the voices of far-left activists and young Muslims in Europe and "the West". Among others, the Palestinian question is a seminal event that reactivates some Islamic practices of remembrance among the respondents. However, they were quick to condemn radical and extremist plots, and were found to be completely detached from old anarchist or radical ideas inspired by anti-colonial waves of protest (Korenkov et al. 2022:114). As a matter of fact, left-wing political parties began moving away from the unprivileged and multicultural cities where the fieldwork was carried out. The "leftist vibes" have almost faded away in most multicultural neighbourhoods, which are now under massive transformation plans that advocate neoliberal policies and exclusionary practices for a "new city" (see Chapter 7). Hence, those respondents who were committed to party politics always pointed out as standing for moderate, centre-left values and being affiliated to centre-left youth organisations on a city level.[2]

2 The principles of solidarity, mutual aid and communal ways of life brought Max Weber to describe the Soviet revolution as "the contemporary Islam" (mentioned by Allievi 2017:119).

In triangulating other answers from in-depth interviews and different data across the four countries of this study, it turned out that respondents determined independently how to participate in, and when to speak about, politics and their political sensitivities. Overall, they are most likely keen on engaging in "unconventional participation" (Van Deth 2016:3): from attending educational programs to volunteering in the NGO sector, from supporting actions of solidarity to engaging in social media campaigns about issues of poverty, children rights and underdevelopment. This type of civic action takes the shape of what Azabar and Van Aelst (2023) similarly define as "non-institutional participation". The latter does not only depend on the different urban dynamics observed during the fieldwork, but also on a wealth of community-led variants. Only a few with Bosniak roots verbalised their sporadic yet genuine engagement in political participation, recalling personal involvement in student protests and green actions in Antwerp, initiatives in support of women's rights in Warsaw and solidarity campaigns at the university and at the offices of political parties in Bremen. While discussing general issues of political participation for young Muslims with a migration background, respondents are eventually more oriented to value the right to vote in fair and free elections. By "political participation", they did not only allude to "simply voting", but rather to the civic duty to get informed about political issues and become aware of the potential danger of political parties, institutional figures and local politicians. Just as exerting the right to vote "for someone" and "for vested interests" was

---

The universal concept of the *ummah*, which does not acknowledge people along ethnic, national and/or national lines, also resonates with the Marxist principles of brotherhood and unity. These affinities were strategically politicised during the period of decolonisation; Islam was thought to represent a natural and complementary ally of the orthodox socialist forces to resist capitalist imperialism in the Global South (Bakić-Hayden 1995:925), thereby offering the potential for an anti-imperialist struggle (Jomo 1992:246). To a certain extent, this political legacy continues to inspire some postulates of solidarity among major countervailing forces of radical left and Muslims against neo-colonial capitalism (Byrd 2017:286). Interestingly, the more spiritual branches of today's alt-right culture, to use Benjamin R. Teitelbaum's paradigm (2020), have also a fascination with Islam. Intolerance toward diversity, glorifications of violence and anti-American, anti-Semitic, anti-democratic messages along with misogyny and homophobia, are all prominent elements shared with the militant Islamist ideologies. The esoteric-gnostic intellectual, René Guénon, and the figure of the traditionalist, Julius Evola, are central in the philosophy of the alt-right (Allievi 2017:117; Rose 2021). This fascination with the mystique of Islam does not necessarily fuel Islamophobia (Geisser 2014:37). Certain political themes, such as antisemitism and pro-Palestinian stances, the "Jewish lobby" plotting behind and supporting the Western plutocracy (some affinities with the radical left here), are shared among alt-/far-rightists and radical Muslims. The emphasis on the glorification of the soldier and the warrior, as well as of his spiritual life understood as an orthopraxis and *jihad*, the cult of war and imperialism, both accepted as appropriate ways of organising social relations around the leader, the *Khalifa* (spiritual head of all Muslims worldwide), and the conception of moral behaviour with passion for chivalry life similar to the *futuwah* in Mediaeval time, reflect and overlap traditional Christian values that have been largely employed and rhetorically used in the Western world. Among others, the "God-Motherland-Family" motto, which is the ideological benchmark of Italy's right-wing party Brothers of Italy (See De Giorgi et al. 2023), echoes a certain traditional system of values among Muslims.

depicted as a negative practice, so aligning with any specific political party in their place of birth and upbringing was considered depreciable. Many admitted to having no serious interest in making inroads into politics as they were rather busy in dealing with "other priorities", such as economic instability, education and looking after their future careers. Alienation from politics and disillusionment in party politics was salient especially among most respondents with Albanian family heritage, who were found to be outspoken about the lack of efficacy of party politics and particularly disappointed about their marginal position in the political party arena.

Throughout, personal and collective identities are conceived through universal Islamic values of social justice and equality, as well as human rights and anti-racism. Their "being Muslim" could not be completely detached from Islam's idea of social justice and the concept of the "right to life", which exhorts Muslims to be active in their individual and social lives (Jomo 1992:24). Their Muslimness is more about generosity and charity, *zakat*, both paramount to practising Islam and counteracting greed (Robinson-Bertoni 2017:10) rather than engaging in some "ideological tenets [through which] to see and understand politics" or "express personal opinions" about public affairs. Unlike in francophone Belgium, where some Muslim women identify political participation as a religious obligation (Easat-Daas 2020:53), religious proximity between the groups under study and other coreligionists barely influence the political opinions of the former. Even zealous Muslims were found to be barely involved in dogmatic, sectarian and fundamentalist practices of political Islam. If anything, they were engaged in contributing to religious associations in their area of residence where they felt a stronger sense of belonging (Cesari 2013:194). Put simply, Islam plays a rather private and discrete role in shaping respondents' political identity – even when Islamophobia heightens the public debate and intensifies intolerance in their place of residence. Nonetheless, young mosque-goers were particularly worried about the electoral successes of the far-right or, alternatively, populist parties. Their concerns were verbalised in relation to the fact that their potential engagement in politics could be paradoxically seen as a cause to inflame the already tense atmosphere, further inciting Islamophobia and violent actions against Muslims.

Unlike in Belgium and Germany, respondents born and bred in Italy did not particularly perceive the rise of intolerant discourse despite the political mood following the landslide victory of the national-conservative and right-wing populist party "Brothers of Italy" (in Italian, *Fratelli d'Italia*) and the widespread Islamophobic tweets published particularly in Northern Italy (Mullol Marin 2023:358). In this regard, respondents verbalised a newer, stronger, more confident voice about their "being Muslim" in comparison with the older generation. Their Islam guides them towards what they can do for human needs (Byrd 2017:148), while feeling a sense of solidarity toward the other, Muslim and non-Muslim (Sofos and Tsagarousianou 2013:134). When needed, they are more likely to retreat into a hyper-personalised and private space where Islam's social potential and commitment do not (seem to) encroach upon the future of society.

Here, family context is central. Most respondents' awareness and genuine interests in politics are enhanced by the (hi)story of their family, especially in relation to a wide range of past experiences that motivate them to become aware of transnational and domestic political issues. Since an early age, they have been listening to unpleasant (hi)stories and events of political discrimination and genocidal violence that their family members and coreligionists endured in economically exploited and war-torn Balkan countries. When some respondents justify their low-profile political engagement through the explanation of "being Muslims originally from the Balkans", it was clear that religious legacies are transmitted across generations and nurtured through cultural practices and traditions of "Balkan Islam" since the time of socialism. In retrospect, it is clearer that the long-lasting legacies of pragmatic attitudes have been passed down by their (grand)parents, who navigated systemic practices of surveillance and scapegoating since the socialist years (see Chapter 3). This perspective contributes to explaining the main reason for which respondents are rather selective in taking action and allowing themselves to consider a course of political action. It also helps explain why they verbalised discomfort and frustration over the pleas of the *ummah*, as the latter largely resonate with their (grand)parents' experiences of war and injustice.

At the same time, however, family heritage also motivated the majority of respondents to discuss the most debated issues of today's (il)liberal democracy in their place of residence and their parental country of origin. Although disengaged from political activism, respondents did not struggle to validate their liberal, secular and democratic values. As shown in Easat-Daas's study (2020:36), grievance-based motivations are important for Muslims to take small but significant actions, or at least have a critical say, in political affairs. To paraphrase Achille Mbembe's words here (2019:51), respondents' convictions and certainties remain personal and private, largely acquired throughout a long "spiritual path", pertaining neither to a feeble fanaticism nor to barbaric madness or disillusion. On the contrary, their practical acts of care manifest an "inner experience" that can be shared only by those who, professing the same faith, obey the same law, the same authorities and the same commandments.

During a few in-depth interviews, two main themes were verbalised – namely, citizenship and diaspora politics. Both are often seen as suspicious because of the political links that could exist between "new citizens" and the network of diaspora's lobbying organisations, NGOs or even other radical groups seeking to emerge from inside the European Union (Scott 2005:103). At the time of these interviews, some respondents had not yet received, nor voluntarily acquired, the citizenship of their country of birth and residence. Others born around the 2000s have renounced their Bosnian, Albanian or Bulgarian citizenship for "better future prospects" and for "exerting their right to vote during the presidential elections". Although they did not specify particular issues at stake, the political atmosphere in Germany was not favourable when compared with the three aforementioned countries. Although naturalisation tripled in Germany between 1988 and 1998, some cultural controversies began to burden the generation born after December 31, 1999, because of the strict requirement connected to having at least 15 years' probationary residence in the country and the final cultural text (Mushaben 2008:509, Cesari 2013:91, Leiken 2012:243–250). In Italy, a similar issue was also raised by a male respondent of Montenegrin origin, born in Germany and now residing in nearby Piacenza.

> "I became a member of a local political party, but they did not involve me in future plans. I also participated in political elections at the university, and I have been quite active in organising events, public meetings. The issue of citizenship is always debated in very radical discourse: there is no discourse on integration because in Italy there is no political representation of ethnic minority issues on an institutional level. The discourse of *ius sanguinis* unravels a racialisation of the issue of citizenship in Italy. Italy has to invest in us – and the other non-Italian communities residing here."

Those holding double citizenship admitted to having been invited to vote in their parental country of origin. Another young Bosnian born in Italy even recalled having been personally contacted by some politicians from Sarajevo with a view to bringing the diaspora closer to the motherland. He also verbalised his sense of embarrassment after deciding to give up on such an opportunity as he felt deeply detached from the political affairs of his parent's country of origin. Likewise, others admitted lacking a general understanding of Bosnia's complicated institutional and political landscape, while accusing ethnonationalism and separatism of spoiling the future of the Balkans. Two respondents, residing in Rome and Warsaw, employ an ethical perspective while explaining how they find it "hypocritical deciding to participate or influence politics in Bosnia [since they do not] live there" and that they "do not understand Bosnians' problems because [they] have never experienced" living there. In Warsaw, another said, "I have never voted. Although I am very attached to Sandžak, I do not know much about the law there, and, to be honest, I do not feel responsible for what is happening in that country". An 18-year-old respondent, whose parents arrived in Bremen in 1999 from Preševo, stated that he was "willing to go back to Kosovo and vote. . . . This is why", he pointed out, "I do not hold German citizenship, but only a Kosovo passport". Tellingly, he was taken by surprise when, during the in-depth interview, he was made aware that the Albanian-majority area of Serbia is not part of Kosovo. In Antwerp, two male respondents admitted that:

> "There are lots of commonalities between my interests and the political parties [here in Germany, but] I do not have one party really representing me . . . [in Bosnia, instead,] most parties are nationalistically oriented, so I don't feel represented by any of them".

> "My father is really into politics, not me. Once he told me to go to the Bosnian embassy in Brussels and vote. I knew everything: whom to vote for, which party, what the latter wanted to do in Bosnia. Yet I had to play in my football team that Sunday, so I did not go. Afterward, I felt bad for my father, who did not complain much, though".

This ethical baggage was also commonly seen, or perceived, as not only linked to Islam, but also part and parcel of the European canon of solidarity and altruism. Foregrounding the latter, many respondents expressed their "good will" in caring and pursuing actions of solidarity among the needy, especially when it comes to the *zakat* and even other charity campaigns organised outside Europe. Mainly among young female respondents, the cause-specific act of the *zakat* was not only presented as one of the pillars of Islam but also associated with the philosophy of human rights. This full or partial connection between European and Islamic values inspires respondents to take actions in the public arena, and it also echoes the findings of similar studies in France and Belgium (Easat-Daas 2020) and in Great Britain (O'Toole et al. 2013). Respectively, both illustrate how Muslim participation and responses are guided by altruistic motivations and the notion of social justice, as well as Islamic moral understanding. In effect, it is through "the other", especially in the case of "the poor" and "the marginalised", that a sense of care motivates respondents to abide by the divine laws and dictates of the Qur'an in being-with-others and being-for-others. In addition, respondents freely chose altruistic commitments that stressed the absolute need for social justice, social equity and social harmony, all instances superseded by the objective needs of the community and motivated by personal desire to raise awareness over injustice and the lack of recognition of fellow Muslims.

## White Habitus, Whiter Habits

On the train to Piacenza, Italy, I was looking for some local news covering the Balkan Muslim diaspora. While scrolling down the headlines, one got my attention: it read, in English, "The Muslims with Blue Eyes and the Liberal Islam of Bosnians in Piacenza".[3] Although the article did not say much about the Bosnian community (Gasparini 2022), the description indirectly reinforces the constantly recurring image depicting Muslims outside the non-European, strictly practising, backward-looking Muslim communities from the Middle East and North Africa. "Bosnian Islam", to allude knowingly to the mischaracterisation of Tone Bringa's work (1995), was described as modern and progressive as well as liberal, open to the dialogue and permeable to the local customs of the host-country. Bosnians themselves were depicted as "white

3 My translation from Italian, "I Musulmani dagli Occhi Azzurri. L'Islam Liberale dei Bosniaci di Piacenza" (See Gasparini 2022)

Muslims" – literally, "blonde and blue-eyed, without the salt-and-pepper, unkempt beard, nor wearing long vests or traditional headgear".

During the interviews in the different European cities, the issue of "whiteness" and "otherness" emerged relevantly. As already shown in other qualitative studies (Colic-Peisker 2005; Grünenberg 2005, among others), respondents reiterate the mainstream self-identification with "white Muslim Europeans" born and living in a "white European country". Whiteness was usually mixed in with other forms of rhetoric and ideologies (Sofos and Tsagarousianou 2013:19) and rarely expressed in purely religious terms. If anything, it was verbalised as the everyday condition under which they go unnoticed and thereby manage to avoid any potential experience of racism. While there was consensus among young Muslims with Bosnian roots about the duality of being in/visible as a non/white Muslim is a dis/advantage in avoiding/experiencing racist encounters, those born in Albanian families and veiled young Muslims pointed out that whiteness often has nothing to do with skin colour. In Antwerp and Dortmund, female respondents argued that "having neither blond hair nor blue eyes" or even "being a veiled young woman" has an impact on their social interactions. To their mind, whiteness can reduce opportunities to gain employment or a traineeship for the university, especially when "the surname is not native". The same goes for establishing social networks "when [the] dress code is not too Western" and "the job position" or "language skills" do not meet external expectations. These answers are congruent with what Zubair reports in Germany (2023:272–273), where Muslim women with a Turkish name, or simply wearing a headscarf, have to apply four times as often to be invited for as many interviews as applicants with a German name who do not wear a headscarf.

These subtle forms of discrimination make Islamophobia even more salient and pertinent when national and local media outlets report petty and organised crimes, or even anti-terrorist policing riots against radical plots. During fieldwork in Antwerp, a Bulgarian citizen was detained for planning a terrorist attack during the period of Ramadan. According to the media in Belgium and Bulgaria, he was arrested along with other young radicalised Belgian nationals and a Turkish citizen because they were all linked to jihadists from the Islamic State claiming responsibility for the attacks in Brussels on March 22, 2016 (Atasanov 2023).

The tandem of whiteness and Islamophobia finds only young Muslims with Bosnian roots who speak slightly differently. During an in-depth interview, a young Muslim with Bosnian roots took his phone from his pocket, showing me a "meme that has gone viral on social media: Bosnians be like: Muhammed Islamović", depicting a blond hair and blue-eyed young man. More seriously, many other respondents recollected the histories of their family members fleeing Bosnia or escaping from genocidal violence organised on the basis of ethnicity/religion that had nothing to do with racial visibility (see Chapter 3). Aware of rampant Islamophobia, they claimed to remain "invisible" or foreign to most techniques of racialisation and minoritisation in comparison with same-age peers of Turkish and Moroccan origin. In Belgium and Germany, national traditions of multiculturalism undoubtedly helped them avoid being singled out in town. However, their personal concerns seemed intensified due to rampant far-right discourse winning ground over domestic issues, or when anti-Muslim discourse echoes the nationalist rhetoric that forced the family to flee Bosnia and escape from the war. These two interview insights are instructive:

> "[Bosnian Muslims] are a small community and the far-right does not target us directly, but they do target Muslims, so we fall under this category. And, yes, we do feel it".
>
> "My mom told me that in Yugoslavia no one used to be really religious. Then, after the collapse of socialism, everything was radicalised and religion became a matter of difference. . . . Yet if it becomes an issue, people look at you differently. . . . This is the kind of sentiment of many people I know and close to my family. What many cannot think possible, can happen for my parents. For example, neighbours can turn against us very soon".

In theory, the complex and subtle discourse of Islamophobia is generally not associated with a form of racism. Among so-called "free thinkers", who take a rather culturalist perspective on the social position of Islam (Van Leuven et al. 2023:62), the Turkish-born German scholar, Necla Kelek, argues that Islam is not a race but rather a culture (quoted by Özyürek 2015:10). In practice, Tawseef Khan argues that contemporary Islamophobia is indeed a type of racism because of the ways Muslims are racialised. Although Islamophobia appears in a markedly different form of "traditional" racism, it cannot be uncritically restricted to ugly, abusive language and behaviour against Muslims. Islamophobia often enables actual racism, one which is far more subtle and sophisticated because it uses innuendoes and suggestions rather than insults, thereby allowing racist messages to pass as harmless (2022:14) in spite of conveying the long legacy of Europe's racialisation.[4] By the same token, Monika Bobako (2017) highlights that certain strategy discourses embedded in anti-Semitic, anti-immigrant and anti-Muslim rhetoric often converge and feed off one another. Associating Islamophobia more easily with a form of structural cultural and epistemic racism is linked to the coloniality of power, knowledge and being, intrinsic to the modern/colonial world system. Muslimness is thus a racialised state of being from which Muslims (or those ascribed as Muslims) manage barely to escape. Questioning issues of racialisation of Roma, refugees and Muslims (in some cases a group could be all three) highlights frequently ignored racialised hierarchies that after socialism (as a result of the imitation of Western modernity) are anchored in the contemporary

4 Interview with Prof. Yasemin Karakaşoğlu, Bremen University (Germany), 25 May 2023.

rise of racism as a simple outcome of post-socialist Europeanisation (Kancler 2021:166). Elana Resnick argues that in the Balkans, such a denial unravels a form of white supremacy and asserts the existence of racialised hierarchies. The entanglement of modern racism and power is not only appropriate to studying the chronological history of Europe, but also paramount for rejecting the issue of racist politics as an unfortunate and unexpected identification with whiteness (quoted by Trupia 2022:27).

Observing the urban clusters chosen for this study helps one understand that the groups of respondents may endure different experiences from other racialised Muslim minorities and generations of (former) migrants who arrived earlier to Western countries (Yuval-Davis 2011:7). The discourse on sameness and otherness changes according to the status of being a refugee or not wearing European clothing or having (not) light skin colour (Grünenberg 2005). In the same vein, the different places where the fieldwork was conducted showed different nuances of Islamophobia and how public debates are constructed around Islam in general. As introduced earlier, "whiteness" was explicitly expressed as an opportunity to avoid being externally ascribed to terrorism and even Islam. Choosing to identify primarily as "white Muslim Europeans" was as much about claiming full inclusion into "a white country" as a socio-psychological mechanism of gaining "advantages" over other Muslim refugees (Colic-Peisker 2005:624). This "white = unthreatening" association erases, explicitly or implicitly, Muslimness from the recognisable identity of respondents, which provides invisibility since they are dissociated from being a potential threat to democracy or even being occasionally associated with Christianity (Amer 2018). The identity of "white Muslims" also influences how they position and see themselves, and how they themselves are positioned and seen by others (Amer and Howarth 2018). However, these identity dynamics are always at the intersecting crossroads of inclusion and exclusion. Rather than associating themselves with direct racial references, the respondents self-reiterate whiteness as a form of social "privilege", which grants them the image of a good, white and secular Muslim. From their perspective, respondents wear a "white habitus" (Piela and Krotofil 2023) in an urban context where "whiteness" is the dominant ethnicity as it appears from the "inside".

> "I also think that looking 'white' helped me avoid facing racism. If there has been some pre-judgment, it came from my name, [which] does not sound Belgian".
>
> "It is easier to avoid and manage with some situations, because we are European Muslims and we visually look Europeans".
>
> "I have never experienced any anti-Muslim rhetoric because I do not look like a person who does not come from this country".
>
> "Once I was asked about my name, and I replied that it has an Arabic meaning and then people told me [that I did] not look like an Arab, ignoring the fact that there were European Muslims who were part of

> this continent for quite a long time; it was difficult to internalise and digest the idea that, for those people, realising that Muslims have lived in Europe for centuries was a new piece of information".
>
> "When people meet us and come to know that we're a Muslim Bosnian family, they say 'it's not visible'. They mostly associated Islam and 'being Muslims' with terrorism. But we all know this is banal and malignant political rhetoric".

Rather than interrupting the continuities of the postsocialist racial and colonial practices and policies of state institutions (Rexhepi 2023:18), all of these answers clearly debunk the myth of racelessness over former socialist citizens arriving in the West after 1989. At the same time, however, most respondents deployed the same tactics that delegitimise dissenting Muslims, lest they be accused of sympathising with the pleas of the *ummah* or even directly supporting "jihadists" or "religious extremists". In Antwerp, some young Bosnian respondents recalled some awkward experiences where their interlocutors did not know they were, in fact, talking to a young Muslim, associating all Muslims with the stereotyped and oriental image of the Muslim attire, such as the *hijab* or the long vest, as well as the long length of beard. Muslimness was not here simply referred to as a process of "othering", but also as a mischaracterisation of cultural features that Muslims (are supposed to) possess. In this regard, two respondents in particular lamented that debates on Islam are too often driven by stereotypical images of Muslimness. Respectively,

> "I [did] not fit their stereotype of a Muslim woman, perhaps because I am not devoutly practicing Islam, and I am not secular either, and this is confusing for people, as I do not fit people's stereotypes about 'being Muslim', and all of these debates about 'laicism' and 'the veil' made me mad about the ways they stereotype Muslim women".
>
> "I feel Islamophobia. I see people here who are genuinely racist . . . and when I am with them, they do not even understand that I am Muslim, and they make racist comments".

Although Amer and Howarth identify descendants of families from the Balkan regions as "white Muslims" (2018:614), not all interviewees are dressed up with a "white habitus". Often through jokes and allusions, most interviewees of Bosnian origin admitted that their "Slavic looks" produce a certain degree of "white-passing", whereas hijab-wearing women, primarily with Albanian or Turkish heritage, are deprived of such a "privilege". Hence the universality of whiteness generally shows how issues of sexuality and freedom (or lack thereof) are embedded in the current Islamophobia mulling over Muslim women's cultural rights. More precisely, whiteness plays the role of an unavailable condition for male and non-veiled interviewees while remaining deeply embedded in the gendered nature of Islamophobia (Smits 2023:94). An interviewee explains that "the headscarf makes [her] visible [and she] had to resign from job positions for it", while another feels the "fiery glances downtown". Among unveiled female interviewees, some felt "lucky to be white and not dark-skinned, such as Pakistani women", even though "non-white looks" are not always associated with "being veiled".

According to those respondents born in the early 2000s in Germany, the distinction between Germanness and Muslimness self-perpetuates logics of anti-Semitism and racism. Although a respondent argued that Germans got used to welcoming refugees and economic migrants after Angela Merkel's iconic "We can do it" (in German, *Wir schaffen das*) amidst the 2015 Syrian refugee crisis, the rampant rise of "Alternative für Deutschland" has helped insidious racism re-emerge from the depths of the fringes of German society. Since the tense political atmosphere of the post-1989 reunification period,[5] Islam has remained the domain of populist politicians, as well as of scholars and intellectuals (Cesari 2013:86). The public debate over the "Leitkultur" (in English, *leading culture*), a term coined by Bassam Tibi (2002), who advocated cultural pluralism based on values of consensus and modernity, brought the centre-right Christian party to demand stricter control over immigration and campaign on an assimilation policy. Germany's "Leitkultur" has been recently dismissed by Björn Höcke from Alternative für Deutschland, who warned Germans about a "war of displacement" in light of the fact that Germans were regarded as living an unworthy life (in German, *Lebensunwertes Leben*). Höcke used a similar term to Adolf Hitler's program of "racial hygiene" by which the Nazis justified the killing of hundreds of thousands of mentally ill and disabled people (Zubair 2023:277–278). Höcke's case also followed the publication of "Deutschland Schafft Sich Ab" (in English, *Germany Abolishes Itself*) in 2020, whose author, Thilo Sarrazin, described Germany as a country where Germans themselves – clearly alluding to white, ethnic Germans – could become "strangers in their own country". Likewise, in Belgium, the far-right extremist Filip Dewinter from the political party "Vlaams Belang" (in English, *Flemish Interest*) introduced his new book, "Omvolking", a word that derives from the German word "Umvolkung" alluding to the great replacement theory. The Dutch version of "Omvolking" is still currently used by right-wing groups and political parties to refer to a general fear of a "great replacement", of a perceived "indigenous" people by a perceived "other" population (Smits 2023:97). Similar theses went viral in Italy after the publication of another book, "Il Mondo al Contrario" (my translation in English, *Topsy Turvy World*) published by Italian General Roberto Vannacci, exposing his racist ideas over issues of diversity, multiculturalism and blackness.

5 The so-called "Baseball bat years" (in German, *Baseballschlagerjahre*) recall the period following Germany's reunification after 1989. Nazi gangs began to dominate the streets by beating, threatening, insulting and even killing dozens of people against refugees and people with migration background (Bangel 2019). In 1992, Sadri Berisha, a Kosovar Albanian guest worker, was beaten to death by seven neo-Nazis in his home near Stuttgart (Ferizaj 2023).

Needless to say, respondents perceived Islamophobia as classifying all Muslims as one single monolithic community. This taxonomy goes beyond the "white habitus" and the abstract idea of the supposedly egalitarian *ummah*. According to almost all interviewees, Islamophobia is simply part and parcel of racism and the nativist discourse that they sadly encounter on a daily basis. Achille Mbembe argues that racial thinking (or indeed, racism) more than class thinking has been the ever-present shadow hovering over Western political thought and practice, especially when the point was to convey the idea of foreign peoples and the sort of domination to be exercised over them (2019:71).

> "We [Albanians] look different from Germans. [I] have the feeling that they will never accept me and I have the impression that they still do not accept me. At [anonymised place] when patients come to see me, some racism pops up . . . at school, sometimes teachers grade me differently, although I was good at the German language".
>
> "My fiancé and I were about to take a train in first class. . . . The train assistant started to yell at me because she thought I did not have a first-class train ticket. She did not even check my ticket, but she assumed that we did not have one for the first-class wagon, clearly judging us from the way I and my fiancé looked".
>
> "Once I was walking with my parents and someone stared at us. Indeed, my parents do not look German. I tend to just ignore this stuff because I can't change [people's minds], and when I try to engage in some discussions, I just receive even harsher replies".
>
> "[As a] man, I do not talk about [discrimination]. . . . [B]ut you hear more and more people making comments of 'going back to your country' or 'I'll kill you curly-headed boys and girls'".
>
> "Some elderly German women were complaining about some veiled Muslim women waiting at the same bus stop . . . and I confessed to being a Muslim woman. Although I am not particularly religious, I played the 'Muslim card' to show them that even though they may not notice some Muslims, we are still nearby".

The latter interview's insight interestingly resonates and resembles Ferruh Yilmaz's conversion to Islam, which had nothing to do with religious faith but with opposing the hegemony of right-wing discourse (Bobako 2015:52). In fact, that respondent clearly stated having only a Muslim family background rather than a strong religious identity. However, she added that she had "reacted spontaneously against those racial innuendoes because [she had had enough] of hearing such comments more and more recently toward non-German people". That assertive response also displays the strong civic identity of young Muslims usually reappearing as a colonial vestige at all levels – from local politics to intra-*ummah* dynamics (Rexhepi 2023). To counter Islamophobia and the illiberal methods of political actors, many verbalise respectfulness and education as paramount in helping Muslims come to terms with the post-secular society as well as non-Muslims to educate themselves about Islam. As discussed at various points of Chapter 5, zealous Muslim respondents refer to respectfulness as one of the pillars of Islam, which teaches how to navigate between different ideas and religious doctrines with tolerance and refusal of any source of conflict. Islamophobia affects Europeans' attitudes towards immigrants, becoming an instrument of specific, politically conditioned practices of categorisation of human diversity (Bobako 2015:43). In addition, the state-endorsed manufacturing of "moderate Islam" has not opened dialogical public spaces (Merdjanova 2013:110) whereby Muslims can legitimise and normalise their positions by promoting an idea of Islam that is both truer to itself and to European values of equality, freedom and democracy (Özyürek 2015:37–38). Nonetheless, configurations of power vis-à-vis Muslim communities continue to dominate the depoliticisation and secularisation of the "good Muslims" that Europe seeks for. The promotion of a "liberal Islam" has been lodged with an assumption that the politicality of Muslims is usually epiphenomenal, i.e. a divergence and/or infringement upon neutral secular public space (Hurd 2008:117). In it, potential conflicts can be viewed as stemming collectively from Islam (Cesari 2013:5). In turn, both de-politicisation and secularisation have become so ingrained in Western thought that a potential reference to Muslim values and practices is often assumed as a "non-secular" and carried out by *populi extranei* (Hurd 2008:31; Orr-Ewing and Orr-Ewing 2002:79).

## Rainbow Flags and Gendered Encounters

During the month of Ramadan in 2023 in Antwerp, the music venue De Roma and Merhaba, a charity that supports LGBTQIA+ Muslims with a migration heritage, planned a "queer iftar" in the Borgerhout neighbourhood. Having a meal after sunset to break the fasting together would have provided an opportunity for LGBTQIA+ Muslims to celebrate an *iftar* evening in a safe place. Yet a grim atmosphere descended after some activists pointed out that the "queer iftar" was not only about the queer experience of potential participants, but also about their religious identity. They were stressed out about bearing the brunt of attacks from many different sides: not only from the intolerant voices of Belgian citizens, but also from those of the same Muslim communities. What they asked for was "not even respect, nor acceptance, but just the right to exist".

Within a few days the event was eventually cancelled due to the negative comments that quickly flooded different social media platforms, directly threatening the LGBTQIA+ Muslims. The Mayor of Antwerp, Bart De Wever, nationalist leader of the New Flemish Alliance, commented that the multitude of online negative opinions were simply freedom of speech (Flandersnew.be 2023). The event left a bitter aftertaste as the police reported no danger against the event organisers and potential attendees.

The mayor later also accused the LGBTQIA+ local community of not collaborating with the police who were investigating potential physical threats against them. Some activists dismissed De Wever's accusation by saying that the refusal to collaborate with police had nothing to do with the event itself (Van Renterghem 2023). On the contrary, they pointed out that the anger that ignited around the "queer *iftar*" evening was as much about their personal identity as religious experience, which had been attacked from different sides. Some local politicians and civil society organisations had provided alternative options for the *iftar* evening, yet De Roma and Merhaba unequivocally declined any alternative plan. In the meantime, an underlying rhetoric spread anti-Muslim stereotypes and narratives by promoting the idea that it was the Muslim community's intolerance toward the LGBT people that was the main reason the "queer *iftar*" had been cancelled (Sanctorum 2023). Notwithstanding, as already studied in Europe (Jones 2021:112), the "queer *iftar*" provided the grounds to dismiss mainstream prejudices toward Muslims, who are often seen and depicted by conservatives, elders and far-rightists as homophobic and anti-democratic. As a matter of fact, the "queer *iftar* event" in Borgerhout presented a picture of active Muslim engagement in addressing those thorny questions that hit the nerves of their coreligionists, as well as tackling societal challenges that are much debated in today's multicultural societies.

While talking to a Brussels-born citizen with Albanian family heritage, he said had "heard about the queer *iftar* in Antwerp". He also explained:

> "to not even understand how you can fast for Ramadan and be gay knowing what Islam does to gays . . . but if they want to, they should have the right to worship, of course! This is the reason I am not that religious [and into] Balkan politics, I do not even often go to Kosovo either, because I'm gay, [so] knowing the amount of homophobia there, I prefer to wait for a change in their mentality".

A female interviewee, who happened to be a freelancer in journalism at the time of the interview, commented on the event by admitting that

> "feminism and LGBTQ rights are issues that most journalists and less progressive politicians use as a means to talk badly about Islam, both indirectly and directly. It is complicated, because one can support feminism and LGBT and still be Muslim".

Other in-depth interviews in Antwerp brought to light a certain degree of mistrust and discomfort toward the lyonisation of "LGBT culture". As already shown in previous studies (Kwon and Hughes 2018:658), primarily male interviewees express personal distress about complying with mainstream institutions and their discourse over gay rights. The abundance of the "LGBT buzzword" and "gender labelling" were considered as having a negative effect on of politics, the labour market, education, welfare and sport, and therefore criticised accordingly.

> "Where does it end? I mean – this attention to [LGBT], parades, and official dates of celebration . . . especially in business. Is it [about people] or about marketing?"
>
> "LGBTQ culture is about forcing society to comply with it. . . . In Borgerhout someone even painted a zebra with the rainbow colours, seriously? They force everyone to comply with that, and I am ok, but you can't force me to teach my kids 'your' beliefs, nor can you criticise me for not complying with 'your' differences. It is about mutual respect".

When in-depth conversations delved into discussing gender politics, LGBT rights were often presented as a divisive issue. A gender perspective is important to unpack here. While female respondents considered the "gender debate" an issue among Muslims and also within wider society, male respondents held a more outspoken position with a lower degree of compromise over the issue. From what they argued, it seems that they had partially retreated from multicultural policies and practices. Without directly mentioning it, respondents blamed "muscular liberalism" and its methods of undertaking politics, which unleashes a side effect. Put simply, they claimed that marginalised communities and people at risk, who are supposed to be recognised and protected, end up being made vulnerable as "muscular liberalism" erodes democracy and pluralism (Rippin 2001; Leiken 2012; Triadafilopoulos 2011; Van Deth 2016; Allievi 2017; Kwon and Hughes 2018). This critical response does not mean that respondents opposed, let alone refused, liberal norms or multiculturalism per se. Rather, they underlined the paradoxical effects of multicultural public policies and the insufficient outcomes of "organised secularism" that arise around the issues of LGBT rights. Here, Muslimness intensifies amidst the backlashes that multiculturalism has created, becoming the broken promises that right-wing populist discourse speaks about to support the need for a "fortress Europe" against the dominant threats of Muslims.

Yet again in Antwerp, male respondents expressed a mixture of apparently welcoming policies that are de facto committed to even-handedness, engaging with distinctive concerns among ethnic and religious groups. However, their implementation often employs hostile, confrontational and intentionally inflammatory vocabulary against Muslims (Jones 2021:13), whose traditional gender values are contested on legal grounds. In it, "too much freedom" could disrespect and endanger people's culture and traditions under the guise of freedom of expression and free speech. The latter in particular is not only criticised for giving too much freedom but also for not regulating the public sphere. A few examples where given, such as: "Is burning the

Qur'an freedom of expression in Sweden?",[6] and "what about children having different gender identifications, is that a right?" In this regard, most male respondents reversed the dilemma of tolerance in liberal democracy from a Muslim perspective, thereby arguing that the respect they pay to non-Muslim cultures and people is not often reciprocated when it comes to them being heard and respected. Regardless of how much they can adjust and restrict their Muslimness, there is an asymmetry between speakers and listeners (Asad 2003:184). This is why, many argue, "being too liberal" and "too modern" has not only already endangered society, but also led to polarisation among newer generations. Relatedly, secularism seems often operating selectively (Khan 2022:51), while the philosophy of laicism is understood as "never neutral but rather restrictive for Muslims" (see Peyrard 2017). In this regard, "being a feminist" or "a progressive woman" count only as long as the woman in question is not veiled, otherwise she cannot verbalise abstract discourses of emancipation and cultural autonomy in the eyes of other "female liberals" and "feminists" who essentially reify her Muslim culture and tradition.

In analysing the interview insights, the issues at stake allow us to undertake a political and philosophical analysis. The first questions the assumption that liberal democracy ushers in a direct-access society, especially in light of the fact that the ideology of political representation in liberal democracy makes it difficult, if not impossible, to represent Muslims as Muslims (Asad 2003;173). The second questions the assumption that tolerance is understood through the relationship between political interests and values and the logic of identity. The latter, according to Giacomo Marramao (2012:43), should be set out in terms of understanding the former as a pluralism of interests, values and identities. This entails that political interests and values are no longer structuring the dynamics of social order and conflicts. Rather, the conflict and pluralism of interests and values, which persist as sharply as before, are inextricably caught up within the dynamic of conflicts and pluralism of identity. Thus, in democracy, the articulation of interests and values appears as an independent variable in the process of symbolic (self-)identification.

Although focusing on the logic of identity may endanger the political arena, in which reality can be exaggerated and stereotypes reinforced (Mansbridge 2003:358), respondents' critical responses and ideas often, albeit not always, take on the shape of neo-traditionalism and find commonality in anti-Western conservatism typical of the far-right discourse (Bobako 2015:49). Put simply, respondents raised their critical views by reiterating the accusations of those who are often found to be uncomfortable with multiculturalism and have expressed their vitriol specifically against some coreligionists. Respondents

6 Here, the respondent referred to the Quran-burning that occurred in Stockholm, Sweden, in January 2023. There, Rasmus Paludan, founder and leader of the right-wing political party Stram Kurs, burned a copy of the Quran outside of the Turkish embassy.

themselves did not only reiterate this language, but they also relied on Islam's horizon of upholding respect toward everyone while maintaining their faith almost uncritically (Byrd 2017:3). While in Antwerp a young Muslim of Bosnian origin spoke of how important a traditional marriage is, a same-age male interviewee of Albanian origin in Dortmund describes the "gender debate" as the elephant in the room of German society. In particular, he pinpoints the banalisation of the "LGBT buzzword" and how certain messages have "gone too far", undermining the values and philosophy that institutions and activists stand for. Similar to a same-age respondent in Antwerp, who ironically depicted the new rainbow-branding of the pedestrian zone in Borgerhout as pointless, the one in Dortmund complained about the double standards applied to Muslims and other Germans (clearly non-white citizens) while referring to the "politicisation of the rainbow armband in German football".

> Do we really think that [wearing a rainbow armband for football matches] is going to support LGBT rights? Those who say do not bring religion and ethnicities into sport are now imposing a certain message which legitimises sexual differences? . . . I always talk with my friends about how LGBTs are looked at badly. Everyone has a duty to respect them [but] it is also different when you, as a non-Muslim, discuss and criticise LGBT; the debate is much calmer and critical viewpoints are more likely to be accepted than when I, a Muslim, discuss and criticise LGBTs. In that situation, everyone says – 'of course, you are Muslim!'

Among the four groups of interviewees, two dilemmas of (post)modernity (Berger 1977:70) arise clearly. First, "individuation" – namely, the separation of the individual from any sense of the collective entity; second, the "liberation" of fate over choices in the realm of everyday life. Respectively, these two dilemmas are clearly experienced while respondents navigate between personal worldviews and the Muslim community in their place of residence and parental country of origin. While attempting to come to terms with respecting everyone's choice, female interviewees in Dortmund also admitted to having struggled to comply with gendered division within their family and the Muslim Albanian community. While most argue that Muslim women with migration heritage struggle more than German women or other German-looking second generations, such as Americans, Dutch and Russians, only one woman spells out the actual issue at stake: patriarchy and gendered performance.

In European studies, Albanian men are often referred to as "violent, primitive, traditional and patriarchal" (Schwandner-Sievers 2003), ascribing upon women the role and status of mothers bearing children – boys in particular (Çaro et al. 2018:51). Moreover, a combination of misleading and overlapping tropes of the veiled, oppressed and mysterious Muslima (Muslim woman), the head-covered "pious mother" and "ultimate proletariat" (Byrd 2017:18; Neuberger 2004:117–119), contributed to reinforce the seemingly hidden layers of oppression upon the second-classed Albanian and Roma citizens since the time of Yugoslavia (Rexhepi 2023:48). Patriarchal values marked the sudden emancipation of women during socialism (Mančić 2020:87), and the legacies of traditional norms and heteronormative roles have been transferred after the emigration experiences passed down across generations. Hence, most patriarchal values and the subjective sense of superior masculinity clearly depend on the social fabric of regions, cities and villages where the parents of the German-born generation of Albanian Muslims come from (Çaro et al. 2018:51). In Bremen, two sisters lamented the fact that in their "Albanian family . . . men treat women differently and mix up culture with religion [and vice versa] to convince [them] that 'this is Islam'". However, they were conscious of the fact that "this was not really Islam". In Dortmund, another younger respondent explained feeling the pressure of "get[ting] a husband and having kids [because] the older you get, the more they talk about this". As discussed in Chapter 2, this specific condition not only relates to Muslim identity, but is precisely inscribed on the bodies of Muslim women, reducing "women" to their specific positionality of specifically gender-coded experiences in public and political affairs (Mansbridge 1991:133).

Tellingly, male respondents were also found to be outspoken about family-laden dynamics, yet were discussing things from a different perspective. A married male respondent pointed out that it "would be unlikely for a Muslim Albanian woman [to have] male friends", and that it "is harder for women than men" to live as a Muslim in Germany. Most interview insights among male Albanian Muslims resulted in discussing the role of women through the prism of stereotypes that German society ascribes to them in general, but to Albanian families as well.

> "There is always a cliché about the Albanians and the Turks, and how we do not respect women – they do not say it openly, but you feel it".
>
> "Germans misunderstand how we treat women at home. One of my aunts is married to a German man, and he was surprised to see how women were in charge of the house during festivities and dinners . . . that atmosphere dispelled some of his stereotypes".
>
> "On social media, there are jokes targeting the looks of 'Albanian women' and especially about the infidelity of 'young Albanian women'. I think this is given by the fact that Albanians are loyal just to Albanians and no one else, so perhaps these stereotypes are the result of some negative experiences with Albanians here and there".

During participation-observation, mosques remained a physically divided space between men and women, dominated by (hegemonic) male norms. In Antwerp, the Bosnian cultural centre spatially constitutes the social network where common language, cultural practices and experiences make it easier for people to gather and worship. During a youth-organised *iftar* evening, tasks and the praying space were not strictly divided along gender lines: while sharing the same space during prayer time, men just stepped ahead of women.

After breaking the fasting, both young males and females helped each other while organising the tables, handing out food and sitting next to each other. A few days later, I attended an open *iftar* evening organised by the local Albanian Muslim community. However, I could not help but notice that no women from the Albanian diaspora were present among the participants.

## References

Allievi, S. (2017) *Conversioni: verso un nuovo modo di credere? Europa, Pluralismo, Islam* [Conversions: Towards a New Way of Believing? Europe, Pluralism, Islam]. Napoli: Guida Editori.

Amer, A. (2018) When Racialised Assumptions Don't Fit: White Muslims and the Contestation of Threat, October 24th, *LSE Blog*. Available at: https://blogs.lse.ac.uk/religionglobalsociety/2018/10/when-racialised-assumptions-dont-fit-white-muslims-and-the-contestation-of-threat/ (Accessed: 20 April 2021)

Amer, A. and Howarth, C. (2018) Constructing and Contesting Threat: Representations of White British Muslims across British National and Muslim Newspapers. *European Journal of Social Psychology*, 48, pp. 614–628. https://doi.org/10.1002/ejsp.2352

Andriof, J., Waddock, S., Husted, B. and Rahman, S. (2002) *Unfolding Stakeholder Thinking: Theory, Responsibility and Engagement*. Sheffield: Greenleaf.

Asad, T. (2003) *Formations of the Secular. Christianity, Islam, Modernity*. Stanford: Stanford University Press.

Atasanov, S. (2023) Bulgarian Arrested for Terrorist Attack Plot in Belgium, *BNR – Radio Bulgaria*. Available at: https://bnr.bg/en/post/101801266/bulgarian-arrested-for-terrorist-attack-plot-in-belgium#:~:text=A%20Bulgarian%20citizen%20 (Accessed: 30 March 2023)

Azabar, S. and Van Aelst, P. (2023) Religion Works in Different Ways: An Intersectional Approach to Muslims' Noninstitutionalized Participation. *Acta Politica*, 59, pp. 416–438. https://doi.org/10.1057/s41269-023-00300-y

Bakić-Hayden, M. (1995) Nesting Orientalisms: The Case of Former Yugoslavia. *Slavic Review*, 54 (4), pp. 917–931. https://doi.org/10.2307/2501399

Bangel, C. (2019) Neo-Nazis: The Baseball Bat Years, *Zeit Online*. Availbale at: www.zeit.de/gesellschaft/2019-11/neo-nazis-youth-east-germany-after-berlin-wall-english (Accessed: 19 May 2023)

Basheska, E. and Kochenov, D. (2024) Migration and Citizenship in Europe – Does 'Illiberalism' Matter? Eurowhiteness Solidarity from the EU and Hungary to the UK, *The Centre on Migration, Policy & Society*. Available at: https://papers.ssrn.com/sol3/papers.cfm?abstract_id=4742900 (Accessed: 12 April 2024)

Berger, P. (1977) *Facing Up to Modernity: Excursion in Society, Politics and Religion*. New York: Basics Book.

Bobako, M. (2015) Inventing Muslims in Europe. Religion, Culture and Identity in the Time of Neoliberalism. *Przegląd Religioznawczy – The Religious Studies Review*, 4 (258), pp. 43–55.

Bobako, M. (2017) The Palestinian Knot: The 'New Anti-Semitism', Islamophobia and the Question of Postcolonial Europe. *Theory, Culture and Society*, 35 (3), pp. 99–120. https://doi.org/10.1177/0263276417708859

Bougarel, X. (2008) 'Balkan Muslim Diasporas and the Idea of a European Islam', in T. Dulić, R. Kostić, R., I. Maček, and J. Trtak (eds.) *Balkan Currents. Essays in Honour of Kjell Magnusson*. Uppsala: Uppsala University Press, pp. 147–165.

Bringa, T. (1995) *Being Muslim the Bosnian Way: Identity and Community in a Central Bosnian Village*. Princeton: Princeton University Press.

Byrd, J. D. (2017) *Islam in a Post-Secular Society. Religion, Secularity and the Antagonism of Recalcitrant Faith*. Leiden and Boston: Brill.

Çaro, E., Bailey, A. and Van Wissen, L. (2018) 'I Am the God of the House': How Albanian Rural Men Shift Their Performance of Masculinities in the City. *Journal of Balkan and Near Eastern Studies*, 20 (1), pp. 49–65. https://doi.org/10.1080/19448953.2017.1375272

Carrim, N. and Paruk, Z. (2020) Do We or Don't We? Muslim Women Wearing the Hijab in the South African Work Environment. *Journal of Religion in Africa*, 50 (1/2), pp. 11–31.

Cavenaugh, K. (2018) 'Policing the Public Sphere: Regulating Religion in Europe', in A. Biró (ed.) *Populism, Memory and Minority Rights. Central and Eastern European Issues in Global Perspectives*, Leiden: Brill, pp. 313–341.

Ceretti, A. and Cornelli, R. (2018) *Oltre la Paura. Affrontare il Tema della Sicurezza in Modo Democratico* [Beyond Fear. Facing the Issue of Securty in a Democratic World]. Milano: Feltrinelli.

Cesari, J. (2013) *Why the West Fears Islam. An Exploration of Muslims in Liberal Democracies*. New York: Palgrave Macmillan.

Colic-Peisker, V. (2005) At Least You Are the Right Colour: Identity and Social Inclusion of Bosnian Refugees in Australia. *Journal of Ethnic and Migration Studies*, 31 (4), pp. 615–638. https://doi.org/10.1080/13691830500109720

De Giorgi, E., Cavalieri, A. and Feo, F. (2023) From Opposition Leader to Prime Minister: Giorgia Meloni and Women's Issues in the Italian Radical Right. *Politics and Governance*, 11 (1), pp. 108–118. https://doi.org/10.17645/pag.v11i1.6042

Della Porta, D. and Diani, M. (2006) *Social Movements. An Introduction*. Malden, MA: Blackwell.

Easat-Daas, A. (2020) *Muslim Women's Political Participation in France and Belgium*. Cham: Palgrave Macmillan.

El-Tayeb, F. (2011) *European Others: Queering Ethnicity in Postnational Europe*. Minneapolis: University of Minnesota Press.

El-Tayeb, F. (2012) 'Gays Who Cannot Properly Be Gay': Queer Muslims in the Neoliberal European City. *European Journal of Women's Studies*, 19 (1), pp. 79–95. https://psycnet.apa.org/doi/10.1177/1350506811426388

Ferizaj, A. (2019) Othering Albanian Muslim Masculinities: A Case Study of Albanian Football Players. *OCCHIALÌ – Rivista sul Mediterraneo Islamico*, 5, pp. 71–93.

Ferizaj, A. (2023) The Desperate Desire to Be Europeans, *Kosovo 2.0*. Available at: https://kosovotwopointzero.com/en/the-desperate-desire-to-be-european/ (Accessed: 3 December 2023)

Fileva, L. (2023) *Активността в ромските секции не донесе на никоя партия силен резултат* [The Participation in the Roma Polling Stations Did Not Bring Any Party a Strong Result]. Available at: www.dnevnik.bg/izbori-2023/2023/04/04/4468216_aktivnostta_v_romskite_sekcii_ne_donese_na_nikoia/ (Accessed: 25 April 2023)

Finkelstein, K. (2023) *Moderne Muslimas – Kindheit – Karriere – Klischees* [Modern Muslim Women – Childhood – Carries – Stereotypes]. Berlin: Verlagshaus Jacoby & Stuart.

Flandersnew.be (2023) Antwerp Police Find No Evidence of Threat to Iftar Event, Mayor Slams Organisers, *Flandersnew.be*. Available at: www.vrt.be/vrtnws/en/2023/03/28/antwerp-police-find-no-evidence-of-threat-to-iftar-event-mayor/#:~:text=ISOPIX-,Antwerp%20police%20find%20no%20evidence%20of%20threat%20to%20Iftar%20event,Borgerhout%20district%20of%20the%20city (Accessed: 28 March 2023)

Fleischmann, F. and Phalet, K. (2018) Religion and National Identification in Europe: Comparing Muslim Youth in Belgium, England, Germany, the Netherlands, and Sweden. *Journal of Cross-Cultural Psychology*, 49 (1) pp. 44–61. https://doi.org/10.1177/0022022117741988

Gasparini, G. J. (2022) I Musulmani dagli Occhi Azzurri. L'Islam Liberale dei Bosniaci di Piacenza [Blue-Eyed Muslims. The Liberal Islam of the Bosnians in Piacenza], *Corriere Padano.* Available at: www.corrierepadano.it/i-musulmani-dagli-occhi-azzurri-lislam-liberale-dei-bosniaci-di-piacenza/ (Accessed: 10 November 2022)

Geisser, V. (2014) 'Islamophobia in Europe: From the Christian anti-Muslim Prejudice to a Modern form of Racism, Keynote Speech', in I. Ramberg (ed.) *Islamophobia and Its Consequences on Young People.* Budapest: European Youth Centre Budapest, pp. 29–35. Available at: www.coe.int/en/web/youth/-/islamophobia-and-its-consequences-on-young-people?inheritRedirect=true (Accessed: 12 December 2022).

Gerlach, J. (2006) *Zwischen Pop und Dschihad. Muslimische Jugendliche in Deutschland Frankfurt* [Between Pop and Jihad. Muslim Young People in Frankfurt, Germany]. Berlin: Verlag Ch. Links.

Grünenberg, K. (2005) Constructing "Sameness" and "Otherness": Bosnian Diasporic Experiences in a Danish Context. *Balkanologie – Reveu d'études pluridisciplinaires,* IX (1–2), pp. 173–193. https://doi.org/10.4000/balkanologie.587

Halilovich, H., Hasić, J., Karabegović, D., Karamehić-Muratović, A. and Oruč, N. (2018) *Mapping the Bosnian-Herzegovinian Diaspora (BiH Migrants in Australia, Austria, Denmark, Germany, Italy, Netherlands, Slovenia, Sweden, Switzerland, and the United States of America): Utilizing the Socio-Economic Potential of the Diaspora for Development of BiH.* Available at: www.mhrr.gov.ba/PDF/MAPPING%20BIH%20DIASPORA%20REPORT.pdf (Accessed: 10 May 2023).

Harris, S. and Nawaz, M. (2015) *Islam and the Future of Tolerance. A Dialogue.* Cambridge, MA: Harvard University Press.

Hess, M. and Korf, B. (2014) Tamil Diaspora and the Political Spaces of Second-Generation Activism in Switzerland. *Global Networks,* 14 (4), pp. 419–437. https://doi.org/10.1111/glob.12052

Hurd, S. (2008) *The Politics of Secularism in International Relations.* Princeton: Princeton University Press.

Izetbegović, A. (1990) Islamic Declaration, *Sarajevo.* Available at: https://archive.org/details/3IslamicDeclarationEng/mode/2up?view=theater (Accessed: 3 October 2022).

Jomo, K. S. (1992) *Islamic Economic Alternatives: Critical Perspectives and New Directions.* London: Macmillan Academic and Professional.

Jones, H. S. (2021) *Islam and the Liberal State. National Identity and the Future of Muslim Britain.* London: I.B. Tauris.

Kancler, T. (2021) 'Speaking against the Void: Decolonial Transfeminist Relations and Radical Potentialities', in R. Koobak, M. Tlostanova, and S. Thapar-Björkert (eds.) *Postcolonial and Postsocialist Dialogues. Intersections, Opacities, Challenges in Feminist Theorizing and Practice.* London: Routledge, pp. 155–170.

Karabegović, D. (2014) Sto Te Nema? Transnational Cultural Production in the Diaspora in Response to the Srebrenica Genocide. *Nationalism and Ethnic Politics,* 20 (4), pp. 455–475. https://doi.org/10.1080/13537113.2014.969151

Karabegović, D. (2019) Who Chooses to Remember? Diaspora Participation in Memorialization Initiatives. *Ethnic and Racial Studies,* 42 (11), pp. 1911–1929. https://doi.org/10.1080/01419870.2019.1577473

Khan, T. (2022) *Muslim, Actually. How Islam Is Misunderstood and Why It Matters.* London: Atlantic Books.

Khankan, S. (2018) *Women Are the Future of Islam. A Memoir of Hope.* London: Penguin.

Khiari, S. (2016) 'The People and the Third People', in A. Badiou, P. Bourdieu, J. Butler, G. Didi-Huberman, S. Khiari, and J. Rancière (eds.) *What is A People?* New York: Columbia University Press, pp. 87–100.

Koinova, M. and Karabegović, D. (2016) Diasporas and Transitional Justice: Transnational Activism From Local to Global Levels of Engagement. *Global Networks*, 17, pp. 212–233. https://doi.org/10.1111/glob.12128

Korenkov, O., Balatska, O. and Rashchupkina, Y. (2022) Separatism and Jihadism: Interaction in the Context of Terrorist Activity. *Studia Polityczne*, 50 (2), pp. 111–138. https://doi.org/10.35757/STP.2022.50.2.05

Kwon, R. and Hughes, E. (2018) Multiculturalist Policies in an Age of Imimigration: Do Multiculturalist Policies Influence Negative Immigrant Attitudes toward Homosexuality? *Ethnicities*, 18 (5), pp. 655–691. https://doi.org/10.1177/1468796817752013

Law, I., Easat-Daas, A., Merali, A. and Sayyid, S. (2019) *Countering Islamophobia in Europe*. Cham, Switzerland: Springer.

Leiken, R. (2012) *Europe's Angry Muslims: The Revolt of The Second Generation*. Oxford: Oxford University Press.

Mančić, I. (2020) Outside the Memories We Belong, Women of Yugoslavia. *Journal of Politics, Gender and Culture*, 17 (1–2), pp. 82–88. https://doi.org/10.51151/identities.v17i2-3.460

Mansbridge, J. (1991) 'Democracy, Deliberation and the Experience of Women', in B. Murchland (ed.) *Higher Education and the Practice of Democratic Politics: A Political Education Reader*. Dayton: Kettering Foundation, pp. 122–135.

Mansbridge, J. (2003) Anti-Statism and Difference Feminism in International Social Movements. *International Feminist Journal of Politics*, 5 (3), pp. 355–360. https://doi.org/10.1080/1461674032000122713

Mark, J., Iacob, B., Rupprecht, T. and Spaskovska, L. (2019) *1989. A Global History of Eastern Europe*. Cambridge: Cambridge University Press.

Marramao, G. (2012) *The Passage West. Philosophy after the Nation State*. New York: Verso.

Mbembe, A. (2019) *Necropolitics*. Durham and London: Duke University Press.

Merdjanova, I. (2013) *Rediscovering the Umma. Muslims in the Balkans between Nationalism and Transnationalism*. Oxford: Oxford University Press.

Metodieva, A. (2020) The Radical Milieu and Radical Influencers of Bosnian Foreign Fighters. *Studies in Conflict & Terrorism*, 46 (9), pp. 1725–1744. https://doi.org/10.1080/1057610X.2020.1868097

Mishev, M. (2023) Къде е бъдещето на ромското движение? [Where Is the Future of Roma Movement], *дВЕРСИЯ*. Accessbile at: https://dversia.net/7549/romsko-dvizhenie/?fbclid=IwAR1aKwQriqD6ud6mlgswvha5ha-ojxrET5dOcP6ZddUHe6sCsi0mK7pdyrQ (Accessed: 14 May 2023)

Mullol Marin, A. (2023) 'Islamophobia in Italy', in E. Bayraklı and F. Hafez (eds.) *European Islamophobia Report 2022*. Vienna: Leopold Weiss Institute, pp. 347–363.

Mushaben, J. M. (2008) Gender, HipHop and Pop-Islam: The Urban Identities of Muslim Youth in Germany. *Citizenship Studies*, 12 (5), pp. 507–526. https://doi.org/10.1080/13621020802337931

Neuberger, M. (2004) *The Orient Within: Muslim Minorities and the Negotiation of Nationhood in Bulgaria*. Ithaca and London: Cornell University Press.

Orr-Ewing, F. and Orr-Ewing, A. (2002) *Holy Warriors. A Fresh Look at the Face of Extreme Islam*. Bletchley: Authentic.

O'Toole, T., DeHanas, D., Nilsson, H., Dilwar, K. and Malik, M. (2013) *Taking Part: Muslim Participation in Contemporary Governance*. Bristol: University of Bristol.

Özyürek, E. (2015) *Being German, becoming Muslim: Race, Religion, and Conversion in the New Europe*. Oxford: Princeton University Press.

Peyrard, C. (2017) *Politique, religion et laïcité* [Politics, Religion and Laicism]. Aix-en-Provence: Presses universitaires de Provence.

Piela, A. and Krotofil, J. (2023) White Habitus among Polish White Female Converts to Islam. *Sociology of Religion: A Quarterly Review*, 84 (1), pp. 72–94. https://doi.org/10.1093/socrel/srac021

Posłuszny, Ł. (2019) 'Memory, Landscape and Biography: Non-Places and Sites of Perished Communities', in A. Haapala, B. Frydryczak, and M. Salwa (eds.) *Moving from Landscapes to Cityscapes and Back: Theoretical and Applied Approaches to Human Environments*. Łódź: Officyna Publishing House, pp. 59–72.

Rexhepi, P. (2015) Mainstreaming Islamophobia: The Politics of European Enlargement and the Balkan Crime-Terror Nexus. *East European Quarterly*, 43 (2–3), pp. 189–214. Available at SSRN: https://ssrn.com/abstract=2706058

Rexhepi, P. (2023) *White Enclosures. Racial Capitalism & Coloniality along the Balkan Route*. New York: Duke University Press.

Rippin, A. (2001) *Muslims. Their Religious Beliefs and Practices*. London: Routledge.

Robinson-Bertoni, S. (2017) Re-Territorializing Religiosity in Wholesome Muslim Praxis. *Religions*, 8 (7), pp. 1–31. https://doi.org/10.3390/rel8070132

Rose, M. (2021) *A World after Liberalism: Philosophers of the Radical Right*. New Haven: Yale University Press.

Roy, O. (2005) The Crisis of the Secular State and the New Forms of Religious Expression, *France Diplomatique*. Available at: www.diplomatie.gouv.fr/IMG/pdf/0101Roy_gb.pdf (Accessed: 19 October 2021)

Roy, O. (2013) Secularism and Islam: The Theological Predicament. *The International Spectator: Italian Journal of International Affairs*, 48 (1), pp. 5–19.

Rubin, H. J. and Rubin, I. S. (1992) *Community Organizing and Development*. New York: Macmillan.

Sadriu, B. (2017) Grasping the Syrian War, a View from Albanians in the Balkans. *The Journal of Nationalism and Ethnicity*, 45 (4), pp. 540–559. https://doi.org/10.1080/00905992.2017.1292498

Sahadžić, M. (2021) Bosnian Diaspora in Belgium (and beyond), *Online Lecture at the University of Antwerp* (Accessed: 9 March 2023).

Sanctorum, J. (2023) Geen iftar voor holebi's: moslims cancelen 'inclusief' feestje. *Doorbraak*?Availableat:https://doorbraak.be/geen-iftar-voor-holebis-moslims-cancelen-inclusief-feestje/ (Accessed: 30 March 2023)

Schwandner-Sievers, S. (2003) 'Albanians, Albanianism and the Strategic Subversion of Stereotypes', in A. Hammond (ed.) *The Balkans and the West*. Ashgate: Aldershot, pp. 46–64.

Scott, T. (2005) *The Global Resurgence of Religion and the Transformation of International Relations. The Struggle for the Soul of the Twenty-First Century*. New York: Palgrave Macmillam.

Smits, A. (2023) 'Islamophobia in Belgium', in E. Bayraklı and F. Hafez (eds.) *European Islamophobia Report 2022*. Vienna, Leopold Weiss Institute, pp. 83–106.

Sofos, Spyros A. and Tsagarousianou, R. (2013) *Islam in Europe. Public Spaces and Civic Networks*. New York: Palgrave Macmillian.

Teitelbaum, B. (2020) *War for Eternity: Inside Bannon's Far-Right Circle of Global Power Brokers*. London: Penguin.

The Economist (May–June 2021) *Gay People Are Reclaiming an Islamic Heritage*. Available at: www.economist.com/middle-east-and-africa/2021/05/27/gay-people-are-reclaiming-an-islamic-heritage (Accessed: 10 June 2021)

Tibi, B. (2002) Leitkultur als Wertekonsens. Bilanz einer missglückten deutschen Debatte, *Bundeszentrale für politische Bildung*. Available at: www.bpb.de/shop/zeitschriften/apuz/26535/leitkultur-als-wertekonsens/#:~:text=Leitkultur%20als%20Wertekonsens%20Bilanz%20einer%20missgl%C3%BCckten%20deutschen%20Debatte&text=Im%20Rahmen%20eines%20Versuchs%2C%20eine,jede%20Gro%C3%9Fgruppe%20eine%20kollektive%20Identit%C3%A4t (Accessed: 10 May 2023)

Tlostanova, M. and Mignolo, W. (2012) *Learning to Unlearn: Decolonial Reflections from Eurasia and the Americas*. Columbus: Ohio State University Press.

Torrekens, C. (2021) The Non-Impact of Religious Practices on the Process of Inclusion and Participation of Belgian Muslims. *Journal of Muslim Minority Affairs*, 41 (1), pp. 141–156. https://doi.org/10.1080/13602004.2021.1894384

Triadafilopoulos, T. (2011) Illiberal Means to Liberal Ends? Understanding Recent Immigrant Integration Policies in Europe. *Journal of Ethnic and Migration Studies*, 37 (6), pp. 861–880. https://doi.org/10.1080/1369183X.2011.576189

Trupia, F. (2022) 'Speaking of Race in Bulgaria', in N. Chanta-Martin, I. Briscu, and F. Trupia (eds.) *Balkans of Colour. A Handbook for Decolonial Encounters*. Gabrovo: Forum for Glocal Change, pp. 27–30. Available at: https://glocalchange.org/2022/08/10/balkans-of-colour-a-handbook-for-decolonial-encounters/ (Accessed: 25 November 2022)

Trupia, F. (2024) 'Beyond Multiculturalism. Minority Intellectuals in the Postsocialist Predicament of Southeast Europe', in S. Petkovska (ed.) *Decolonial Politics in European Peripheries*. London: Routledge, pp. 129–144. https://doi.org/10.4324/9781003246848-12

Van Deth, J. W. (2016) 'What Is Political Participation?', in *Oxford Research Encyclopedia of Politics*. Oxford: Oxford University Press. https://doi.org/10.1093/acrefore/9780190228637.013.68

Van Leuven, A., Mertens, S., D'Haenens, L. and Mekki-Benada, A. (2023) 'The Political and Intellectual Discourse on Islam and Muslims in Flanders', in L. d'Haenens and A. Mekki-Berrada (eds.) *Islamophobia as a Form of Radicalisation. Perspectives on Media, Academia and Socio-political Scapes from Europe and Canada*. Leuven: Leuven University Press, pp. 59–74.

Van Renterghem, B. (2023) Organisatoren afgelaste 'Queer Iftar': 'Wij vragen niet eens respect, gewoon het recht om te mogen bestaan', *Staandard*. Available at: www.standaard.be/cnt/dmf20230322_95754178 (Accessed: 22 March 2023)

Yuval-Davis, N. (2011) 'Power, Intersectionality and the Politics of Belonging', in W. Harcourt (ed.) *The Palgrave Handbook of Gender and Development*. London: Palgrave Macmillan, pp. 367–381. https://doi.org/10.1007/978-1-137-38273-3_25

Zubair, A. (2023) 'Islamophobia in Germany', in E. Bayraklı and F. Hafez (eds.) *European Islamophobia Report 2022*. Vienna: Leopold Weiss Institute, pp. 261–284.

# 7 City(zens) of Silence

After the rapid industrialisation of the 1950s, Western Europe's post-industrial societies became home to Muslim populations arriving from Yugoslavia and Eastern Europe, among others. Intensively recruited as a temporary foreign workforce, most "guest workers" (in German, *Gastarbeiter*) helped reconstruct and eventually contribute to the take-off of post-war national economies. Many decided to stay and reunite with their families in "the West", thereby continuing to live as inconspicuous members of religious minority groups – something they were used to under socialism. Although they were not particularly exposed to anti-migration discourse and far-right violence, West Germany imposed a recruitment ban (in German, *Anwerbestopp*) in 1973 (Canan and Foroutan 2016:162). Austria followed in 1979 with a reenactment of the law introduced to govern "guest workers" from Socialist Yugoslavia and Turkey.

By the 1980s, about 63,000 and 58,000 Albanians and Bosniaks, respectively, resided outside Yugoslavia. According to the 1953 population census in Yugoslavia, many had Muslim family backgrounds, while 93.6% of Albanians and 97.7% of those living in Macedonia had declared to be either active or passive members of Islamic religious communities (Bougarel 2008:3). At the end of the 1990s, a similar pattern could be discerned for over 1 million Muslims from the Balkans who were displaced and expelled to various countries of the European Union in the wake of the dissolution of socialism and the Yugoslavian wars in particular. Muslims comprised around 665,000 Bosniaks and 380,000 Albanians from Kosovo and today's North Macedonia. Another 800,000 from Albania proper (a quarter of the total population) left the country for Greece (500,000), Italy (200,000), and other European countries (50,000), joining the other 20,000 Turks from the Thrace region (Merdjanova 2013:104; Bougarel 2005:5; Mai and Schwandner-Siever 2003:941), along with those 360,000 Muslims and Turks who fled Bulgaria in the wake of the Communist assimilation campaign (see Kamusella 2019).

As mentioned previously in Chapter 4, a sense of homeliness and strangeness was captured among respondents. At the same time, however, their attachment towards their birthplace and the Balkans fades away at times, and it is only nurtured by a range of pragmatic attitudes towards space and Islam.

DOI: 10.4324/9781003589624-8

The latter and the former overlap, providing yet another vantage angle of investigation. If Chapter 5 shows that most respondents rely on a space of mutuality and support to comply with *halal* rigour, a further triangulation of this qualitative data with field notes confirms that Islamophobia shifts gears spatially. In other words, Islamophobia hits the so-called "*halal* neighbourhoods" the hardest by exploiting the already-existing issues of (post-) migrant urban space to depict Islam as an obstacle to the development of the city and as a threat to liberal democracy. Within Muslim-majority neighbourhoods or where people with migration background reside, Islamophobia resonates with Frantz Fanon's description of the colonised "zone of non-being" – namely:

> a place of ill fame, peopled by men of evil repute . . . born there, it matters not where, or how. It is a world without spaciousness; men live there on top of each other, and their huts are built one on top of another . . . it is a town of niggers and dirty Arabs.
>
> (1967:20)

Undoubtedly, it is no longer plausible or feasible from a scholarly standpoint to keep a space-blind approach to the different manifestations of Islamophobia across Europe. During the fieldwork, a *glance inward* the neighbourhoods under observation debunks the idea that infra-/inner city problems are to be primarily attributed to the widespread presence of Islam and the growing number of Muslims in migrant urban spaces (Roy 2013). Instead, it was noticed that gentrification thrives within "Muslim neighbourhoods". Under the guise of modernisation and innovation, gentrification echoes far-right and anti-Muslim discourse by advocating untapped potentials within problematic urban migrant spaces, thereby evincing a logic of nesting inequalities and self-exclusion that stem from the archaic, rural and peripheral customs of Muslim residents.

This final chapter addresses the under-researched nexus of young people with a migration background living in multicultural neighbourhoods (Driezen 2023:15) where the most significant manifestations of gentrification go hand in hand with subtle expressions of Islamophobia. Inspired by Antonio Gramsci's paradox of Italian "cities of silence" (1971:90–92), the fieldwork sites were not chosen as particular "ethnic enclaves" of European cities (Bunse 2019), where potential respondents might suffer much harsher economic disadvantages and inequalities than political alienation and marginalisation. Nor were they believed to be "the crucibles of secularisation" (Driezen 2023:34) where newcomers would relinquish their religious beliefs and practices due to modernisation and urbanisation. If anything, neighbourhoods were understood as constituting a new geography of religious space in which spirituality retains a significant role (Najib and Teeple Hopkins 2020:42). As discussed throughout Chapter 5, the most significant manifestations of capitalism and forms of exploitation stemmed from the ways Islamophobia manifests itself spatially, thereby shaping inner-city "migrant areas" and the so-called "*halal* neighbourhoods".

These areas are being restructured by the uncontrolled growth of investments. The consequent extension of consumption, dilution and pollution, driven by gentrification, couples with the movement of higher-income households into lower-income neighbourhoods (Swanstrom and Plöger 2022), uprooting any spirit of sociality and conviviality in the name of "innovation" (Bourriaud 2002). The following sections aim to show that Muslim-majority areas of cities are being changed and transformed, not only by new physical materialities and related investments resulting from gentrification, but also by a spatialised Islamophobia (Najib 2022) taking inroads simultaneously through all levels – e.g., education, housing, the job market, surveillance media and so forth (Sant'Angelo 2004:58). This twofold process develops on the "entanglements" or "intertwinings" of anti-Muslim discourse and violence into urban spaces and their Muslim inhabitants (Najib 2022:47, Najib and Teeple Hopkins 2020:51). Therefore, this chapter contends that gentrification and Islamophobia occur reciprocally; hence, both follow one other and develop into new forms of inequality and the urban breakdown of social ties between the core (white) society and the peripheral (Muslim) suburbs.

## The City and its Discontents

Urbanisation has not simply been synonymous with diversity and transformation. At its very core, "a city in the making" has also conceived the idea of dwellers fostering, holding and nurturing multiple relations to enhance the circulation of ideas, materials and practices, which also encompasses leisure time, religious faith, community spirit and so forth (Glenn and Weedon 1995; Thorstensen et al. 2021; Aboumaliq 2010; Allievi 2017). With cities becoming more multicultural, people have come together to seek a sense of community, affirm their culture and feel more at home as a coping mechanism after the experience of (forced) migration.

European cities have been stratified and developed around living streets and quarters thanks to ethnic restaurants and shops where day-to-day business is conducted in Chinese, Arabic, Turkish and other non-European languages. "Balkan corners" or "Balkan areas" are also present, albeit inconspicuous or assimilated into much bigger diaspora communities. They have all contributed to the transformation of the post-industrial cityscapes in France (Leiken 2012), Belgium (Devaux 2017) and Germany (Swanstrom and Plöger 2022), producing a multiplicity of spatiality (King 2004:57–60) that has constantly transformed the urban context. The so-called "ethnic quarters" – whose organisation deepens on apparent self-sufficiency from the core society – have taken the name of *globurbs* because of the highly fragmented and contiguous worlds that they constitute from within the city. By definition, Anthony King (2004:103) gives validity to such a term for having identified forms and settlements on the outskirts of the city, the origin of which – be it economic, social, cultural, or architectural – is generated less by developments inside the city, or even inside the country, and more by external forces beyond its boundaries. Among others, migratory and global capital flows generate such globurbs.

At the roots of the cluster of post-colonial studies, social scientists and geographers pay attention to the strongly interwoven interrelations between physical, spatial, symbolic, visual and material environments with culture, identity, ethnicity and religion in everyday life (Knox and Pinch 2010; King 2004:57; Lefebvre 1991). Yet these relationships between urban spaces and their inhabitants are increasingly complex due to the impact of gentrification on (post) migrant and racialised communities, and the growth of racial capitalism and its financialised economy (Bale 2021). Although the literature shows how neoliberal restructuring and rescaling of cities depend on the parallel phenomena of capital accumulation and global migration (Schiller and Ayse 2009:177–178), the discourse over gentrification remains vague and wide. The phenomenon is in itself complex, and the term would be used to refer to much more than simply the movement of higher-income households into lower-income neighbourhoods (Swanstrom and Plöger 2022:527). In this regard, the interrelation of the power struggle over gentrifiers and inhabitants has been largely under-addressed (Erkan 2022:19).

After Islam emerged as an urban practice embedded in transnational networks, Muslim organisations began playing a role in the political and public sphere by operating as welfare providers and important civil society actors that could activate collective mobilisation. In the post-9/11 era, a wealth of pressing issues regarding Muslims and Islam have exacerbated public anxiety over Islamist extremism, urban disorders and terrorist attacks (Najib 2022:42). Hence, "being Muslim" in the banlieues of Paris or the working-class estate of Malmö's Rosengård changes from the daily experiences of "being Muslim" in a more affluent middle-class suburb of West London or the centre of Frankfurt in Germany. Moreover, "no-go zones" have dominated headlines, and Muslim-majority urban spaces have quickly been considered the hotbed of radicals, rioters and terrorists. Samuel Huntington contended that Islamic radicalisation is both a product of and an effort to come to grips with modernisation, which undermines traditional village and clan ties, leading to alienation and identity crises (mentioned in Leiken 2012:198). That said, new studies rebut Huntington's approach. The continuously changing urban fabric of super-diverse cities is driven by global processes of transformation that are centrally paramount to understanding (and revisiting the history of) "the city" as a site of contention and protest (Driezen 2023:37, Domaradzka and Hamel 2024:3). In fact, "the city" has become the most appropriate scale level and framework for enabling people and groups with a migration background to participate in society actively.

In Belgium, for instance, Muslims have in the past effectively mobilised against the rise of far-right neopopulism. The assumed foreignness and incompatibility of Islam and Muslim minorities with Belgian culture (especially

Flemish) has gone hand in hand with the rise of the xenophobia and Islamophobia expressed by Vlaams Belang and other mainstream politicians (Sofos and Tsagarousianou 2013:88). However, what Henry Lefebvre theorised as a "right to the city" (1991), namely, an emancipatory struggle to unite and cultivate practices of community-based resistance against predatory capitalism, thereby reclaiming residential areas and defending the political agency, has recently been hijacked and instrumentally used by far-right parties and Islamophobes. This is what keeps young Muslims away from downtown and compartmentalises the social fabric through the *logic of continuous ghettos* (Marramao 2012:44) that in turn intensifies a sense of remoteness among the post-migrant generation of young Muslims and the core urban society (Fleischmann and Phalet 2018:47).

In all neighbourhoods where in-depth interviews were held, gentrification manifests itself as an aspect of spatialised Islamophobia. Ghent is instructive in this regard. Muslim Roma from Bulgaria are low-income residents of Sleepstraat and Dampoort, two migrant-majority areas where a certain urban binarism develops along the lines of "autochthonous" (native) and "allochtonen" (non-native) dwellers (Driezen 2023:4). Likewise, Northern Germany's problematic neighbourhoods are referred to as *kiez* – literally, "the hood", a word of possibly Slavic origin if compared with the Slovak *chyža*, which connotes orientalising and exclusivist imagery of Turks and Turkey. While the image of the country is associated with the figure of Recep Tayyip Erdoğan and his ideological stances contradicting secularism and, by extension, liberal democracy, the presence of the Turkish diaspora seems to pose an "Islamic challenge" to Germany and Europe as a whole (Hurd 2008:93). Similar intra-/inner-city dynamics were also observed in Antwerp and Dortmund, where Muslim communities are considered suspect (Najib and Teeple Hopkins 2020:452). In contrast, Piacenza and Warsaw do not have "Arab quarters" and "Muslim areas", yet derogatory and pejorative connotations are used to associate a given residential area with its density of immigrants and non-natives.

The participation-observation method came to show an urban crisis underway on the edge of most European cities. Here, the term "crisis" is used under its Greek etymological term *krísis*, from "krínein" – namely, "to separate" or "to discern," meaning the root of a "caesura" (Marramao 2012:115). This urban caesura not only reinforces the colonial discourse that Muslims do not belong to European cities and that their presence is conditional; it also highlights a racial discourse circulating around European cities that are already being driven by and connected with international economic and cultural processes. At the same time, it is deepening spatial and economic exclusion and increasing surveillance (Domaradzka and Hamel 2024:4) against those "unwanted citizens" in town.

Antonio Gramsci's historical analysis of urbanism provides a more sophisticated, albeit not theorised, approach to the theoretical and practical issues of urban transformation, modernisation and people's agglomeration. His quasi-ontological claims about the urban/rural dichotomy explain the appeal

*Figure 7.1* The Turkish Fatih Mosque overshadows the other minor local mosques of Bosnian and Albanian Muslims in the Gröpelingen. Photo by the author.

of his work in analysing the historical development of imperialism, colonisation and racialisation in Europe and Muslim-majority countries (see Khaldoun 2005). In his *Prison Notebooks* (1971), the Italian Marxist did not see the city as automatically synonymous with progress, modernisation and revolutionary politics (Urbinati 1998:378), nor with democracy, freedom and secularisation (Ekers et al. 2012:98). Gramsci referred to post-unification Italy's "cities of silence" to explain the historical struggle between hegemonic and subaltern forces from the great industrial cities in the North and the great rural agglomeration in the South, respectively. Hence, the paradox unfolds: both groups complement one another in a new urban type of living, which soon shapes a "city of silence" – meaning, a city with a glorious past but now of secondary importance, some of them little more than a village with a magnificent monumental centre as a relic of its bygone splendour, in which the newcomers are submerged, oppressed and crushed by the urban core society (Gramsci 1971:92). Gramsci's description of this paradox follows coherently the theory of hegemony, the role of subalterns and the formations of organic and traditional intellectuals on political and cultural grounds.

However, we can expand the horizon of philosophical investigation to foreground Europe's North/South migration trends and their implications for the issues of political representation of newcomers in today's liberal democracy. Just as the Italian "borgate" – literally, the residential areas on the edge of the city – received the great masses of labourers and landless peasants from economically exploited rural areas, so have today's peripheral neighbourhoods of most northern European cities become home to post-migrant generations and newcomers originally from Europe's southern and eastern states. Within today's cities of silence, newcomers are submerged, oppressed and crushed by the urban core society and its urban (hegemonic) ideology. The latter targets Muslims and newcomers in general as a "category of non-fellows" – a status given to the defeated, exploited racialised (non-)citizenry on the edge of the city, who cannot be part of the latter and have no rights to have rights (Mbembe 2019:27). As discussed in Chapter 2, this urban condition prevents most respondents from connecting with the *ummah*, lest the former be identified with the pleas of the latter (Rexhepi 2023). Islamophobia and gentrification intensify a pervasive caesura between the core society and the city's edges – be it Gröpelingen in Bremen, Rabat and Sleepstraat in Ghent, Durne and Borgerhout in Antwerp, and so forth. Within these neighbourhoods, Islamophobia stokes people's fear and heightened emotions while simultaneously gentrification attempts to reorder, manage and discipline "the Others". Islamophobia manifests itself at various interrelated spatial scales (e.g., global, nation, urban, neighbourhood, body and mind) by shaping new spatial settings through, and according to, the racial organising logics of modernity (Ali et al. 2023:81) coupled with gentrification.

## A Glance Inwards *the City*

After wrapping up an interview in Bremen, I stood across an unusual inscription sprayed on the wall of a middle school in Gröpelingen. The unusual combination of Latin and Cyrillic letters related some gossip from Bulgaria, apparently from 2022. Next to a red heart was written, "Aiin sleeps with Turks". That sprayed inscription was instructive to intercept a visual replication of Islamophobic tropes by those who are apparently already the target of ethnic-related stereotypes, reinforcing already-existing social class, race, migration or education determinants (Kazi 2015:119). That "semantic landscape" provided a sensitive diagnostics of the groups under study throughout the intense dynamics of urban transformation in superdiverse neighbourhoods such as Gröpelingen (Blommaert and Rampton 2011; Barni and Bagna 2008). Since images and representations are central to any study on the Muslimisation of urban areas (Thorstensen et al. 2021:4), that inscription shows how Islamophobia is spatialised - and self-reiterated (my emphasis) – at various scales: from the globe to the body and mind (Najib 2022:46), coupled with taboo topics, such as sex and ethnic markers (the Turks, often likened to Muslims) in a country like Bulgaria where Islamophobia has never really ceased influencing society at large.

*Figure 7.2* Graffiti in Gröpelingen, "Aiin sleeps with Turks". Photo by the author.

Another interesting vignette deserves to be recalled here. While waiting in Geempoort-Ghent on my train back to Antwerp, I decided to help myself to a *banitsa* – a typical Bulgarian pastry. A Bulgarian-coloured kiosk stood out in the cloudy weather, attracting my attention. Once inside, I noticed that the young person at the checkout spoke Turkish with his father while serving his primarily Bulgarian clients, apart from me. A piece of Qur'an hung on the wall, barely visible from the outside and ignored by the clients. The Cyrillic-inscribed menu and Bulgarian-coloured kiosk facade were strategically used to associate the pastry shop with "Bulgarian owners" in Ghent and transpose political and religious stigmatisation.

The vast array of publicly visible signs, billboards and advertisements were instructive in illuminating the complex, often ambivalent and rapidly evolving nature of the urban fabric and its plethora of identities. Thus, semantic landscapes are not simply bits and pieces of insignificant evidence placed, readjusted or occasionally hidden from the public eye (see Duncan and Duncan 2009). Although we avert our eyes from seeing what we do not want to see (Groys 2024), the appearance of details is not insignificant but rather an accurate angle of investigation into the nature and direction of social processes (Blommaert 2014; Scollon and Scollon 2003). Semantics and signifiers help us capture what is consciously kept hidden, thereby shining a light on symbols and signs of otherness. In the multi-sited fieldwork that this study relies on, visual ethnography was essential in grasping better knowledge "from below" (Swartz 1989; Angrosino 2007) to employ a less elitist and less Eurocentric approach toward the combination of visual indications and interview insights. This emic perspective more effectively reveals what respondents highly valued concerning "the city" (Stone 2013:26), helping the triangulation of data from specific yet different groups of respondents who might feel reluctant to reach out to, such as Muslim Roma originally from Bulgaria and the former Yugoslavia.

Although the neighbourhoods under observation were expected to generate similar patterns of gentrification, the specific conditions brought to light features and characteristics that defy the paradigms of migration, mobility and new widespread technologies of communication among residents of the groups under study (Blommaert 2014:2). During the fieldwork, the linguistic landscapes signalled the impact of urbanisation, especially in relation to evolving mobility, improved technology, globalising markets and alienation from politics – all instances that shine a light on inconspicuous "spatial practices" that can easily be explained and seen (Van Leuven et al. 2023:137).

Yet again, Antwerp and Dortmund are here instructive. As the Dutch capital of Belgian Flanders, Antwerp hosts projects of care for those who are excluded (Huybrechts et al. 2022:37) and considered incapable of responding to the mismatch of zoning plans and the current reality. Daily centres and NGOs were usually found within immigrant neighbourhoods, such as Borgerhout and Durne, both recipients of a large number of governmental projects (Hoops 2021:95). Meanwhile, anti-immigration stances and anti-Islam sentiments are rather palpable (Driezen 2023:3). In Germany, old post-industrial cities are

*Figure 7.3* The "banicharnitsa" in Geempoort-Ghent. Photo by the author.

undergoing deep processes of economic restructuring with new knowledge workers moving into neighbourhoods adjacent to expanding tech clusters (Swanstrom and Plöger 2022). Dortmund suffers from a massive socioeconomic imbalance and is, at the municipal level, Germany's most segregated city when considering indices of ethnic and social segregation (Sürig and Wilmes 2015:102). Unlike Sleepstraat in Ghent, Innenstadt-Nord remains remarkably resistant to gentrification and is often portrayed as an example of failed integration due to low-income housing and crime-ridden incidents that occur in this (post)migrant neighbourhood. In it, the immense diversity of residents originally from Turkey, the former Yugoslavian and Balkan countries, who arrived in the 1980s and are now joined by other newcomers from Syria and the Middle East after 2015, is often depicted as problematic (Ilter et al. 2020).

The urban realm of everyday life sheds light on hidden signs of relational conflicts and solidarities derived from higher activities. Particular local spaces are invested with meanings and significance assigned by inhabitants. As discussed largely in Chapters 3 and 4, "the neighbourhood" is more likely than "the city" to provide the youngest respondents with a safe space and a sense of homeliness. While lingering on these urban nuances, I raised the question: who knows better than those who live and work there about gentrification, intra-neighbourhood dynamics and hidden divisions? Therefore, the following sections of this chapter draw upon the combination of qualitative data collected from in-depth interviews and a wide range of urban issues shared and verbalised by respondents addressing their concerns over "being Muslim". This analysis also considers n=12 in-depth interviews conducted with NGO practitioners and social workers who were met working in the neighbourhoods under observation in Belgium and Germany. According to what was discussed in Chapter 2, both groups can be considered two "epistemic communities" that hold, possess and employ "endogenous knowledge" to deal with community practices in the specific locality of "the city".

## The Right in the City

While conducting in-depth interviews in Belgium and Germany, some respondents divided the city along the spatial binary of "here and there" in terms of "us and them". Often unknowingly, they referred to "there and them" as the white, non-Muslim space of natives, and to "here and us" as the notably brown, Muslim urban space where locals with a migration background are perceived as struggling to catch up with the "Western", "liberal" and "secular" values of gender equality, freedom of speech, neutrality, individual freedom and laicism. In contrast, Warsaw and Piacenza were less likely to exhibit such trends.

Among young Muslims with Bosnian family heritage in Antwerp, Islamophobia does not deny access to any urban space in their everyday life. As discussed in Chapter 4, Antwerp is at first described as the capital of the Bosnian diaspora, where "the Bosnian Muslim community lives in different districts without any major problem". Yet the tense anti-Muslim atmosphere in town brings respondents to get "much closer to the community rather than the different districts", unlike the "much bigger and louder Turkish and Moroccan diaspora who settled down much earlier in Oud-Berchem". A male respondent added, "yes, we are proud of being Antwerpians, but Durne is the historical area where the first Yugo club was opened in the 1990s, the same place which today hosts the Bosnian mosque and cultural centre".

There is no doubt that the city's multicultural environment usually helps the group under study avoid unpleasant encounters with violent racists and Islamophobes. However, Islamophobia manifests itself through structural and institutional discrimination in neighbourhoods such as Borgerouth and Durne. The latter are often depicted as the hotbed of passivity, male chauvinism, religious fanatism, "*halal* apartheid", alienation from public affairs and the ever-present threat of terrorist plots. The extreme-right Dutch *Vlaams Belang* and *PVV* (respectively, in English, the "Flemish Interest in Belgium" and the "Party for Freedom in the Netherlands") used to carry out "islam-safaris" within Muslim-majority districts to prove how immigrant communities are slowly but surely taking over Western "native" society. In Dortmund, some respondents likewise complained about "the rampant growth of the far-right party Alternative for Deutschland" (herein AfD). In-depth interviews conducted with young Muslims of Albanian origin provided eye-opening perspectives. Many depicted Dortmund as quite divided, adding that "Innenstadt-Nord is where Muslims live and hang around"; hence, "the AfD usually organises rallies to show off and mark their territory by waving fascist flags to provoke [non-German] locals". While two male respondents argued that "the atmosphere is more alarming in Dorstfold – an area not that far from Innenstadt-Nord, popular for hosting the Neo-Nazi community living there", a same-age female Muslim was particularly concerned about Nordstadt after reading the news about a pig's head being hung on the Turkish mosque's entrance and some swastika-like graffiti sprayed overnight (Daily Shaba 2019). Yet another concern was raised about the great danger posed by "AfD, which is now able to influence people who previously had no political affiliation, nor an anti-Muslim position, before". Likewise, the multicultural neighbourhoods in Bremen are no exception to such dynamics. In Gröpelingen, the director of the city library pointed out that the neighbourhood is "unfortunately known for drugs, prostitution, overrepresentation of semiskilled workers in the secondary segment of the job market and substandard premises leading to segregation in housing".

It here seems that Lefebvre's "right to the city" (1991) is more likely exerted by Islamophobic, far-right and racist organisations rather than locals subjected to otherisation and gentrification. Hence, spatialised Islamophobia hits the physiological and emotional dimension of young respondents as they themselves are put on alert by potential escalations of anti-Muslim actions in town. Moreover, spatialised Islamophobia leads to frictions within one's community vis-à-vis the manifestations of gentrification that restructure the urban areas by displacing communities with similar living standards and religious backgrounds. As discussed in Chapter 5, the mushrooming of "*Halal* environments" reinforces the perception of exclusion from certain urban places (Najib 2022:40). Moreover, Islam and Muslim signifiers came to challenge what secularism did not eradicate – namely, the visual elements of Christianity. In Ghent, for instance, different religious markers outweigh the previous heritage in the neighbourhoods under observation. There, respondents pointed out that "most [white] locals have gone to live outside because they prefer living apart from the multicultural atmosphere". The neighbourhood is not only considered a safe (*halal*) space, where moral and ethical considerations are often subjected to pragmatic choices to avoid wrongdoings (*haram*), but also an urban arena of self-contestation and self-confrontation, where the sense of otherness is forged and continually tested, confirmed and revised (Sofos and Tsagarousianou 2013:93). Within the Innenstadt-Nord in Dortmund, a young Muslim of Albanian origin admitted to "visiting the Turkish mosque rather than the Albanian, otherwise I pray at home, [thereby] avoiding the judging eye of family friends and community members who also came from my parents' hometown in [North] Macedonia".

This example from everyday life is important for shedding light on the complexity of hidden (hi)stories and the carriers of social, cultural and political agencies. Among others, language is quite often overlooked in studies of social conduct in urban space, and more attention has been paid to the material-infrastructural and spatial-architectural (topographic or cartographic) features of the city (for a critique, see Koch and Latham 2012). In Germany, however, language is a means to forge solidarities in a specific context. When interviewing Fitore and Denisa – two sisters whose parents escaped Kosovo just before the NATO bombing in 1999 – the same-age female Turkish Muslim who came to the interview to translate suggested the two respondents "speak in Kanaken". Although the latter carries a mostly derogatory aspect of describing the lack of fluency in German of migrants and newcomers from the Balkans, "the East" and Africa, this street language seemed to help respondents avoid issues of communication and stigmatisation. In Bremen, the conversation went as follows:

*Me:* "What does Kanaken mean?"

*Fitore:* "When we do not know how to say something in German, or we lack understanding with each other due to some language barrier, we use certain street words . . . this is Kanaken!"

*Denisa:* "Oh yeah, let's be the way we are! After all, we are Kanaken. In the eyes of Germans, we are still missing some German part of [their culture]".

In Dortmund, another same-age Muslim with a similar family heritage touched upon the issue of the German language. She was upset about her "colleagues complimenting her on her German" because they knew the respondent had been born, raised and had always lived in Germany. Then, I followed up with the question, "Do you also speak Kanaken?", she promptly replied, smiling:

> "Of course, I do speak Kanaken! When you speak 'Kanaken', you feel like you are not left alone, especially when you [need to make an] important decision . . . because it is very difficult to speak up in public in Germany. For example, in Germany, we do not have what Muslim women have in the US. Perhaps in Berlin, but [Muslim women] have collectives and can talk about women's topics unlike in other German cities".

## The City/Zens of Silence

The alarm bells of Islamophobia do not stir respondents to action, nor do they seem to convince most of them to make inroads into politics. As discussed in Chapter 6, however, a few exceptions can be found among second and third generations of former refugees and economic migrants from the Balkans (Karabegović 2024). Yet the general form of alienation is interrupted by global events, such as Israel's military response against Hamas within Gaza following October 7, 2023. After the fieldwork, it was unsurprising that non-conventional forms of participation followed the geopolitical upheaval in the Middle East. Respondents picked a side in defence of Palestine, and Gazans in particular, after perceiving the widespread Islamophobia emanating from systematic racism in the places where they live in Europe. The genocidal violence inflicted on Palestinians in Gaza reactivated memories of the past among the groups under study, whose generational identities are forged by the glocal dynamics of war, violence and the forced migration of Muslims (Posłuszny 2019:60).

Nonetheless, this remains an expectation in the four countries under observation. The widespread form of alienation captured among most respondents during the fieldwork echoes what Antonio Gramsci would have related to the paradox of the "cities of silence". Respondents' "silent position" in the political arena ontologically reveals a lack of political representation. Paraphrasing Gramsci's famous quote on the "organic crisis" (1971:210), the old city is dying, and a new one cannot be born. In this interregnum, a great variety of morbid symptoms appear. Among others, Islamophobia and gentrification are two of the symptoms that feed one another by excluding post-migrant communities and newcomers from the democratic arena. While the latter hits "migrant neighbourhoods" the hardest, the former exploits the already-existing issues of inequalities, exclusion and underdevelopment to advance new urban projects under the watchword of modernisation and innovation. Among the groups under study, those young Muslims whose parents fled Bulgaria, Kosovo and North Macedonia were the most difficult to reach out to. The few met, especially those with Roma family heritage, were not only subjected to nesting racism and discrimination as people coming from Eastern Europe (De Kock et al. 2022:139) but also as residents of non-white and working-class neighbourhoods (De Cesari and Dimova 2018; Devaux 2017). They were found to be targeted by the trans-local specificities of Islamophobia, which reduces them to "city/zens of silence" on the edge of the city. Housing issues, high unemployment and school dropout were all instances that continued to impact their urban predicament in the form of "crisis", which resembles its Greek etymological term, "krísis", from "krínein" – namely, "to separate" or "to discern", meaning the root of a "caesura" (Marramao 2012:115). The criterion by which this urban caesura manifests itself shows how the political space of post-migrant communities is rendered lifeless and exposed to a process of racialisation that suppresses critical voices.

At the time of fieldwork, Sleepstraat – a Turkish-majority area in downtown Ghent – was undergoing a profound urban transformation. Gentrification was aestheticising the neighbourhood and increasing levels of surveillance, as well as changing the old model of "ethnic enterprise" (Blommaert 2014) to forge a shiny, new neighbourhood centred around the IT sector and international finance corporations. Moreover, skyrocketing housing prices and new forms of heritagisation had already begun deepening the infra-urban inequalities between the much better-established Turkish diaspora and Balkan Roma families. The latter are exposed to the pendulum of migration that postpones their full integration since European Union enlargement eastwards in 2004. Since then, the public image of Roma workers in town has been sullied, putting their modest entrepreneurial activities at stake. While eventually displaced by gentrification, the new approach of state agencies may marginalise them even further. A social worker and NGO practitioner working near Sleepstraat confirmed that

> "After focusing on the role of neighbourhood stewards to prevent urban nuisance, Belgium has stopped contacting families in precarious situations. The process has been reversed: newcomers or decades-long refugee groups need to approach the regional offices to begin their integration process. [Now] Ghent's authorities focus on the integration of children from migrant communities, giving priority to education, employment and cohabitation while being ready to provide a new integration package to those who can pay for it".

According to what the same two social workers pointed out, "gentrification is the primary concern [because] the transformation of new residential areas and working spaces are further marginalising the Roma working in the service economy". In Ghent, the Roma community risks moving away from a precariat to complete isolation, which would soon push them away from downtown and worsen their unqualified, low-skill positions in the job market of Sleepstraat. A third social worker analysed the urban transformation caused by gentrification. Within the Turkish urban space, gentrification has already motivated those few white, native people in two ways: either to take advantage as landlords or directly move out and live outside a crowded and devalorised

*Figure 7.4* New housing models in Sleepstraat. Photo by the author.

environment (Erkan 2022:65). Post-migrant communities from today's "elitist creative class" move away from central areas like Sleepstraat, looking for new entrepreneurial ideas away from the low living standards of the surrounding areas. Unlike Sleepstraat, the Muslim-majority area of Rabat does not have the same consumer trends, vibrant nightlife and ethnic restaurants. There, however, young Muslims with Balkan family heritage live and work close to the more considerable Turkish diaspora, remaining disengaged from the core society and seemingly disinterested in speaking up about day-to-day worries and related issues they might face in their everyday life. Yet again, gentrification seems to be taking a toll.

> "We are from Razgrad. My parents came here many years ago. Turks and Bulgarians live close to each other. We go back to our hometown every summertime during the vacation period. What we really miss is the social life. Young people here do not have a social life – just home and work. This country produces robots, not people".
>
> "There is a multi-faceted form of racism against Roma from Bulgaria here in Rabat because of their migration background, their closeness with other Muslims and Turkish households and the general portrayal of backward people in the media landscape. . . . Most of them have problems in speaking Dutch as, at home, they just speak Bulgarian or Turkish, therefore struggling at school. In class, some cases of intolerance often occur. When they apply for jobs, they often ask our centre for help. They do not know how to design a CV, and the other requested documentation is full of spelling mistakes, or simply empty as they do not know how to fill it out".

In both neighbourhoods, semantic landscapes helped identify Balkan small businesses, such as cafeterias, kiosks and pastry shops. Their facades also displayed the linguistic hierarchies and communicative resources used publicly (Blommaert 2014:9). While most young Roma speak and write in Bulgarian and Turkish along with occasional Dutch and French to address locals, the visual organisations of languages and the conditional ways they were spoken provided an often-overlooked and inconspicuous geography of migration, identities and integration (or lack thereof). Along the streets, every sign targets an audience, and such a selection in turn shows the symmetrical or vertical organisation of bilingualism and trilingualism in relation to space and power dynamics. Beyond the facade, semantic landscapes also speak of the pragmatic actions of self-identification, belonging and the much larger social and political history of the people in that given neighbourhood.

The large concentration of precariat workers from Bulgaria and Roma communities was not found in other neighbourhoods in Italy, Germany and Poland. In the case of the latter, however, a few Roma vendors were met at the renowned marketplace on Bakalarska Street in the Włochy District of Warsaw. There, multicultural networks give street vendors and small entrepreneurs the ideal opportunity to come into contact with others, such as people of different ethnic, religious and racial backgrounds, as well as presenting a chance for them to enjoy themselves, alone or with their friends and family, etc, and express their identity during their everyday leisure activities. However, the marketplace itself is being modernised and undergoing a facelift, which could, ultimately, transform the area into a high-quality space for local businesses and street sellers. Yet again, such small-scale gentrification is hitting Roma the hardest. Two young Roma of Bulgarian origin pointed out that many have "already left for Belgium and the Netherlands" or "moved their business to other Polish cities where they are not constantly asked to reorganise their stands".

## References

Aboumaliq, S. (2010) The Social Infrastructures of City Life in Contemporary Africa, *Uppsala: Nordiska Afrikainstituet*. Available at: www.diva-portal.org/smash/record.jsf?pid=diva2%3A357359&dswid=3187 (Accessed: 10 February 2023).

Ali, N., El-Sherif, L. and Mire, H. (2023) Islamophobia and Proximities to Whiteness: Organising Outside of the Brown Muslim Subject. *ReOrient*, 8 (1), pp. 78–100. https://doi.org/10.13169/reorient.8.1.0078

Allievi, S. (2017) *Conversioni: verso un nuovo modo di credere? Europa, Pluralismo, Islam* [Conversions: Towards a New Way of Believing? Europe, Pluralism, Islam]. Napoli: Guida Editori.

Angrosino, M. (2007) *Doing Ethnographic and Observational Research*. London: SAGE Ltd. Available at: https://methods.sagepub.com/book/mono/doing-ethnographic-and-observational-research/toc (Accessed: 4 March 2023).

Bale, R. (2021) The Impact of Gentrification on Ethnic Communities, *Law Blogs – University of Oxford*. Available at: https://blogs.law.ox.ac.uk/housing-after-grenfell/blog/2021/05/opinion-impact-gentrification-ethnic-communities (Accessed: 20 September 2024).

Barni, M. and Bagna, C. (2008) 'A Mapping Technique and the Linguistic Landscape', in E. Shohamy and D. Gorter (eds.) *Linguistic Landscape. Expanding the Scenery*. New York: Routledge, pp. 126–141.

Blommaert, J. (2014) Infrastructures of Superdiversity: Conviviality and Language in an Antwerp Neighbourhood. *European Journal of Cultural Studies*, 17 (4), pp. 431–451. https://doi.org/10.1177/1367549413510421

Blommaert, J. and Rampton, B. (2011) Language and Superdiversity, *Max Planck Institute for the Study of Religious and Ethnic Diversity*. Available at: https://pure.mpg.de/rest/items/item_1615144_3/component/file_1615143/content (Accessed: 3 January 2023).

Bougarel, X. (2005) *The Role of Balkan Muslims in Building a European Islam*. Available at: https://shs.hal.science/halshs-00143385/ (Accessed: 19 November 2022).

Bougarel, X. (2008) 'Balkan Muslim Diasporas and the Idea of a European Islam', in T. Dulić, R. Kostić, R., I. Maček, and J. Trtak (eds.) *Balkan Currents. Essays in Honour of Kjell Magnusson*, Uppsala: Uppsala University Press, pp. 147–165.

Bourriaud, N. (2002) *Relational Aesthetics.* Dijon: Les Presses du Reel.

Bunse, A. (2019) *Migrant Entrepreneurship Network Structures.* Wiesbaden: Springer Gabler.

Canan, C. and Foroutan, N. (2016) The Paradox of Equal Belonging of Muslims. *Islamophobia Studies Journal*, 3 (2), pp. 160–176. http://dx.doi.org/10.18452/22484

Daily Shaba (2019) *Increasing Anti-Muslim Attacks Worry Islamic Community in German.* Available at: www.dailysabah.com/politics/2019/06/15/increasing-anti-muslim-attacks-worry-islamic-community-in-germany (Accessed: 28 June 2023).

De Cesari, C. and Dimova, R. (2018) Heritage, Gentrification, Participation: Remaking Urban Landscapes in the Name of Culture and Historic Preservation. *International Journal of Heritage Studies*, 25 (9), pp. 863–869. https://doi.org/10.1080/13527258.2018.1512515

De Kock, C., Decorte, T., Schamp, J., Vanderplasschen, W., Hauspie, B., Derluyn, I., Sacco, M. and Jacobs, J. (2022) Substance Use among People with a Migration Background: A Community-based Participatory Research Study, *Ghent University.* Available at: https://biblio.ugent.be/publication/8503482 (Accessed: 20 May 2023).

Devaux, U. (2017) Ghent as a Second Home for Many Bulgarians Analysis of the City's Policy Regarding Intra-European Migration and the Life of Bulgarians, *Ghent University.* Available at: https://lib.ugent.be/en/catalog/rug01:002375913 (Accessed: 14 January 2023).

Domaradzka, A. and Hamel, P. (2024) *Handbook on Urban Social Movements.* Cheltenham: Edward Elgar Publishing Ltd.

Driezen, A. (2023) Youth Navigating the Superdiverse City of Antwerp: Constructing and Negotiating Ethnic and Religious Symbolic Boundaries, *University of Antwerp.* Available at: https://repository.uantwerpen.be/docman/irua/986f79motoM53 (Accessed: 2 March 2024).

Duncan, N. and Duncan, J. (2009) *Doing Landscape Interpretation. The SAGE Handbook of Qualitative Geography.* London: SAGE Publications.

Ekers, M., Hart, G., Kipfer, S. and Loftus, A. (eds.) (2012) 'City, Country, Hegemony', in *Gramsci. Space, Nature, Politics.* Oxford: John Wiley & Sons. https://doi.org/10.1002/9781118295588.ch4

Erkan, D. (2022) When Urban Transformation Becomes Gentrifcation: Policies and Perceptions In(m)migrant Neighborhoods of Istanbul, Vienna and Paris, *Université Panthéon- Sorbonne – Paris I and Universität Wien.* Available at: https://theses.hal.science/tel-03771819 (Accessed: 15 May 2024).

Fanon, F. (1967) *The Wretched of the Earth.* New Work: Grove Press.

Fleischmann, F. and Phalet, K. (2018) Religion and National Identification in Europe: Comparing Muslim Youth in Belgium, England, Germany, the Netherlands, and Sweden. *Journal of Cross-Cultural Psychology*, 49 (1), pp. 44–61. https://doi.org/10.1177/0022022117741988

Glenn, J. and Weedon, C. (1995) *Cultural Politics: Class, Gender, Race and the Postmodern World*. Hoboken: Wiley-Blackwell.
Gramsci, A. (1971) *Selections from Prison Notebooks* (Q. Hoare and G. N. Smith, Ed. and Trans.). New York: International Publishers.
Groys, B. (2024) Critique and Complaint, *E-Flux Notes*. Available at: www.e-flux.com/notes/599788/critique-and-complaint (Accessed: 2 June 2024).
Hoops, J. F. (2021) Discourses of Integration in Antwerp. *Southern Communication Journal*, 86 (2), pp. 92–106. https://doi.org/10.1080/1041794X.2021.1882544
Hurd, S. (2008) *The Politics of Secularism in International Relations*. Princeton: Princeton University Press.
Huybrechts, L., Devisch, O. and Tassinari, V. (2022) *Re-Framing the Politics of Design*. Antwerp: Public Space.
Ilter, E., Koç, H. E., Korkou, M., Alagöz, S. Ö. and Rachdan, S. (2020) Seeing Dortmund from the South Boundaries and Socio-Spatial Segregarion: How to Transfrom Socially Constructed Boundaries into Multicultural Spaces, *Technische Universität Dortmund*. Available at: www.researchgate.net/publication/341120480_Seeing_Dortmund_from_the_South_Boundaries_and_Socio-Spatial_Segregation_How_to_Transform_Socially_Constructed_Boundaries_into_Multicultural_Spaces (Accessed: 15 April 2024).
Kamusella, T. (2019) *Ethnic Cleansing during the Cold War: The Forgotten 1989 Expulsion of Turks from Communist Bulgaria*. London: Routledge.
Karabegović, D. (2024) Fixing Things from Outside? Diaspora Politicians and Transnational Political Engagement, in *Globalisation*, pp. 1–18. https://doi.org/10.1080/14747731.2024.2336647
Kazi, N. (2015) Ahmed Mohamed and the Imperial Necessity of Islamophilia. *Islamophobia Studies Journal*, 3 (1), pp. 115–126. https://doi.org/10.13169/islastudj.3.1.0115
Khaldoun, I. (2005) *The Muqaddimah: An Introduction to History*. Princeton: Princeton University Press.
King, A. (2004) *Spaces of Global Cultures. Architecture, Urbanism, Identity*. London: Routledge.
Knox, P. and Pinch, S. (2010) *Urban Social Geography. An Introduction*. London: Routledge.
Koch, R. and Latham, A. (2012) Rethinking Urban Public Space: Accounts from a Junction in West London. *Transactions of the Institute of British Geographers*, 37 (4), pp. 515–529. https://ui.adsabs.harvard.edu/link_gateway/2012TrIBG.37.515K/doi:10.1111/j.1475-5661.2011.00489.x
Lefebvre, H. (1991) *The Production of Space* (D. Nicholson, Trans.). Oxford: Blackwell Publishers Limited.
Leiken, R. (2012) *Europe's Angry Muslims: The Revolt of The Second Generation*. Oxford: Oxford University Press.
Mai, N. and Schwandner-Sievers, S. (2003) Albanian Migration and New Transnationalisms. *Journal of Ethnic and Migration Studies*, 29 (6), pp. 939–948. https://doi.org/10.1080/1369183032000171302
Marramao, G. (2012) *The Passage West. Philosophy after the Nation State*. London: Verso.
Mbembe, A. (2019) *Necropolitics*. Durham and London: Duke University Press.
Merdjanova, I. (2013) *Rediscovering the Umma. Muslims in the Balkans between Nationalism and Transnationalism*. Oxford: Oxford University Press.
Najib, K. (2022) *Spatialised Islamophobia*. London: Routledge. https://www.routledge.com/Spatialized-Islamophobia/Najib/p/book/9781032111186?srsltid=AfmBOorGVQFR75D8Ao1saxpxof8w4H6SHGewjOgpgonPWoJHE5Oy9V7q
Najib, N. and Teeple Hopkins, C. (2020) Geographies of Islamophobia. *Social & Cultural Geography*, 21 (4), pp. 449–457. https://doi.org/10.1080/14649365.2019.1705993

Posłuszny, Ł. (2019) 'Memory, Landscape and Biography: Non-Places and Sites of Perished Communities', in A. Haapala, B. Frydryczak, and M. Salwa (eds.) *Moving from Landscaes to Cityscapes and Back: Theoretical and Applied Approaches to Human Environments.* Łódź: Officyna Publishing House, pp. 59–72.
Rexhepi, P. (2023) *White Enclosures. Racial Capitalism & Coloniality along the Balkan Route.* New York: Duke University Press.
Roy, O. (2013) Secularism and Islam: The Theological Predicament. *The International Spectator: Italian Journal of International Affairs*, 48 (1), pp. 5–19.
Sant'Angelo, F. (2004) 'The Council of Europe and the Work against Islamophobia: Existing Instruments and Standards', in I. Ramberg (ed.) *Islamophobia and Its Consequences on Young People.* Budapest: European Youth Centre Budapest, pp. 29–35. Available at: www.coe.int/en/web/youth/-/islamophobia-and-its-consequences-on-young-people?inheritRedirect=true (Accessed: 12 December 2022).
Schiller, N. G. and Ayse, Ç. (2009) Towards a Comparative Theory of Locality in Migration Studies: Migrant Incorporation and City Scale. *Journal of Ethnic and Migration Studies*, 35 (2), pp. 177–202. https://doi.org/10.1080/13691830802586179
Scollon, R. and Scollon, W. (2003) *Discourses in Place. Language in the Material World.* London: Routledge.
Sofos, S. A. and Tsagarousianou, R. (2013) *Islam in Europe. Public Spaces and Civic Networks.* New York: Palgrave Macmillian.
Stone, G. (2013) Visual Ethnography for Community Participation in Urban Development, *Uppsala University.* Available at: www.diva-portal.org/smash/get/diva2:629912/FULLTEXT01.pdf (Accessed: 28 February 2024).
Sürig, I. and Wilmes, M. (2015) *The Integration of the Second Generation in Germany Results of the TIES Survey on the Descendants of Turkish and Yugoslavian Immigrants.* Amsterdam: Amsterdam University Press.
Swanstrom, T. and Plöger, J. (2022) What to Make of Gentrification in Older Industrial Cities? Comparing St. Louis (USA) and Dortmund (Germany). *Urban Affairs Review*, 58 (2), pp. 526–562. https://doi.org/10.1177/1078087420975203
Swartz, D. (1989) Visual Ethnography. Using Photography in Qualitative Research. *Qualitative Sociology*, 12 (2), pp. 119–154. https://doi.org/10.1007/BF00988995
Thorstensen, E., Hagen, A. L. and Brattbakk, I. (2021) Images of Place, Secularity and Gentrification: On Urban Religious Belonging in an Inner City Neighbourhood in Oslo. *Secularism and Nonreligion*, 10 (1), pp. 1–16. https://doi.org/10.5334/snr.144
Urbinati, N. (1998) From the Periphery of Modernity: Antonio Gramsci's Theory of Subordination and Hegemony. *Political Theory*, 26 (3), pp. 370–391. https://doi.org/10.1177/0090591798026003005
Van Leuven, A., Mertens, S., D'Haenens, L. and Mekki-Benada, A. (2023) 'The Political and Intellectual Discourse on Islam and Muslims in Flanders', in L. d'Haenens and A. Mekki-Berrada (eds.) *Islamophobia as a Form of Radicalisation. Perspectives on Media, Academia and Socio-political Scapes from Europe and Canada.* Leuven: Leuven University Press, pp. 59–74.

# Conclusion

This qualitative study cannot provide a complete picture of the generations of young Muslims born to émigrée families who fled the Balkans after the demise of socialism. Nor can it exhaustively explore the wide range of issues and everyday worries evident in a time of deep political, ideological and cultural polarisation on the themes of Islam, multiculturalism and democracy in "the West". Needless to say, a more in-depth combination of qualitative and quantitative research would better identify Muslims' sensitivities and related concerns that this study may have overlooked. Nonetheless, the triangulation of detailed and extensive interview insights and field notes collected during fieldwork provides some telling perspectives.

To begin with, the *generation after* proves that Muslim Balkan communities have endured radical transformations. Since the early 1990s, at least two generations of young Muslims were born outside the Balkans and raised in families of former emigres in Western countries. Both have achieved higher educational attainment and acquired critical thinking to deal with the challenges of contemporary society. They have also been deeply influenced by street culture and come up with their own vision of Islam, which, if properly adhered to, provides a spiritual compass to navigate a wealth of identity and cultural dilemmas in today's post-secular society.

At the same time, this *generation after* has lived through the ebbs and flows of the post-9/11 period. If it is still true that Muslims in and from the Balkans remain barely exposed to political Islam and its malign influences, some have already carried out disloyal actions in and beyond Europe. During the fieldwork, however, respondents held balanced and progressive stances towards "the West" and its political affairs. Those who grew up throughout the 1990s speak up less about Islamophobia and experiences of exclusion than those born in the early 2000s. Along this intra-generational divide, the first group of respondents tend to privatise their Muslimness, although Islam does play an essential role in their everyday lives. The second group of respondents instead openly embrace and praise Islam for tackling, when needed, the reverberations and everyday consequences of anti-Muslim discourse and other manifestations of Islamophobia. Hence, the latter are not afraid of contesting nationalism,

DOI: 10.4324/9781003589624-9

positing themselves along the pleas of the *ummah* and having a say in the political upheavals in the Balkans.

When both groups of respondents were found to be connected with the *ummah*, such a connection did not seem to take the shape of a "rediscovery". Within multicultural cities and neighbourhoods in particular, personal relations with same-age and non-European Muslims are more likely to be held and nurtured than those established by older generations of Balkan Muslims. The *generation after* appreciates the different shades and nuances of Islam; that said, the *ummah* is not a benchmark to a global movement of coreligionists seeking justice and supporting political actions. Nor does it convey the image of a joint radical enterprise or the hotbed of plotters and potential terrorists. In the eyes of younger respondents, the *ummah* is a transnational and centreless safety network of friends, mates and neighbours where they can easily share their worries, a place they can receive advice without judgment. The *ummah* is, in fact, the venue where family stories match and connect with those of other Muslims, and where the burden of family traumas and painstaking integration (or lack thereof) can be understood without raising any particular alarm. In this regard, however, qualitative data also suggest that most respondents yearn to present themselves as the bearers of "European Islam" to claim full membership to Europe as a whole. This is why many respondents, primarily young males, often reject, elude or at times even give up on human relations with other local Muslims, lest they face stigmatisation as Muslims and as city dwellers residing in non-white, "poor" and "backward" neighbourhoods. Although this self-identification and coping mechanism may sound banal and trite, respondents' constant reference to Europeanness reveals a series of privileges and disadvantages from within Balkan Muslim communities. As often verbalised during in-depth interviews, some are able to shed the idiosyncrasies of being Muslims from the Balkans thanks to a "white habitus" – here meaning being taken for white, Christian Europeans – that eludes otherisation "out there". Otherwise, others fall victim to such a self-reiteration of Europeanness that they cannot distance themselves from this racialised, gendered and class-based vision of Islam. These respondents are those who are often racialised by the Western gaze, which ascribes them the identity of newcomers or "people of colour" because they are veiled women or non-white people, respectively.

Tellingly, this subtler form of whiteness operates in tandem with the nesting phenomena of gentrification, which spatialise anti-migration and nativist discourse by penetrating the urban fabric and the psychological and emotional dimensions of most young Muslims in town. Across the different cities where fieldwork was conducted, subtler manifestations of spatialised Islamophobia nonetheless provide different venues for postulates of solidarity to emerge and a wealth of political and religious sensitivities to be verbalised and heard. Although the same fieldwork results from a male bias study, interview insights from female Muslim respondents reveal gender dynamics within the *generation after*. Informed and guided by old-fashioned heteronormative gender roles, male and younger respondents care about maintaining solid ties with older generations. Hence, history, national culture and kinship are often associated with "their own Islam", i.e. one that complies with Europe and liberal democracy. In contrast, female Muslims are more inclined to criticise family culture and customs, negotiating their own cultural belonging to find pragmatic solutions to postmodern (identity) dilemmas. Without rejecting Islam, they are likely to speak up on the misinterpretation of the Qur'an by community members and family members as a means to patronise wives, daughters, sisters and women in general. Actions and practices of solidarity are thus much more common for women than men outside their family circles and diaspora communities; the former attempt to seek support from other female Muslims and find untapped solutions to their everyday worries and dilemmas.

This study has also addressed the particular dilemma of belonging. Paraphrasing Aleksandar Hemon's words (Bronwyn and Hemon 2020), the groups under study are close enough to belong to Europe to keep perpetually failing at actually being Europeans. Qualitative data suggest that the further back in time the parents' mo(ve)ment of settling in "the West" is, the stronger the respondents' sense of otherness and remoteness to their birthplace and the Balkans. Connections with the country are less fulfilling than local or ethnic ties, and family legacies supplant that of community at times, especially when minority roots continue to matter more than political and mainstream self-identification. Put simply, it seems that the groups under study do not belong to any locality. However, if one delves deeper, respondents feel much more strongly connected with the city they were born and reside in than the locality their parents came from. As discussed in Chapter 4, the condition of *atopicality* (Marramao 2012:70) stems from family history and the causes of migration (or displacement), and it impacts quotidian choices, values and different strategies when negotiating their religious identity "out there". Yet again, here the social function of Islam guides respondents as a moral compass in times of uncertainty and dilemmas, shaping their human relations outside their communities with non-Muslim dwellers.

Aleksander Hemon's idea of "concentric motherlands" (2019:41) visualises what has been discussed throughout this study in terms of religious identity and belonging. Among the groups of respondents, attachment to the Balkans is activated in the first familial and private circle of belonging. In it, Islamic practices and values are passed down through generations, and later acted out within the urban fabric where the family and other Muslim communities have settled over time. Born outside the Balkans, the latter remain somewhat unavailable, except for the parental birthplaces that respondents visit regularly. A wide range of localities paves the way to the second circle of belonging. After Yugoslavia fell apart and its would-be successor states were brutalised and divided by war, the legacies of migration and traumas of displacement were passed down to the *generation after*, thereby burdening young Muslims with Balkan roots born somewhere else. They know that family heritage and

Islam are precious for their parents, who endured exploitation, genocide and violence of all sorts, but these values are not equally important for their generation. They are aware that their connections with the Balkans (may) fade away over time. Simultaneously, their Muslimness continues to evoke the endless (hi)story vicious circles of nationalism and hatred that family members endured. Seemingly paradoxically, the precedent circles of spatial belonging continue to stretch away. Meanwhile, Islam increases its values in a new circle defined by the markers of nostalgia around the past and, at times, the present critiques of post-modern society. In this last circle, the *generation after* comes to terms with the desire to belong to the Balkans as unassailable while a constellation of memories, music, storytelling and customs linger over their generation through their own family histories and community dynamics. Yet here a paradox unfolds: almost all respondents position themselves in between their birthplace and residence and that of their parents: both places are interconnected and interdependent, but at the same time equally distant from one another and never fully tangible.

Another critical dimension that this study aimed to explore was the domain of political participation. When trying to detect the latter by strategically discussing political sensitivities that may activate respondents' political participation, it was noticed that political opinions and sensitivities were readily detectable in connection with family traumas and heritage. Put simply, the higher the level of political engagement among some groups of respondents, the harsher the experiences and causes of dislocation in the family history. Unlike those who actually endured violence and displacement, however, the *generation after* is more outspoken about the past and the painstaking process of integration in highlighting Europe's age-old systemic racism and injustice toward Muslims and people with a migration background. Most respondents with Bosnian and Kosovar heritage consciously refer to themselves as the byproduct of the genocidal violence against Muslims in the Balkans. If Islam was the last thorn to be ripped out by nationalists in the region, their Muslimness is today understood as part and parcel of the cityscape and Europe's post-migrant society. Specific political sensitivities are activated by the "Islam of the young", which plays a pivotal role in the processes of healing and nurturing at the personal and community level, as well as in respecting and caring for "the other".

Moreover, the *generation after* was found to be particularly concerned about the current instability of liberal democracy. Islamophobia is understood as a manifestation of the crisis of liberal institutions, which is in turn portrayed as a multi-faceted phenomenon of ubiquitous nationalism, colonial legacies and systemic discrimination, among others. When some respondents (particularly males) occasionally disagreed with the West's societal model of multiculturalism and secularism, they neither advocated nor supported disloyal actions to counteract Islamophobia. Tellingly, they also address political Islam as denigratory to most Muslims worldwide, but they have a low opinion of feminism and LGBT rights. In this regard, the creation of a "post-national European Islam" would more likely follow up on the desire of young Muslims to comply with the Qur'an's teachings in the everyday life rather than their uncritical acceptance of multiculturalism, gender discourse and alarmist rhetoric over Islamic radicalism. In other words, these most debated political themes remain the litmus test for a multicultural society; however, according to many respondents, polarisation will not ease by only promoting a principle of mutuality, which, when it comes to respecting Islam and Muslims, is presented as a concrete means to build resilience and respect among all fellow human beings in Europe and beyond.

It is also important to note that data triangulation shows how the current geopolitical turmoil in Ukraine and the Middle East shapes different political sensitivities. The fieldwork was carried out in the wake of Russia's full-scale invasion of Ukraine in 2022, the reverberations of which could not help but put respondents on high alert. Postulates of solidarity and words of support toward Ukrainians were widespread among those groups under study, whose families had sought and found refuge in the West in the 1990s. At the same time, critical stances were also directed against the West-based values and double standards on foreign affairs. Since the "Palestinian question" was one of the significant themes verbalised by respondents, Israel's military operations in Gaza in response to Hamas' mass killing mobilised through protests an unprecedented wave of Muslims from and in the Balkans. Although data collection ended right after the events of October 7, 2023, it was no longer possible to ignore how quickly and unequivocally previous respondents and respective communities picked a side and expressed their pessimism and frustration over Israel's genocidal violence within Gaza. Everyone called for an immediate ceasefire, while others followed the South Africa v. Israel case closely before the International Court of Justice, often joining forces with leftist organisations that historically held a pro-Palestinian position over its territorial dispute with Israel. Tellingly, the pro-Palestinian stance drastically changed the positionality of respondents in the public eye. While previous support for Ukraine had provided the groups under study recognition in the public sphere, their "white habitus" was removed by their political engagement, boycotting campaigns and public interventions in solidarity with Palestine and Palestinian civilians in particular. Significantly, the previously entitled status of "acceptable", "good" and "Westernised Muslims" who rightfully supported Ukraine vanished in a puff of smoke.

Compared with the Russian-Ukrainian war and its implications for the Western orbit, the situation in Gaza ruptured, once again, wounds of unhealed traumas among young Muslims in and from the Balkans. The new postulates of solidarity activated by the resurfacing of the past would warrant separate research to sufficiently unravel the genealogy of these new forms of activism, political participation and criticism. Undoubtedly, these *generations after* will lay claim to the Muslim world and have a critical say in European public affairs.

## References

Bronwyn, J. and Hemon, A. (2020) The Balkans Is Just Close Enough to Being Europe to Perpetually Fail at Being Europe, *Kosovo 2.0*. Available at: https://kosovotwopointzero.com/en/aleksandar-hemon-the-balkans-is-just-close-enough-to-being-europe-to-perpetually-fail-at-being-europe/ (Accessed: 5 October 2022).

Hemon, A. (2019) *My Parents: An Introduction/This Does Not Belong to You*. New York: MCD Books.

Marramao, G. (2012) *The Passage West. Philosophy after the Nation State*. London: Verso.

# Index

www.ingramcontent.com/pod-product-compliance
Lightning Source LLC
LaVergne TN
LVHW021128300926
849160LV00010B/910
* 9 7 8 1 0 3 2 9 6 4 8 2 9 *